D0019543

266.001
R 399 m

MISSION BETWEEN THE TIMES

Essays by
C. RENÉ PADILLA

GRAND RAPIDS, MICHIGAN
WILLIAM B. EERDMANS PUBLISHING COMPANY

75253

Copyright © 1985 by Wm. B. Eerdmans Publishing Co.
255 Jefferson Ave. S.E., Grand Rapids, Mich. 49503
All rights reserved
Printed in the United States of America

Library of Congress Cataloging in Publication Data:

René Padilla, C.
Mission between the times.

1. Mission of the church — Addresses, essays, lectures.
2. Evangelistic work — Addresses, essays, lectures.
3. Christianity — Latin America — Addresses, essays, lectures. I. Title.
BV601.8.R46 1985   266' 001   85 10130

ISBN 0-8028-0057-2 (pbk.)

CONTENTS

Preface

All the essays included in this volume have been written within the last decade and reflect my involvement in a number of conferences beginning with the International Congress on World Evangelization held in Lausanne, Switzerland, 16-25 July 1974. All of them have appeared in various publications in English; some of them were part of a collection of essays published in Spanish under the title *El Evangelio Hoy* (Buenos Aires: Ediciones Certeza, 1975). Except for slight changes, they are printed here in their original form.

The 1974 Lausanne Congress was described by *Time* magazine as "a formidable forum, possibly the widest-ranging meeting of Christians ever held." What the reporter who wrote these words probably had in mind was the fact that the Congress had gathered 2,473 participants and close to 1,000 observers representing 150 countries and 135 Protestant denominations. More important than that, however, was the impact that the Congress produced around the world. As evangelist Leighton Ford has put it, "If there has ever been a moment in history when evangelists were in tune with the times, it surely must have been in July of 1974. Lausanne burst upon us like a bombshell. It became an awakening experience for those who attended and thousands of Christians in numerous countries who read about it."

The first part of the first essay in this collection, "Evangelism and the World," was one of the papers circulated in English, Spanish, French, German, and Indonesian to delegates in preparation for the Congress. The second part of this essay was one of the main presentations at the Congress, an attempt to respond to questions and observations that had come to me from all over the world. The two parts were previously published in the official reference volume *Let the Earth Hear His Voice*, edited by J. D. Douglas (Minneapolis: World Wide Publications, 1975). A section of the first part was also included in *Mission Trends No. 2: Evangelization*, edited by Gerald H. Anderson and Thomas F. Stransky (New York: Paulist Press; Grand Rapids: William B. Eerdmans, 1975).

One of the most valuable results of the Congress was the Lausanne Covenant, a 2,700-word, fifteen-point document drafted under the leadership of John Stott. With this Covenant, Evangelicals took a stand against a mutilated gospel and a narrow view of the Christian mission. In keeping with the desire that the Congress be regarded as a process more than an event, a number of us undertook the task of carrying on the debate that had taken place at Lausanne. For that purpose we put together a symposium dealing with the fifteen sections of the Covenant; the results were published under the title *The New Face of Evangelicalism* (London: Hodder & Stoughton; Downers Grove, Ill.: InterVarsity Press, 1976). The second essay in this volume, "Spiritual Conflict," was my contribution to that symposium.

I originally presented "What Is the Gospel?" (the third essay herein) in August of 1975 at the IX General Assembly of The International Fellowship of Evangelical Students, a student movement within which I have sharpened my theological reflection on the Christian mission for over two decades. It was previously published in preparation for that event in *The Gospel Today* (London: IFES, 1975).

To that same year belongs "The Contextualization of the Gospel," a paper I originally read at an international consultation on evangelical literature for Latin America held in June at the Pinebrook Conference Center in Stroudsburg, Pennsylvania, under the sponsorship of Partnership in Mission and the David C. Cook Foundation. It was subsequently included in the collection *Readings in Dynamic Indigeneity*, edited by Charles H. Kraft and Tom N. Wisley (Pasadena: William Carey Library, 1979). A part of it was also included in "Hermeneutics and Culture — A Theological Perspective," a paper I read at the

Consultation on Gospel and Culture (another outgrowth of the 1974 Lausanne Congress), which was held at Willowbank, Bermuda, in January of 1978. This consultation was sponsored by the Theology and Education Group and the Strategy Working Group of the Lausanne Committee for World Evangelization (LCWE), and its proceedings appeared in *Gospel and Culture*, edited by John Stott and Robert T. Coote (Pasadena: William Carey Library, 1979).

In November of 1979 the Latin American Theological Fraternity held CLADE II (the Second Latin American Congress on Evangelization) in Lima, Perú. In sharp contrast to CLADE I (which was held in Bogota in November of 1969), this Congress viewed evangelization as inseparable from social and political concerns. Under the motto "Let Latin America Hear His Voice," it took the Lausanne Covenant as its frame of reference but sought to relate its message to the concrete reality of poverty and oppression, moral corruption and abuse of power in this area of the world. "Christ and Antichrist in the Proclamation of the Gospel" (essay five herein) was the paper I read on that occasion. It was originally published in Spanish in *Pastoralia* magazine (vol. 2, nos. 4-5, November 1980). The English translation appeared in the *Theological Fraternity Bulletin* (January-March 1981).

"The Fullness of Mission" was circulated at the Fourth Conference of the International Association for Mission Studies held at Maryknoll, New York, in August of 1978. It was a sort of presentation card with which I became a member of an association that has given me many satisfactions since then. It was later published in the *Occasional Bulletin of Missionary Research* (January 1979).

The Lausanne Covenant is critical of the worldliness involved in compromising the Christian message, manipulating hearers through pressure techniques, and becoming "unduly preoccupied with statistics or even dishonest in our use of them" (par. 12). That critique took up an objection I raised in my Lausanne paper to the use of the so-called "homogeneous unit principle" as a basis for church growth. In order to have the whole issue openly debated, the LCWE Theology and Education Group organized a consultation that took place at the headquarters of the Fuller School of World Mission in Pasadena, California, in June of 1977. At that conference I read a paper entitled "The Unity of the Church and the Homogeneous Unit Principle." It appeared later in a revised form in the *International Bulletin of Missionary Research* (January 1982) and was reprinted in a book edited by Wilbert R. Shenk, *Exploring Church Growth* (Grand Rapids: William B. Eerdmans, 1983). It is included as the seventh essay in this volume.

Another concern expressed in the Lausanne Covenant provided the subject matter for a worldwide consultation sponsored by the LCWE Theology and Education Group and the Ethics and Society Unit of the Theological Commission of the World Evangelical Fellowship. The signatories of the Covenant living in affluent circumstances had accepted their "duty to develop a simple lifestyle in order to contribute more generously to both relief and evangelism" (par. 9). The meaning of that commitment was explored at the Consultation on Simple Lifestyle held in Hoddeson, England, in March of 1980. My paper "New Testament Perspectives on Simple Lifestyle" (essay eight herein) · was read at that consultation and later published as part of the proceedings in *Lifestyle in the Eighties: An Evangelical Commitment to Simple Lifestyle*, edited by Ronald J. Sider (Exeter: Paternoster Press, 1981; Philadelphia: Westminster Press, 1982).

The ninth and final essay in this collection, "The Mission of the Church in Light of the Kingdom of God," previously appeared in the April-June 1984 issue of *Transformation* magazine. Before that I had delivered a slightly different version of the essay at the Consultation on the Relationship between Evangelism and Social Responsibility (Grand Rapids, Michigan, June 1982), another conference organized by the group that had sponsored the conference on Christian lifestyle. The purpose of the conference was to generate a face-to-face discussion among people stressing two different statements made in the Lausanne Covenant—that "evangelism and socio-political involvement are both part of our Christian duty" (par. 5) and that "in the church's mission of sacrificial service evangelism is primary" (par. 6). My assignment was to respond to a major paper read by Arthur P. Johnston on "The Kingdom in Relation to the Church and the World."

PREFACE

It will by now be very obvious to the reader that most of the essays in this volume reflect the international theological dialogue that has been taking place in evangelical circles since the 1974 Lausanne Congress. As a matter of fact, I doubt that they would ever have been written had the promoters of that dialogue, notably John Stott and Ronald Sider, not kindly drawn me into it. To them and to the many partners in this exciting dialogue, I am deeply grateful. I also want to thank my wife and colleague, Catharine Feser Padilla, for all her encouragement and help throughout these years.

In his prologue to *The New Faces of Evangelicalism*, John Stott says that in his view the face of evangelicalism presented at Lausanne was still the true evangelical face but that it was wearing a different expression. "The old face now wears a new seriousness," he concludes; "it is lit with a new smile of joyful confidence in God, and is newly turned in the direction of the contemporary world's agony and need." Ever since the Lausanne Congress I have seen myself as a highly privileged witness to what the Spirit of God has been doing to give his people a renewed sense of holistic mission. If with these essays I have contributed in a small way toward turning the face of evangelicalism in the direction of a suffering world, let God be praised!

Buenos Aires   C. R. P.
October 1984

Evangelism and the World

The gospel of Jesus Christ is a personal message — it reveals a God who calls each of his own by name. But it is also a cosmic message — it reveals a God whose purpose includes the whole world. It is not addressed to the individual per se but to the individual as a member of the old humanity in Adam, marked by sin and death, whom God calls to be integrated into the new humanity in Christ, marked by righteousness and eternal life.

The lack of appreciation of the broader dimensions of the gospel leads inevitably to a misunderstanding of the mission of the church. The result is an evangelism that regards the individual as a self-contained unit — a Robinson Crusoe to whom God's call is addressed as to one on an island — whose salvation takes place exclusively in terms of a relationship with God. It is not seen that the individual does not exist in isolation, and consequently that it is not possible to speak of salvation with no reference to the world of which he is a part.

In his high priestly prayer, Jesus Christ pleaded thus for his disciples: "I am no more in the world, but they are in the world, and I am coming to thee. . . . I do not pray that thou shouldst take them out of the world, but that thou shouldst keep them from the evil one. They are not of the world, even as I am not of the world" (John 17:11, 15-16). The paradox of Christian discipleship in relation to the world is placed before us — to be *in* the world but not to be *of* the world. This essay may be regarded as an attempt to explain the meaning of that paradox in its bearing on evangelism. The study is divided into three parts. The first is an analysis of the various usages of the term *world* in the New Testament. The second shows in what sense evangelism deals with a separation from the world, inasmuch as the disciples of Christ are not *of* the world. The third, finally, views evangelism from the perspective of involvement with the world, an involvement that reflects the fact that the disciples of Christ are *in* the world.

PART ONE: THE WORLD IN BIBLICAL PERSPECTIVE

A simple observation of the important place that the term *world* (Greek: *cosmos*) has in the New Testament (especially in the Johannine and Pauline writings and passages relating to the history of salvation) should suffice to demonstrate the cosmic dimension of the gospel. God's work in Jesus Christ deals directly with the world as a whole, not simply with the individual. Thus, a soteriology that does not take into account the relationship between the gospel and the world will not do justice to the teaching of the Bible.

But what is the world?

I cannot here attempt an exhaustive study of the topic, but by way of introduction I will try briefly to sort out the various strands of meaning of the complex term *cosmos* in the New Testament.

1. The world is the sum total of creation, the universe, "the heavens and the earth" that God created in the beginning and that one day he will recreate.[1]

What is most distinctive in the New Testament concept of the universe is its christological emphasis. The world was created by God through the Word (John 1:10), and without him nothing that has been made was made (John 1:3). The Christ whom the gospel proclaims as the agent of redemption is also the agent of God's creation. And he is at the same time the goal toward which all creation is directed (Col. 1:16) and the principle of coherence of all reality, material and spiritual (Col. 1:17).

In light of the universal significance of Jesus Christ, the

---

1. See Matt. 24:21; John 1:9-10; 17:5, 24; Acts 17:24; Rom. 1:20; 1 Cor. 4:9; 8:4; Eph. 1:4; Phil. 2:15; Heb. 4:3; 9:26.

Christian cannot be pessimistic concerning the final destiny of the world. In the midst of the changes of history, he knows that God has not abdicated his throne and that at the proper time all things will be placed under the rule of Christ (Eph. 1:10; cf. 1 Cor. 15:24ff.). The gospel implies the hope of "a new heaven and a new earth" (Rev. 21; cf. 2 Pet. 3:13).[2] Consequently, the only true evangelism is that which is oriented toward that final goal of "the restoration of all things" in Christ Jesus promised by the prophets and proclaimed by the apostles (Acts 3:21). Eschatology centered in the future salvation of the soul turns out to be too limited in the face of secular eschatologies of our day, the most important of which—the Marxist—looks forward to the establishment of the ideal society and the creation of a new man. Today more than ever the Christian hope in its fullest dimensions must be proclaimed with such conviction and with such force that the falseness of every other hope should not have to be demonstrated.

2. *In a more limited sense, the world is the present order of human existence, the space-time context of man's life.*[3]

This is the world of material possessions, in which men are concerned for "things" that are necessary but that easily become an end in themselves (Luke 12:30). "Anxiety" for these things is incompatible with seeking the Kingdom of God (Luke 12:22-31). The treasures that man can store up on earth are perishable (Matt. 6:19). It is useless for him to gain "the whole world" and lose or forfeit his own self (Luke 9:25; cf. John 12:25). There is a Christian realism that demands that we take seriously the fact that "we brought nothing into the world, and we cannot take anything out of the world" (1 Tim. 6:7). All material possessions lie under the sign of the transitoriness of a world that advances inexorably toward the end. In light of the end, everything that belongs solely to the present order becomes relative; it cannot be considered the totality of human existence (1 Cor. 7:29-31; cf. 1 John 2:17). To the contrary,

2. It is noteworthy that the New Testament never uses the term *cosmos* to refer to the eschatological world of the Christian hope, for which other expressions are used.

3. See Matt. 4:8; John 8:23; 12:25; 16:33; 18:30; 1 Cor. 7:31; 1 John 3:17; 1 Tim. 6:7.

it forms part of the system of man's rebellion against God (to which we will return later in this study).

To proclaim the gospel is to proclaim the message of a Kingdom that is not of this world (John 18:36) the politics of which cannot for that reason conform to the politics of the kingdoms of this world. This is a Kingdom whose sovereign rejected "the kingdoms of the world and their glory" (Matt. 4:8; cf. Luke 4:5) in order to establish his own Kingdom on the basis of love. It is a Kingdom that is made present among men, here and now (Matt. 12:28), in the person of one who does not come from this world (*tou cosmou toutou*) but "from above," from an order beyond the transitory scene of human existence (John 8:23).

3. *The world is humanity, claimed by the gospel, but hostile to God and enslaved by the powers of darkness.*[4]

Occasionally *cosmos* denotes humanity, with no reference to its position before God.[5] Much more frequently, though, it denotes humanity in its relation to the history of salvation that culminates in Jesus Christ, by whom it is judged.

a. *The world claimed by the gospel.* The most categorical affirmation of God's will to save the world is made in the person and work of his Son Jesus Christ. Let us not deny the universal scope of New Testament soteriology just because we are unable to explain how it is that not all are saved even though it is God's will that his salvation reach all men (1 Tim. 2:4). According to the New Testament, Jesus Christ is not the Savior of a sect but rather "the Savior of the world" (John 4:42; 1 John 4:14; 1 Tim. 4:10). The world is the object of God's love (John 3:16). Jesus Christ is the Lamb of God that takes away the sin of the world (John 1:29), the light of the world (John 1:9; 8:12; 9:5), the propitiation not only for the sins of his own people but "also for the sins of the whole world" (1 John 2:2; cf. 2 Cor. 5:19). To this end he was sent by the Father — not

4. See Matt. 5:14; 13:38; 18:7; 1 Cor. 1:27-28; 3:22; 4:13; 2 Pet. 2:5; 3:6; Heb. 11:7, 38.

5. The texts in which *cosmos* with this connotation appears are numerous in Johannine and Pauline writings. The usage of the term with this meaning is peculiar to the New Testament.

4

to condemn the world, but "that the world might be saved through him" (John 3:17).

Obviously God's salvation in Christ Jesus is universal in scope. But the universality of the gospel must not be confused with the universalism of contemporary theologians who hold that on the basis of the work of Christ all men have received eternal life, whatever their position before Christ. The benefits obtained by Christ are inseparable from the gospel and, consequently, can be received only *in* and *through* the gospel. To preach the gospel is not merely to proclaim an accomplished fact but simultaneously to proclaim the accomplished fact and make a call to faith. The proclamation of Jesus as "the Savior of the world" is not an affirmation that all men are automatically saved but rather an invitation to all men to put their confidence in the one who gave his life for the sin of the world. "Christ does not save us apart from faith, faith does not restore us apart from Christ. He became one with us, we have to become one with him. Without the affirmation of this double process of self-identification and of the results that follow it, there is no complete exposition of the gospel."[6]

From the universality of the gospel is derived the universality of the evangelizing mission of the church. The gospel's claim on the world, initiated in Jesus Christ, is continued through his followers. As the Father sent him, so he has sent them into the world (John 17:18). Repentance and forgiveness of sin in his name must be announced to all nations (Luke 24:47; cf. Matt. 28:19; Mark 16:15). And it is this demand of the gospel that gives meaning to history until the end of the present era (Matt. 24:14).

b. *The world hostile to God and enslaved by the powers of darkness.* The most distinctive usage of *cosmos* in the New Testament is predominately negative. It refers to humanity, but to humanity in open hostility to God: it is personified as the enemy of Jesus Christ and his followers. The Word through whom all things were made came into the world, but "the world knew him not" (John 1:10). He came as the light of the world (John 8:12;

6. Vincent Taylor, *Forgiveness and Reconciliation: A Study in New Testament Theology* (London: Macmillan, 1941), p. 273.

9: 5) to bear witness to the truth (John 18: 37), but "men loved darkness rather than light, because their deeds were evil" (John 3: 19). It was a collective rejection. But it was the only attitude consistent with the nature of the world alienated from God: the world *cannot* receive the Spirit of truth (John 14: 17); the carnal mind *cannot* submit to God's law (Rom. 8: 7). This is the tragedy of the world: it is caught up in the vicious circle of a rejection that leads it to hate Christ and his followers (John 15: 18, 24; 1 John 3: 1, 13) and at the same time leaves it incapable of recognizing the truth of the gospel (John 9: 39-41). The condition of the world in its rebellion against God is such that Jesus Christ does not even pray for it (John 17: 9).

But if we dig a bit deeper in our analysis of the concept of the world in the Johannine and Pauline writings, it becomes obvious that behind this rejection of Jesus Christ lies the influence of spiritual powers hostile to man and to God. "The whole world is in the power of the evil one" (1 John 5: 19). The "wisdom of the world," characterized by its ignorance of God, reflects the wisdom of "the rulers of this age" — the powers of darkness — that crucified Christ (1 Cor. 1: 20; 2: 6, 8). Unbelievers' blindness to the gospel is the result of the action of Satan, "the god of this world" (2 Cor. 4: 4). Apart from faith, men are in subjection to the spirit of the age (the *Zeitgeist*) controlled by the "prince of the power of the air" (Eph. 2: 2). The world is under the domination of the "elemental spirits" (Gal. 4: 3, 9; Col. 2: 8, 20), the principalities and powers (Rom. 8: 38; 1 Cor. 15: 24, 26; Eph. 1: 21; 3: 10; 6: 12; Col. 1: 16; 2: 10, 15).

The picture of the world that emerges from the texts I have cited is confirmed by the rest of the New Testament. In it, as in first-century Judaism, the present age is conceived of as the period in which Satan and his hosts have received the authority to rule the world. The universe is not a closed system in which everything can be explained by an appeal to natural causes; rather, it is the arena in which God — a God who acts in history — is engaged in a battle with the spiritual powers that enslave men and hinder their perception of the truth revealed in Jesus Christ.

This diagnosis of man's plight in the world cannot simply

be dismissed as stemming out of the apocalyptic speculation that was common among the Jews of New Testament times. As Emil Stauffer says, "In primitive Christianity there is no theology without demonology." And without demonology the answer to the problem of sin must be found exclusively in man, without giving due attention to the fact that man himself is the victim of an order that transcends him and imposes on him a detrimental way of life. Sin (singular) is not the sum total of the individual sins (plural) of man. It is, on the contrary, an objective situation that conditions men and forces them to commit sin: "Everyone who commits sin is a slave to sin" (John 8:34). The essence of sin is the lie ("You will be like God" — Gen. 3:5), and lying has its origin in the devil, the "liar and the father of lies" (John 8:44). Sin, then, is a social and even a cosmic rather than merely an individual problem. Personal sins — those sins that according to Jesus come "from within, out of the heart of man" (Mark 7:21-2) — are the echo of a voice that comes from the creation, the creation that "was subjected to futility" and that will be "set free from its bondage to decay" (Rom. 8:20-21).

Unfortunately, much too frequently it has been taken for granted that the concrete manifestation of satanic action among men takes place primarily or even exclusively in those phenomena that fall within the sphere of demonic possession or the occult. Thus we have lost sight of the demonic nature of the whole spiritual environment that conditions man's thought and conduct. The individualistic concept of redemption is the theological consequence of an individualistic concept of sin that ignores "all that is in the world" (not simply in the heart of man) — namely, "the lust of the flesh and the lust of the eyes and the pride of life" (1 John 2:15-16). In one word it ignores the reality of *materialism*, which is to say the absolutization of the present age in all it offers — consumer goods, money, political power, philosophy, science, social class, race, nationality, sex, religion, tradition, and so on; the "collective egoism" (to borrow Niebuhr's phrase) that conditions man to seek his realization in "the desirable things" of life; the Great Lie that man derives his meaning from "being like God" in independence from God.

7

Under the domination of the powers of darkness, the world stands at the same time under the judgment of God. God sent his Son not to condemn the world but to offer it the possibility of salvation through him (John 3:17; cf. 12:47). Nevertheless, the world is judged by its rejection of the light of life that has made its appearance among men. "This is the judgment, that the light has come into the world, and men loved darkness rather than light, because their deeds were evil" (John 3:19; cf. 12:48).

In conclusion, man's problem in the world is not simply that he commits isolated sins or gives in to the temptation of particular vices. It is, rather, that he is imprisoned within a closed system of rebellion against God, a system that conditions him to absolutize the relative and to relativize the absolute, a system whose mechanism of self-sufficiency deprives him of eternal life and subjects him to the judgment of God. This is one of the reasons that evangelism cannot be reduced to the verbal communication of doctrinal content with no reference to specific forms of man's involvement in the world. It is also one of the reasons that the evangelist's confidence cannot rest in the efficacy of his methods. As the Apostle Paul taught, "We are not contending against flesh and blood, but against the principalities, against the powers, against the world rulers of this present darkness, against the spiritual hosts of wickedness in the heavenly places" (Eph. 6:12). The proclamation of the gospel does take seriously the necessity of divine resources for the battle.

PART TWO: EVANGELISM AND SEPARATION FROM THE WORLD

The gospel does not come from man, but from God. Its entrance into the world necessarily leads to conflict, because it questions the absolute nature of "the desirable things" of the old era. Its presence alone means crisis, because it demands that man discern between God and the false gods, between light and darkness, between truth and error. Those who bear the gospel, then, are "the aroma of Christ to God among those who are being saved and among those who are perishing, to one a fragrance from death to death, to the other a fragrance from life to life" (2 Cor. 2:15-16). The gospel unites, but it also separates. And out of this separation created by the gospel springs the church as a community called to be not *of* the world but to be *in* the world.

The concept of the church as an entity "separated" from the world lends itself to all kinds of false interpretations. At the one extreme is the position which holds that there is no real separation but only a simple epistemological difference: the church knows that it has been reconciled to God, while the world does not know—and that is all.[7] At the other extreme is the position which holds that the separation is an impassable chasm between two cities that communicate with each other only as the one sets out on a crusade to conquer the other. Our concept of the nature of the separation between the church and the world inevitably influences our definition of the gospel and our methods of evangelism. We urgently need to recover an evangelism that takes seriously the distinction between the church and the world as it is seen from the perspective of the gospel, an evangelism that is oriented toward breaking man's slavery in the world and does not itself become an expression of the church's enslavement to the world.

1. Evangelism and the Proclamation of Jesus Christ as Lord of All

A brief study of the New Testament is sufficient to show that the essentials of its message are summarized in the oldest creed of the church: "Jesus Christ is the *Kyrios*." Though it is true that only after the resurrection were the disciples able to grasp the importance of this title as applied to Jesus Christ, there is no doubt that for them the one whom God had *made* "Lord and Christ" was none other than the Jesus who had been crucified (Acts 2:36). To say that Jesus Christ is Lord is to say

7. This position is illustrated by Oscar Cullmann's affirmation that "the fundamental distinction . . . between all the members of the lordship of Christ and the members of the Church is that the former do not know that they belong to this lordship, whereas the latter do know it" (*The Christology of the New Testament*, trans. Shirley C. Guthrie and Charles A. M. Hall [1955; Philadelphia: Westminster Press, 1963], p. 231).

that the same Jesus whom God put forward "as a propitiatory offering by his blood" (Rom. 3:25) is now "Lord of all" (Rom. 10:12). Having provided the basis for the forgiveness of sin through the sacrifice of himself, he has occupied the place that is rightly his as mediator in the government of the world (Heb. 1:4).

On the basis of the texts mentioned, to which several others could be added, it is obvious that it is impossible to separate the priestly ministry of Jesus Christ from his kingly ministry. From the New Testament perspective, the work of God in his Son cannot be limited to cleansing from the guilt of sin; it is also a liberation from the powers of darkness, a transference to the messianic Kingdom which, in anticipation of the end, has been made present in Christ (Col. 1:13). The Christ who wrought forgiveness of sins is also the Christ who wrought liberation from slavery to the world. The hour of the Cross was the hour of the judgment of this world and of its "ruler" (John 12:31; 16:11), the hour in which Christ disarmed the principalities and powers and proclaimed their defeat, leading them as prisoners in a triumphal parade (Col. 2:15). Jesus Christ has been exalted as the *Kyrios* of all the universe (Eph. 1:20-22; Phil. 2:9-11; 1 Pet. 3:22), and it is as such that he is able to save all those who call on his name (Rom. 10:12-13). Salvation in Christ involves both forgiveness of sin (1 John 1:9) and victory over the world (John 5:4) by faith.

To evangelize, then, is not to offer an experience of freedom from feelings of guilt, as if Christ were a super-psychiatrist and his saving power could be separated from his Lordship. To evangelize is to proclaim Christ Jesus as Lord and Savior, by whose work man is delivered from both the guilt and the power of sin and integrated into God's plans to put all things under the rule of Christ. As Walter Künneth has pointed out, an individualistic Christology—a Christology that views Christ only in his relation to the individual—leaves the door open to a denial of creation, for the world must then be understood as if it existed apart from the Word of God which gives it meaning.[8] The Christ proclaimed by the gospel is the Lord of all,

8. Künneth, *The Theology of the Resurrection*, trans. James W. Leitch (1965; St. Louis: Concordia, 1966), pp. 161-62.

in whom God has acted decisively in history in order to form a new humanity. The one who places his confidence *in him* is delivered from "the present evil age" (Gal. 1:4) and from the powers by which it is characterized, the world is crucified to him, and he to the world (Gal. 6:14); he cannot submit to false gods as if he still belonged to the sphere of their influence (Col. 2:20).

Obviously, the separation of the church from the world can take place only from a theological, eschatological perspective. It is *before God* that the church takes shape as a community that belongs not to the present age but to the coming age. By vocation it is not *of* the world in the sense that it has rejected the Great Lie implicit in materialism (with its absolutization of "the desirable things" that the world offers). Though the old era is under the dominion of idols that set themselves up as gods and lords, the church holds that there is only one God, the Father, and one Lord, Jesus Christ, the mediator of creation and of redemption (1 Cor. 8:5-6). Here and now, in anticipation of the universal recognition of Jesus Christ as Lord of all creation (Phil. 2:9-11), the church has received him (Eph. 1:22) and lives by virtue of the blessings and gifts which he as Lord bestows (Eph. 1:3-14; 4:7-16). This is the basic difference between the church and the world.

Without the proclamation of Jesus Christ as Lord of all, in the light of whose universal authority all values of the present age become relative, there is no true evangelism. To evangelize is to proclaim Jesus Christ as the one who is reigning today and who will continue to reign "until he has put all his enemies under his feet" (1 Cor. 15:25). New Testament cosmic Christology is an essential element of the gospel proclamation.

2. Evangelism and Worldliness

On the Cross Jesus Christ inflicted a decisive defeat on the prince of this world. The enemy has been mortally wounded. The resurrection has demonstrated that the futility to which creation is subjected does not mean that God has abdicated his rule over it. All creation will be delivered from its bondage to decay (Rom. 8:20-21); the whole universe will be placed under the rule of Christ (Eph. 1:10).

Hope in the final triumph of Jesus Christ belongs to the

essence of the Christian faith; what God did through the death and resurrection of his Son he will complete at the end of time.

We cannot, however, fool ourselves about the actual historic situation of the church in relation to the world. A rapid reading of the New Testament points out the crude reality of the conditioning that the world and "the things that are in the world" exercise over man, whether Christian or not. The victory of Christ over the world and the powers is not a mere doctrine requiring intellectual assent; it is a fact that must become concrete reality in Christian experience through faith. To Jesus' claim "I have overcome the world" (John 16:33) corresponds the believer's "victory that overcomes the world, our faith" (1 John 5:4). In other words, the Christian is called to *become* what he already *is*. The imperative of the evangelical ethic forms an indivisible whole with the indicative of the gospel.

As long as the present age endures, the battle against the powers of darkness continues. Worldliness never ceases to be a threat to the church and its evangelizing mission. In spite of having been delivered from the present evil age (Gal. 1:4), Christians run the risk of returning to the "weak and beggarly elemental spirits" to which this age is subject (Gal. 4:9), the risk of submitting themselves to slavery to human regulations ("Do not handle, do not taste, do not touch") as if they were still of the world (Col. 2:20-22). For this reason, Christians need to be reminded of the liberty that has been given them in Christ. Because he died and rose again, the way has been opened to live here and now in the liberty of the children of God that belongs to the new era. All legalism is, therefore, worldliness — a return to slavery to the powers of darkness. And this is applicable to the prohibitions and taboos that today in many places in the world are part of the "evangelical subculture" and that are often so confused with the gospel that evangelism becomes a call to observe certain religious rules and practices and loses its meaning as proclamation of the message of liberty.

Another form in which worldliness enters the life and mission of the church today is the adaptation of the gospel to the "spirit of the times." Because of the limits of space, I will cite only two examples.

a. *"Secular Christianity."* Already in the first century an attempt was made to accommodate the gospel to the dualism between *spirit* and *matter* that was part of the ideological atmosphere of the day. Thus developed what in the history of Christian thought is known as "Docetism": in the face of a dualistic interpretation of the world, a *new* Christology was proposed that would make the gospel acceptable to those who could not conceive of the possibility that God (good by nature) should enter into direct relation with matter (evil by nature). Such seems to be the heresy to which the Epistles of John refer.

The problem today is not the dualism between spirit and matter, but rather secularism — the concept that the natural world represents the totality of reality and thus that the only possible knowledge is the "scientific." It is the logical consequence of another type of dualism, one derived from the philosophy of Descartes — the dualism between man (the thinking subject) and the world (the object of thought).[9] There is no place for God as the transcendent being who has the power to act in history and in nature. All that exists or happens in the universe can be explained by the laws of cause and effect; what cannot be investigated by empirical methods cannot be real.

All the versions of "secular Christianity" advocated by modern theologians assume the validity of secularism, sometimes under the garb of mere "secularity." They all take as their starting point a world in which man has supposedly come of age (as seen by Dietrich Bonhoeffer) and has no need for supernatural reality, the basic premise of religion. Their purpose is a "re-statement" of the gospel for this modern man who has learned to get along in the world and now presumes that he has no need of supernatural help. The end of "supernaturalism,"

9. The Cartesian dictum "I think, therefore I am" fails to take into account the fact that man is not merely a mind but a mind/body (a psychosomatic being) living and acting in the world, and that the "subjective" and "objective" aspects of reality are therefore inseparable in knowledge. Those burdened with this misperception tend to split reality into two levels: the upper level of the "subjective" (feelings and religion) and the lower level of the "objective" (facts and science) — and in fact this split is behind much of modern thinking in the fields of science, philosophy, and theology.

the end of that old doctrine of transcendence which is part and parcel of a pre-scientific concept of the universe, has arrived. If the Christian faith is to survive, it must be brought up to date; it must throw off every residue of "transcendentalism" and express itself in secular terms, so that no thinking man has to reject it together with accompanying pre-scientific ideas. Far from being an enemy of the Christian faith, secularism is an ally, since (as Friedrich Gogarten has argued) man's responsibility for the world is the very essence of the gospel.

Thus the foundation is laid for man to concentrate *all* his effort in building the earthly city without having to concern himself with reality "beyond" or "above" the natural realm. Man is the author of his own destiny, and his vocation is exclusively historical.

Robert J. Blaikie has demonstrated in detail that in the Cartesian system of reality that underlies "secular Christianity" there really is no place for the concept of man as an "agent" — a person capable of acting freely and introducing intentional changes in the world.[10] Action is the basic characteristic of personal reality. But if man is no more than the thinking subject and the world only the object of his thought, completely determined within a closed system of causes and effects, it follows that man is not personal reality and cannot be considered an active agent. Common sense tells us, nevertheless, that we are in fact beings living and acting in the world and that the concept of reality as something that can only be known "objectively" by means of the scientific method is incomplete, a view based on philosophical premises that, as such, cannot be proven scientifically. In conclusion, "secular Christianity" is not a mere "restatement" of the gospel, but rather a capitulation to a distorted concept of reality that is part of modern secularism.

Man's responsibility for creation is an essential aspect of his vocation according to the biblical definition; the exclusion of God (i.e., the personal God who acts in nature and in human history) is a compromise with "the spirit of the age." It is a form of worldliness. "Secular Christianity" is a man-centered religion

10. See Blaikie, *Secular Christianity and the God Who Acts* (Grand Rapids: William B. Eerdmans, 1970).

that says only what man wants to hear—that he is his own boss, that the future is in his hands, that God is merely something impersonal that he can manipulate. It is a denial of the biblical message, the basic presupposition of which is that God transcends the universe and acts freely within it.

In the final analysis, what "secular Christianity" does is sanctify the secular, replacing God's love manifested in Jesus Christ with love for *the things* of the secular city, as if the present order to which they belong had absolute value. John's admonition to a first-century church threatened by Docetism is relevant today: "Do not love the world or the things in the world. If any one loves the world, love for the Father is not in him" (1 John 2: 15).

b. *"Culture Christianity."* No less harmful to the cause of the gospel than "secular Christianity" is the identification of Christianity with a culture or a cultural expression. In the sixteenth century, Latin America was conquered in the name of the Catholic king and queen of Spain. This conquest was not only military but religious as well. It was concerned with implanting not merely Spanish culture but a "Christian culture." Only in recent years has Rome become aware that the Christianity of the people of Latin America is almost purely nominal. In the nineteenth century, the Christian missionary outreach was so closely connected with European colonialism that in Africa and Asia Christianity became identified as the white man's religion.

Today, however, there is another form of "culture Christianity" that has come to dominate the world scene—the "American Way of Life." This phenomenon is described by a North American Christian writer in these terms: "A major source of the rigid equation of socio-political conservatism with evangelicalism is conformity with the world. We have equated 'Americanism' with Christianity to such an extent that we are tempted to believe that people in other cultures must adopt American institutional patterns when they are converted. We are led through natural psychological processes to an unconscious belief that the essence of our American Way of Life is basically, if not entirely, Christian."[11] This equation in the

11. See David O. Moberg, *The Great Reversal: Evangelism versus Social Concern* (Philadelphia: Lippincott, 1972), p. 42.

United States insures the presence of a large number of middle-class whites in the church. But the price the church has had to pay for quantity is its prophetic role in society. What Tillich called "the Protestant principle" (i.e., the capacity to denounce every historic absolutization) is impossible for "culture Christianity." And this explains the confusion of Christian orthodoxy with socio-economic and political conservatism among evangelicals in the United States.

Because of the powerful influence that this type of Christianity has had in what is known as "the mission field," the gospel that is preached today in the majority of countries of the world bears the marks of "the American Way of Life." It is not surprising that at least in Latin America today the evangelist often has to face innumerable prejudices that reflect the identification of Americanism with the gospel in the minds of his listeners. The image of a Christian that has been projected by some forms of United States Christianity is that of a successful businessman who has found the formula for happiness, a formula he wants to share with others freely. The basic problem is that in a market of "free consumers" of religion in which the church has no possibility of maintaining its monopoly on religion, this Christianity has resorted to reducing its message to a minimum in order to make all men *want* to become Christians. The gospel thus becomes a type of merchandise the acquisition of which guarantees to the consumer the highest values — *success* in life and personal *happiness* now and forever. The act of "accepting Christ" is the means to reach the ideal of "the good life" at no cost. The Cross has lost its offense, since it simply points to the sacrifice of Jesus Christ for us but does not present a call to discipleship. The God of this type of Christianity is the God of "cheap grace"; the God who constantly gives but never demands; the God fashioned expressly for mass-man, who is controlled by the law of least possible effort and seeks easy solutions; the God who gives his attention to those who will not reject him because they need him as an analgesic.

In order to gain the greatest possible number of followers, it is not enough for "culture Christianity" to turn the gospel into a product; it also has to distribute it among the greatest number of consumers of religion. For this, the twentieth century has provided it with the perfect tool—technology. The strategy for the evangelization of the world thus becomes a question of mathematical calculation. The problem is to produce the greatest number of Christians at the least possible cost in the shortest possible time, and for this the strategists can depend on the work of the computer. Thanks to computers, never in the modern era have we been closer to the reestablishment of one culture unified by the Christian faith—the *Corpus Christianum*. The "culture Christianity" of our day has at its disposal the most sophisticated technological resources to propagate its message of success throughout the world and to do it *efficiently*!

Obviously, what is objectionable in this approach to evangelism is not the use of technology in itself. Viewed alone, technology, like science or money, is morally neutral. Nor is the concern that there be more Christians in the world to be questioned. God "desires all men to be saved and to come to the knowledge of the truth" (1 Tim. 2:4). The problem with this "culture Christianity" lies in the fact that it reduces the gospel to a formula for success and equates the triumph of Christ with obtaining the highest number of "conversions." This is a man-centered Christianity that clearly shows itself to be conditioned by the "technological mentality"—that mentality that, as Jacques Ellul has pointed out, regards efficiency as the absolute criterion and on this basis seeks, in all areas of human life, the systematization of methods and resources to obtain preestablished results.[12] It is the "religious" product of a civilization in which *nothing*, not even man himself, escapes technology—a civilization obsessed with its search for the "one best way," which inevitably leads to automation. This is another form of worldliness. The manipulation of the gospel to achieve successful results inevitably leads to slavery to the world and its powers.

As is the case with "secular Christianity," the basic question in relation to "culture Christianity" is the very significance of the gospel. I am afraid, nevertheless, that the proponents of

12. See Ellul, *The Technological Society*, trans. John Wilkinson (1954; New York: Random House-Vintage, 1970).

this type of Christianity are those least able to see the problem, since the majority of them live in the land where the techno- logical mentality exerts its greatest influence. It is not surprising that any criticism of this approach to evangelism should fall on deaf ears or be interpreted as a lack of interest in the propa- gation of the gospel. At this rate we may ask if the day is not close when missionary strategists employ B. F. Skinner's "be- havior conditioning"[13] and "Christianize" the world through the scientific control of environmental conditions and human genetics.

The proclamation of Jesus Christ as Lord of all is a call to turn to God from idols, to serve a living and true God (1 Thess. 1:9). Where there is no concept of the universal sovereignty of God there is no repentance, and where there is no repentance there is no salvation. Christian salvation is, among other things, liberation *from* the world as a closed system, *from* the world that has room only for a God bound by sociology, *from* the "consistent" world that rules out God's free, unpredict- able action. One cannot be a friend of this world without being an enemy of God (James 4:4). To love this world is to reject the love of God (1 John 2:15). The gospel, then, is a call not only to faith but also to repentance, to a break with the world. And it is only in the extent to which we are free from this world that we are able to serve our fellow men.

PART THREE: EVANGELISM AND INVOLVEMENT WITH THE WORLD

The Kingdom of God has arrived in the person of Jesus Christ. Eschatology has invaded history. God has clearly ex- pressed his plan to place all things under the rule of Christ. The powers of darkness have been defeated. Here and now, in union with Jesus Christ, man has within his reach the blessings of the new era.

However, the Kingdom of God has not yet arrived in all its fullness. Our salvation is "in hope" (Rom. 8:24). According to God's promise, "we wait for new heavens and a new earth

13. See Skinner, *Beyond Freedom and Dignity* (New York: Knopf, 1971).

in which righteousness dwells" (2 Pet. 3:13). Ours is the time of the patience of God, who does not wish "that any should perish, but that all should reach repentance (2 Pet. 3:9).

1. *Evangelism and Repentance Ethics*

The gospel is always proclaimed in opposition to an organized lie — the Great Lie that man realizes himself by pretending to be God, in autonomy from God; that his life consists in the things he possesses; that he lives for himself alone and is the owner of his destiny. All history is the history of this Lie and of the destruction it has brought upon man — the history of how man (as C. S. Lewis would aptly express it) has enjoyed the horrible liberty he has demanded and consequently has been enslaved.

The gospel involves a call to repentance from this Lie. The relation between the gospel and repentance is such that preaching the gospel is equivalent to preaching "repentance and forgiveness of sins" (Luke 24:47) or to testifying "of repentance to God and of faith in our Lord Jesus Christ" (Acts 20:21). Without this call to repentance there is no gospel. And repentance involves not merely a bad conscience — the "worldly grief" that produces death (2 Cor. 7:10) — but a change of attitude, a restructuring of one's scale of values, a reorientation of the whole of one's personality. It is not simply giving up habits condemned by a moralistic ethic but rather laying down the weapons of rebellion against God in order to return to him. It is not simply recognizing a psychological necessity but rather accepting the Cross of Christ as death to the world in order to live before God.

This call to repentance throws into relief the social dimension of the gospel. It comes to man enslaved by sin in a specific social situation, not to a "sinner" in the abstract. It is a change of attitude that becomes concrete in history. It is a turning from sin to God not only in the individual's subjective consciousness but *in the world*. This truth is clearly illustrated in John the Baptist's proclamation of the Kingdom (Matt. 3:1-12; Luke 3:7-14), concerning which I will simply make the following observations: (1) It has a strong eschatological note. The time of fulfillment of God's promises given through his prophets has come. The presence of Jesus Christ among men is the evidence that God is active in history to accomplish his purposes: "The kingdom of heaven is at hand" (Matt. 3:2). (2) This new reality places men in a position of crisis; they cannot continue to live as if nothing had happened; the Kingdom of God demands a new mentality, a reorientation of all their values, repentance (Matt. 3:2). Repentance has an eschatological significance: it marks the boundary between the old age and the new, between judgment and promise. (3) The change imposed involves a new lifestyle: "Bear fruits that befit repentance" (Luke 3:8). Without ethics there is no real repentance. (4) Repentance ethics is more than generalizations; it has to do with specific acts of self-sacrifice in concrete situations. To each one who becomes convicted by his message, John the Baptist has a fitting word, and in each case his ethical demand touches the point at which the man is enslaved to the powers of the old age and closed to God's action. To the people in general he says, "He who has two coats, let him share with him who has none; and he who has food, let him do likewise." To the tax collectors he says, "Collect no more than is appointed you." To the soldiers he says, "Rob no one by violence or by false accusation, and be content with your wages" (Luke 3:11-14). The crisis created by the Kingdom cannot be resolved by accepting concepts handed down by tradition ("We are descendants of Abraham"); it must be resolved by obedience to the ethics of the Kingdom.

Where there is no concrete obedience there is no repentance, and without repentance there is no salvation (Mark 1:4; Luke 13:3; Matt. 21:32; Acts 2:38; 3:19; 5:31). Salvation is man's return to God, but it is at the same time *also* man's return to his neighbor. In the presence of Jesus Christ, Zacchaeus the publican renounces the materialism that has enslaved him and accepts responsibility for his neighbor: "Behold, Lord, the half of my goods I give to the poor; and if I have defrauded anyone of anything, I restore it fourfold" (Luke 19:8). This renunciation and this commitment Jesus calls *salvation*: "Today salvation has come to this house" (Luke 19:9). Zacchaeus's response to the gospel call could not be expressed in more concrete or "worldly" terms. It is not merely a subjective experience; it is a moral

20

experience as well — an experience that affects his life precisely at that point at which the Great Lie had taken root, an experience that brings him out of himself and turns him toward his neighbor.

The gospel message, since it was first proclaimed by Jesus Christ, involves a call to repentance (Matt. 4: 17). Repentance is much more than a private affair between the individual and God. It is the complete reorientation of life in the world — among men — in response to the work of God in Jesus Christ. When evangelism does not take repentance seriously, it is because it does not take the world seriously, and when it does not take the world seriously it does not take God seriously. The gospel is not a call to social quietism. Its goal is not to take a man out of the world but to put him into it, no longer as a slave but as a son of God and a member of the body of Christ.

If Jesus Christ is Lord, men must be confronted with his authority over the totality of life. Evangelism is not, and cannot be, a mere offer of benefits achieved by Jesus Christ. Christ's work is inseparable from his person; the Jesus who died for our sins is the Lord of the whole universe, and the announcement of forgiveness in his name is inseparable from the call to repentance, the call to turn from "the rulers of this world" to the Lord of glory. But "no one can say Jesus is Lord except by the Holy Spirit" (1 Cor. 12: 3).

2. Evangelism and "Otherworldliness"

To "secular Christianity," obsessed with the life of this world, the only salvation possible is one that fits within the limits of this present age. It is essentially an economic, social, and political salvation, although sometimes (as in the case of the Latin American "liberation theology") an attempt is made to extend the concept to include "the making of a new man," the author of his own destiny.[14] Eschatology is absorbed by Utopia, and the Christian hope becomes confused with the worldly hope proclaimed by Marxism.

14. On this, see Gustavo Gutiérrez, *Teología de la liberación* (Lima: Editorial Universitaria, 1973), p. 132.

At the other extreme is the concept of salvation as the future salvation of the soul, in which present life has meaning only as a preparation for the "hereafter." History is assimilated by a futurist eschatology, and religion becomes a means of escape from present reality. The result is a total withdrawal from the problems of society in the name of "separation from the world." It is this misunderstanding of the gospel that has given rise to the Marxist criticism of Christian eschatology as the "opiate of the people."

That this concept of salvation is a misunderstanding of biblical soteriology should not have to be demonstrated. Unfortunately, it is a concept rooted so deep in the preaching of so many evangelical churches that we must stop to analyze the question.

In the first place, for Jesus Christ himself the mission entrusted to him by the Father was not limited to preaching the gospel. Matthew for example, summarizes Jesus' earthly ministry in these words: "And he went about all Galilee, *teaching* in their synagogues and *preaching* the gospel of the kingdom and *healing* every disease and every infirmity among the people" (Matt. 4:23; cf. 9:35). Even if evangelism is defined solely in terms of *verbal* communication—a definition that would leave much to be desired in light of the psychology of communication—we still must add, on the basis of the text, that evangelism was only one of the elements of Jesus' mission. Together with the *kērygma* went the *diaconia* and the *didachē*. This presupposes a concept of salvation that includes the whole man and cannot be reduced to the simple forgiveness of sins and assurance of unending life with God in heaven. A comprehensive mission corresponds to a comprehensive view of salvation. Salvation is wholeness. Salvation is total humanization. Salvation is eternal life, the life of the Kingdom of God, life that begins here and now (this is the meaning of the present tense of the verb "has eternal life" in the Gospel and the Epistles of John) and touches all aspects of man's being.

In the second place, Jesus' work had a social and political dimension. The individualism of "culture Christianity" to which I have referred above sees the Lord with only one eye, as an individualistic Jesus who is concerned with the salvation of

22

individuals. An unprejudiced reading of the Gospels shows us a Jesus who, in the midst of many political alternatives (Pharisaism, Sadduceeism, Zealotism, Essenism), personifies and proclaims a new alternative — the Kingdom of God. To say that Jesus is the Christ is to describe him in political terms, to affirm that he is *king*. His Kingdom is not of this world — not in the sense that it has nothing to do with the world but in the sense that it does not adapt itself to human politics. It is a Kingdom with its own politics, marked by sacrifice. Jesus is a king who "came not to be served but to serve, and to give his life as a ransom for many" (Mark 10:45). This service to the point of sacrifice belongs to the very essence of his mission. And this must be the distinctive sign of the community that acknowledges him as king. According to the politics of man, "those who are supposed to rule over the Gentiles lord it over them, and their great men exercise authority over them"; in the politics of the Kingdom of God, he who wants to be great "must be slave of all" (Mark 10:43-44). Thus Jesus confronts the power structures by denouncing their deep-seated ambition to rule and by proclaiming another alternative, based on love, service, dedication to others. He does not take refuge in "religion" or "spiritual things," as if his Kingdom had nothing to do with political and social life; rather, he demythologizes the politics of man and presents himself as the Servant-King, the creator and model of a community that submits to him as Lord and commits itself to live as he lived. The concrete result of Jesus' sacrifice for the sake of others, the culmination of which was reached in the Cross, is this community patterned after the Servant-King: a community in which each member gives according to his means and receives according to his needs, since "it is more blessed to give than to receive" (Acts 2:45; 4:34-35; 20:35); a community in which racial, cultural, social, and even sexual barriers disappear, since "Christ is all, and in all" (Col. 3:11; Gal. 3:28); a community of reconciliation with God and reconciliation among men (Eph. 2:11-22); and a community, finally, that serves as a base for the resistance against the conditioning of "the present evil age" and makes it possible for Jesus' disciples to live *in* the world without being *of* the world.

In the third place, the new creation in Jesus Christ becomes history in terms of good works. In Paul's words, God has "created [us] in Christ Jesus for good works, which God prepared beforehand, that we should walk in them" (Eph. 2:10). Jesus Christ "gave himself for us to redeem us from all iniquity and to purify for himself a people of his own who are zealous *for good deeds*" (Titus 2:14). The New Testament knows nothing of a gospel that makes a divorce between soteriology and ethics, between communion with God and communion with one's neighbor, between faith and works. The Cross is not only the negation of the validity of every human effort to gain God's favor by works of the law; it is *also* the demand for a new quality of life characterized by love — the opposite of an individualistic life centered on personal ambitions and indifferent to the needs of others. The significance of the Cross is both soteriological and ethical. This is so because in choosing the Cross Jesus not only created the indicative of the gospel ("By this we know love, that he laid down his life for us" — 1 John 3:16a) but also *simultaneously* provided the pattern for human life here and now ("And we ought to lay down our lives for the brethren" — 1 John 3:16b). Just as the Word became man, so also must love become good works if it is to be intelligible to men. This is what gives meaning to "worldly goods": they can be converted into instruments through which the life of the new age expresses itself. This is what John means when he says, "If anyone has the world's goods and sees his brother in need, yet closes his heart against him, how does God's love abide in him? Little children, let us not love in word or speech but *in deed and in truth*" (1 John 3:17). God's love expressed in the Cross must be made *visible* in the world through the church. The evidence of eternal life is not the simple confession of Jesus Christ as Lord, but "faith working through love" (Gal. 5:6). Jesus said, "Not every one who says to me, 'Lord, Lord,' shall enter the kingdom of heaven, but he who does the will of my Father who is in heaven" (Matt. 7:21).

In light of the biblical teaching, there is no place for an "otherworldliness" that does not result in the Christian's commitment to his neighbor, rooted in the gospel. There is no room for "eschatological paralysis" nor for a "social strike." There is no place for statistics on "how many souls die without Christ every minute" if they do not take into account how many of those who die are dying of hunger. There is no place for evangelism that passes by the man who was assaulted by thieves on the road from Jerusalem to Jericho and sees in him only a soul that must be saved. "What does it profit, my brethren, if a man says he has faith but has not works? Can his faith save him? If a brother or sister is ill-clad and in lack of daily food, and one of you says to them, 'Go in peace, be warmed and filled,' without giving them the things needed for the body, what does it profit? So faith by itself, if it has no works, is dead" (James 2: 14-17).

Only in the context of a soteriology that takes the world seriously is it possible to speak of the *oral* proclamation of the gospel. If men are to call on the name of the Lord, they must believe in him — "and how are they to believe in him of whom they have never heard?" (Rom. 10: 14). But the "word of reconciliation" entrusted to the church is the prolongation of the act of reconciliation in Jesus Christ. "For our sake he made him to be sin who knew no sin, so that in him we might become the righteousness of God" (2 Cor. 5: 21). It was thus — from within the situation of sinners, in an identification with them that he carried to its final consequences — that God in Christ reconciled the world to himself once and for all. This was the vertical movement of the gospel, the movement that in the Cross reached its darkest point. This is the heart of the gospel. But it is also the standard for evangelism. If God worked out reconciliation from within the human situation, the only fitting evangelism is that in which the Word becomes flesh in the world and the evangelist becomes "the slave of all" in order to win them to Christ (1 Cor. 9: 19-23). The first condition for genuine evangelism is the crucifixion of the evangelist. Without it the gospel becomes empty talk and evangelism becomes proselytism.

The church is not an otherworldly religious club that organizes forays into the world in order to gain followers through persuasive techniques. It is the sign of the Kingdom of God; it lives and proclaims the gospel here and now, *among men,* and waits for the consummation of God's plan to place all things under the rule of Christ. It has been free *from* the world, but it is *in* the world; it has been sent by Christ into the world just as Christ was sent by the Father (John 17:11-18). In other words, it has been given a mission oriented toward the building of a new humanity in which God's plan for man is accomplished, a mission that can be performed only through sacrifice. Its highest ambition cannot and should not be to achieve the success that leads to triumphalism but rather faithfulness to its Lord, which leads it to confess that "We are unworthy servants; we have only done what was our duty" (Luke 17:10). The confession can be made only by those who live by God's grace and desire that all their works result in the glory of the one who died for all, "that those who live might live no longer for themselves but for him who for their sake died and was raised" (2 Cor. 5:15).

Remarks on "Evangelism and the World"

As I begin I would like to express my deep appreciation to those of you who have sent your questions and comments in response to my paper. It has been a great encouragement to me to see that many of you do in fact share my concern for an evangelization that is more faithful to the gospel and less bound to worldly ideologies. Only one of my readers has said that he doesn't understand why my paper was ever written. Others may feel the same way, but they have kindly remained silent about it, and that has led me to believe that on the whole I have before me a rather sympathetic audience. I am therefore going to put all my cards on the table with the prayer that God lead us during these days to a clearer understanding of all that he expects of us as disciples of our Lord Jesus Christ in the twentieth century.

The task of answering all the questions that have been asked and amplifying all the points that have been said to need

amplification is an impossible task. May I plead for your for-
bearance if it looks as if I'm not taking into account a question
or comment you feel very strongly about. I've done my best
to select themes that are not only closely related to my topic
but also of the widest interest among those attending this
meeting.

In the first section of my paper I take a look at the use of
the term *cosmos* (world) in the New Testament. My purpose is
to show that according to the Scriptures the gospel is addressed
not to man as an isolated being called to respond to God with
no reference to his life context but rather to man in relation to
the world. The gospel always comes to man in relation to the
world of creation, the world that was made through Jesus Christ
and that is to be re-created through him. It comes to man
within the present order of existence, immersed in the transient
world of material possessions. It comes to man as a member of
humanity — the world for which Christ died, but at the same
time the world hostile to God and enslaved to the powers of
darkness. The aim of evangelization is, therefore, to lead man
not merely to a subjective experience of the future salvation of
his soul but to a radical reorientation of his life, including his
deliverance from slavery to the world and its powers on the
one hand, and his integration into God's purpose of placing all
things under the rule of Christ on the other. The gospel is not
addressed to man in a vacuum. It has to do with man's movement from the old humanity in Adam, which belongs to this
age that is passing away, into the new humanity in Christ,
which belongs to the age to come.

In the second section of my study I attempt to bring out
the significance of evangelization in relation to separation from
the world. Because Jesus has been made Lord and King over
all things through his death and resurrection, here and now,
in anticipation of the deliverance of the whole creation from
its bondage to decay, those who believe in him are delivered
from slavery to the world and its powers.

Salvation is not exclusively forgiveness of sins; it also involves deliverance from the dominion of darkness to a realm in
which Jesus is recognized as *Kyrios* of all the universe — the
Kingdom of God's beloved Son (Col. 1: 13).

May I here say parenthetically that the whole question of repentance could well have been considered in this second section rather than in the section dealing with evangelization and involvement with the world. Repentance does often have a negative connotation — it is a "turning away from" according to Scripture. If I have preferred to deal with it in the following section, it is simply because I want to emphasize not the act of repentance as such but rather the positive ethical implications of repentance for man's life in the world.

To resume, then, in the second section of my study I illustrate the problem of worldliness in evangelization by referring first to the confusion of the gospel with moralistic rules and practices. In reaction to this, one of my critics asks, "Why is legalism considered worldliness? The Bible is full of negative commands." Biblical negative injunctions taken in the context of salvation history are one thing. They are included in the law that the New Testament describes as "holy and just and good" (Rom. 7: 12). But rules and practices derived from "the tradition of the elders" — they are something else. I am not defending a new (antinomian) morality. What I am doing is pointing out the danger of reducing the Christian ethic to a set of rules and regulations that "have indeed an appearance of wisdom . . . but have no value in checking the indulgence of the flesh" (Col. 2: 23).

That there is a place for the use of the law in the Christian life (which in theology is known as "the third use of the law") no Christian should deny. The problem comes when the Christian life is turned into outward conformity to prohibitions and taboos that have no relation to the gospel. This, according to Paul, is a return to "the weak and beggarly elemental spirits" — a slavery to the world. But then, "aren't some of the negatives necessary safeguards for unstable Christians?" I see the need to raise up fences for the protection of small children. What concerns me is that these fences are often turned into cement walls within which there grows an "evangelical subculture," isolated from the real issues of life in the world.

If we think that we are in fact fostering separation from the world by maintaining a legalistic approach, let us not forget that one may conform to regulations such as "Do not smoke" and "Do not drink beer" and still remain in slavery to the collective egoism that conditions man's life in the world. Whenever we concentrate on "microethics" and slight the problems of "macroethics," we place ourselves under the Lord's judgment. "Woe to you, scribes and Pharisees, hypocrites; for you tithe mint and dill and cummin, and have neglected the weightier matters of the law, justice and mercy and faith; these you ought to have done without neglecting the others. You blind guides, straining at a gnat and swallowing a camel!" (Matt. 23: 23-24).

As a second illustration of the way in which worldliness can affect evangelization, I would like briefly to discuss the question of the adaptation of the gospel to the "spirit of the times." I cite two examples of such an accommodation: "secular Christianity" and "culture Christianity." As was to be expected, no one in this Congress really seems to disagree with my basic conclusion that "secular Christianity" is "not a mere 'restatement' of the gospel but rather a capitulation to a distorted concept of reality that is part of modern secularism." The situation is entirely different when it comes to the question of culture Christianity. One of my critics holds that my description of this type of Christianity is "so patently a caricature as to create static that cannot but block [the transmission of] many insights which people attending the conference will need." Another suggests that "What America is sharing with the world today is a parody of Christianity, tied to a materialistic philosophy and a truncated theology," and that although I come close to saying that, I "have not gone far enough." Whether my description is an overstatement or an understatement is not for me to decide. In view of the conflicting opinions, however, it does seem extremely important for this Congress to come to grips during these days with the theological and practical issues related to the problem of culture Christianity. I, for one, believe that it would be a great pity if by the end of our time together we have done little more than pat one another on the back and tell one another that we have the right theology, that the evangelical churches are on the right track, and that all we need now is the right strategy and the most efficient methods for the evangelization of the world.

Please allow me to underscore the fact that I have no intention of judging the motives of the propounders of North American culture Christianity. It is the Lord who judges; when he comes he will disclose the purposes of the heart and "if anyone builds on the foundation with gold, silver, precious stones, wood, hay, straw — each man's work will become manifest; for the day will disclose it" (1 Cor. 3:12-13).

My duty before God this morning is rather to try to make, with as much objectivity and fairness as I can, a theological evaluation of a type of Christianity that, having as its center the United States, has nonetheless spread widely throughout the world.

Granted, I could have chosen a variety of "culture Christianity" other than "the American Way of Life," as some of you have suggested.

I do not wish to imply that North American Christians are the only ones who may fall into the trap of confusing Scripture and culture. The fact, however, is that because of the role that the United States has had to play in world affairs as well as in the spread of the gospel, this particular form of Christianity, as no other today, has a powerful influence far beyond the borders of that nation. So, for those of you who wonder why I condemn the identification of Christianity with "the American Way of Life" but not with other national cultures, this is my answer. Behind my condemnation of this variety of culture Christianity lies a principle that applies to all varieties of culture Christianity — namely, that the church must be delivered from anything and everything in its culture that would prevent it from being faithful to the Lord in the fulfillment of its mission within and beyond its own culture. The big question that we Christians always have to ask ourselves with regard to our culture is which elements of it should be retained and utilized and which ones should go for the sake of the gospel.

When the church lets itself be squeezed into the mold of the world, it loses the capacity to see and, even more, to denounce the social evils in its own situation. Like the color-blind person who is able to distinguish certain colors but not others, the worldly church recognizes the personal vices traditionally condemned within its ranks but is unable to see the evil features of its surrounding culture. In my understanding, this is the only way one can explain, for example, how it is possible for North American culture Christianity to infuse racial and class segregation into its strategy for world evangelization The idea is that people *like* to be with those of their own race and class and that we must therefore plant segregated churches, which will undoubtedly grow faster. We are told that race prejudice "can be understood and should be made an aid to Christianization." No amount of exegetical maneuvering can ever bring this approach in line with the explicit teaching of the New Testament regarding the unity of men in the body of Christ: "Here there cannot be Greek and Jew, circumcised and uncircumcised, barbarian, Scythian, slave, free man, but Christ is all, and in all" (Col. 3:11); "There is neither Jew nor Greek, there is neither slave nor free, there is neither male nor female; for you are all one in Christ Jesus" (Gal. 3:28). How can a church that deliberately opts for segregation for the sake of numerical expansion speak to a divided world? By what authority can it preach man's reconciliation with God through the death of Christ while at the same time denying man's reconciliation with man through the same death, when both are equally important aspects of the gospel (Eph. 21:14-18)? As Dr. Samuel Moffett put it at the Berlin Congress, "When racial discrimination enters the churches, it is something more than a crime against humanity; it is an act of defiance against God himself."

It is perhaps in this context that I should say a word about the prophetic ministry today, as I have been asked to do. For it is only in the measure in which the church itself is the incarnation of God's purpose to put all things under the Lordship of Christ that it can denounce the evils in society which are a denial of God's original purpose for man. There is an internal connection between the life of the church and its prophetic ministry, and between the prophetic ministry of the church and its evangelization. The church is called here and now to be what God intends the whole of society to be. In its prophetic ministry it lays open the evils that frustrate the purpose of God in society; in its evangelization it seeks to integrate men into that purpose of God the full realization of which is to take place in the Kingdom to come. Consequently, wherever the church fails as a prophet it also fails as an evangelist.

A church that is not faithful to the gospel in all its dimensions inevitably becomes an instrument of the status quo. The gospel is meant to place the totality of life under the universal Lordship of Jesus Christ, not to produce cultic sects; it is an open break with the status quo of the world. Therefore, a gospel that leaves untouched our life in the world — in relationship to the world of men as well as in relationship to the world of creation — is not the Christian gospel, but culture Christianity, adjusted to the mood of the day.

This kind of gospel has no teeth. It is a gospel that the "free consumers" of religion will want to receive because it is cheap and it demands nothing of them. The gospel in the first century was, according to Canon Michael Green, "politically suspect, socially disruptive." The gospel of culture Christianity today is a message of conformism, a message that is easily tolerated even by those who do not accept it, because it doesn't disturb anybody. The racist can continue to be a racist; the exploiter can continue to be an exploiter. Christianity for them will be something that runs alongside life but will not cut through it.

A truncated gospel is utterly insufficient as a basis for churches that want to be able "to generate their own Calvins, Wesleys, Wilberforces and Martin Luther Kings." It can serve as the basis for nothing more than unfaithful churches, strongholds of racial and class discrimination, religious clubs with a message that has no relevance to practical life in the social, economic, and political spheres.

Now perhaps I'm in a position to explain my reservations about the emphasis on numbers in relation to the Christian mission. One of my readers has commented, "I hope the author is not saying that those who advocate church growth and who think that the number of converts is important necessarily fall into the category of those who opt for superficial conversion. Some of us believe that both quality and quantity are important." My answer is that the numerical expansion of the church is a legitimate concern for anyone who takes the Scriptures seriously. As I have stated in my paper, this concern as such should not be questioned. "God desires that all men be saved and come to the knowledge of the truth." John R. Mott's concern to bring the gospel "within the reach of every creature within this generation" is a biblical concern and should be a part of our Christian commitment.

Furthermore, there is nothing to insure that those who win fewer people for Christ will be able to show forth higher-quality Christians as a result of their work. The point, however, is that quality is at least as important as quantity, if not more, and that faithfulness to the gospel should therefore never be sacrificed for the sake of quantity. When the gospel is truncated in order to make it easy for all men to become Christians, from the very outset the basis is laid for an unfaithful church. As the seed, so the tree, and as the tree, so its fruit. It follows that the real question with regard to the growth of the church is not successful numerical expansion — a success patterned after worldly standards — but faithfulness to the gospel, which will surely lead us to pray and work for more people to become Christians. I am for quantity, but for quantity in the context of faithfulness to the gospel. I am for numbers, but for numbers of people who have heard a presentation of the gospel in which the issues of faith and unbelief have been made clear and the choice between grace and judgment has been a *free choice.*

In contrast to the "gospel of the sword," the gospel of the Cross leaves open the possibility for people to reject Christ because they find his claims too costly; the gospel of the Cross admits that there are cases in which it is better not to have certain people in the church, even though that means a smaller membership. Was that not Jesus' attitude in dealing with the rich young ruler (Mark 10: 17-22) and with the multitudes at the peak of his popularity (Luke 14: 25-32)? Furthermore, if a truncated gospel necessarily results in churches that are themselves a denial of the gospel, in speaking of the numerical expansion of the church it is not out of place to ask what kind of church it is that is being multiplied. It may be that such multiplication turns out to be a multiplication of apostasy! Obviously, then, the real question is not numerical growth per se, but faithfulness to the gospel.

In my paper, I state that culture Christianity has not only turned the gospel into a cheap product but has also turned the strategy for the evangelization of the world into a problem of technology. One of my critics describes my reservations with regard to this approach to world evangelization as "a Latin American hangup." This is an *ad hominem* argument. Latin Americans have not made any particular contribution to the definition of the limitations of technology when it comes to man. In fact, it is to a Frenchman, Jacques Ellul, that I appeal when I refer to the "technological mentality" that conditions North American culture Christianity—the mentality according to which *efficiency* is an absolute criterion on the basis of which one should seek, in all areas of human life, the systematization of methods and resources to obtain preestablished results. It is to this absolutization of efficiency at the expense of the integrity of the gospel that I object. Technology has its place in evangelization; it would be foolish for me to deny that. The problem comes when technology is made a substitute for Scripture on the assumption that what we need is a better strategy rather than a more biblical gospel and a more faithful church. The picture of the church that one derives from the New Testament is certainly not that of a powerful organization that has achieved success in its conquest of the world by the masterly use of human devices and techniques. It is rather the picture of a community experiencing a new (supernatural) reality—the Kingdom of God—to which "the Lord called day by day those who were being saved." As Michael Green has put it, "In the early church the maximum impact was made by the changed lives and quality of community among the Christians." Changed lives and quality of community—that is to say, faithfulness to the gospel in practical life—do not come through technology, but through the Word and the Spirit of God. Technology will never make up for our failure to let the gospel mold our lives!

Furthermore, if the strategy for world evangelization is tied to technology, then obviously the ones who have the final word on the strategy that the church is to follow in the future will be those who have the technical know-how as well as the resources to make the necessary investigations. The church in the Third World has nothing to say on the matter. Isn't this again a way to identify the gospel with worldly power, a way to perpetuate the domination/dependence patterns that have on the whole characterized missionary work for the last hundred years? What becomes of the universal character and the unity of the church of Christ? But perhaps these things don't matter after all—perhaps the real problem is to produce the greatest number of Christians at the least possible cost in the shortest possible time!

If I have dealt mainly with North American culture Christianity, it is not because I am unaware of the fact that in other situations Christians may fall into the trap of accommodating the gospel to their own culture. It is rather because of the broad influence of *this* variety of culture Christianity in evangelical circles around the world. But I have no difficulty in accepting the fact that, as someone has put it, "There is a parallel danger in developing countries where national goals and leaders are idolized by mass cult," or that, as someone else has expressed it, "It is questionable whether we can accept in the Christian context some of the cultural aspects of other nations." There is, then, a place for the question of how we non-Americans can avoid creating our own version of culture Christianity. I will, however, attempt to kill two birds with one stone by taking up that question in connection with a similar question raised by an American who acknowledges the problem of culture Christianity in his own situation: "How can I overcome culture Christianity, since I cannot get out of my own culture?"

In the first place, let us recognize the conditioning that the world and "the things that are in the world" exercise over us, even in relation to our service to God. All too often we are ready to condemn the distortions that others have openly allowed to come into their theology through the front door, but we remain blind to the distortions that have come into our evangelization through the back door. The orthodoxy of our creed is no guarantee of our own faithfulness to the gospel in either our life or our service. The key word here is *humility*.

In the second place, let us be aware of the need to place our lives and activities continually under the judgment of the Word of God. We cannot simply assume that we have the truth and that everything else, including our evangelization and our ethics, will just fall in line with that truth. The purpose of theology is not merely to reaffirm what previous generations have said but to bring the whole life and mission of the church into line with God's revelation. All our assumptions and methods must therefore be examined in the light of Scripture. The gospel itself, not success, is the criterion with which we must evaluate our work. The key phrase here is *theological renewal*.

In the third place, let us take seriously the unity of the body of Christ throughout the world. If the church is really one, then there is no place for the assumption that one section of the church has a monopoly on the interpretation of the gospel and the definition of the Christian mission. Those of us who live in the Third World cannot and should not be satisfied with the rote repetition of doctrinal formulas or the indiscriminate application of canned methods of evangelization imported from the West.

I am not advocating here a relativistic approach to theology. I am calling for the recognition of a problem and a change of attitude with regard to the making of theology and the planning of world evangelization. The problem is that one version of culture Christianity based on an inadequate theological foundation and conditioned by "fierce pragmatism" — the kind of pragmatism that in the political sphere has produced Watergate — is being regarded by some as the official evangelical position and the measure of orthodoxy around the world. The change of attitude being called for involves the renunciation of ethnocentrism and the promotion of theological cross-fertilization among different cultures. Under the Spirit of God, each culture has something to contribute in connection with the understanding of the gospel and its implications for the life and mission of the church. North American culture Christianity should not be allowed to deprive us of the possibility that we *all* — whatever our race, nationality, language, or culture — as equal members in the one body of Christ "attain the unity of the faith and of the knowledge of the Son of God, to mature manhood, to the measure of the stature of the fullness of Christ" (Eph. 4: 13). The key word here is *cross-fertilization*.

I believe with all my heart that if with a humble spirit, recognizing our need of deliverance from the world, we come to the Word of God and are willing to learn from one another, the Spirit of God will work in us that we may be not merely a reflection of society with its materialism but "the salt of the earth" and "the light of the world."

The third section of my paper deals with evangelization of and involvement with the world. Here I first propose that repentance, conceived as a reorientation of one's whole personality, throws into relief the social dimension of the gospel, for it involves a turning from sin to God not only in the individual subjective consciousness but *in the world*. Without ethics, I say, there is no repentance. Am I slighting the personal aspect of evangelization, as I have been accused of doing? I don't think I am. What I am doing is recognizing that man is a social being and that there is no possibility for him to be converted to Christ and to grow as a Christian except as a social being. Man never turns to God as a sinner in the abstract; he always turns to God in a specific social situation.

One objection that has been made regarding my emphasis on repentance is that the call to repentance is not an essential aspect of the gospel. Jesus' summons to repent "for the kingdom of heaven is at hand," I am told, "is addressed to the Jews," and we should not confuse Jesus' approach to the Jews with what would apply in the age of grace. "The Jews rejected Jesus' proposals, and he then offered, through his apostles and the Holy Spirit, the salvation to all by grace." When we come to the preaching of the gospel in the Gentile world—so this argument goes—the emphasis should be on faith rather than on repentance.

What we have before us is a very serious question indeed. The argument has to do with nothing less than the very content of the message we are to proclaim to the world. There is no use in assuming that we all agree on the gospel that has been entrusted to us and that all we need now is more efficient methods to communicate it. If we think so, we deceive ourselves. The gospel of repentance is one thing; the gospel of cheap grace is something else. Time doesn't allow me to discuss the question in full. Let me limit myself to the following observations:

1. In the Great Commission as it appears in Luke 24: 47, Jesus himself defines the content of the message that his disciples are to proclaim to the nations as "repentance and for-

giveness of sins . . . in his name." That the early heralds of the message faithfully followed his instructions is attested by the book of Acts. Repentance was an integral part not only of Peter's and the other early apostles' preaching among the Jews (Acts 2:38; 3:19; 5:31) but also of Paul's preaching among the Gentiles (Acts 17:30; 20:21; 26:18). To those who would point to Acts 16:31 ("Believe in the Lord Jesus, and you will be saved, you and your household"), let me point out that verse 31 is followed by verse 32: "And they spoke the word of the Lord to him and to all that were in the home." To those who call my attention to 1 Corinthians 15:1-5 as a passage that contains a full synthesis of Paul's message and yet makes no reference to repentance, let me point out that the passage doesn't make explicit reference to faith either; the emphasis is on the facts of the gospel, not on the appropriation of it.

2. It is true that the words *repentance* and *repent* are not commonly found in the Pauline Epistles (but see Rom. 2:4; 2 Cor. 7:9; and 2 Tim. 2:25). This must not lead us, however, to contrast Paul's emphasis on justification by faith with Jesus' call to repentance. Justification can no more be separated from regeneration than forgiveness can be separated from repentance. Along with all the other writers of the New Testament, Paul holds that the God who justifies and forgives is also the God who delivers from slavery to sin. As Joachim Jeremias puts it, "God's acquittal is not only forensic, it is not 'as if,' not a mere word, but it is God's word that works and creates life. God's word is always an effective word. As an antedonation of God's final acquittal, justification is pardon in the fullest sense. It is the beginning of a new life, a new existence, a new creation through the gift of the Holy Spirit." Justification, therefore, cannot be separated from the fruits of justification, just as faith cannot be separated from works. We do a great disservice to Paul if we fail to see that the same moral transformation to which the Gospels and Acts point when they use the term *repentance* is assumed by his teaching on dying to sin and being raised to life (Rom. 6) and on the new creation in which the old has passed away and the new is come (1 Cor. 5:17) and on the contrast between gratifying the desires of the flesh and walking by the Spirit (Gal. 5).

3. Faith without repentance is not saving faith but presumptuous believism. The aim of the gospel is to produce in us faith, but faith that works through love. Without the works of love there is no genuine faith. If it is true that we are not saved by works, it is also true that the faith that saves is the faith that works. As Luther put it, "Faith alone justifies, but faith is never alone." The indicative of the gospel and the imperative of Christian ethics may be distinguished but must never be separated.

It is hard to avoid the conclusion that the basis for the denial of repentance as an essential aspect of the gospel is not the result of a careful study of Scripture but another expression of the attempt to accommodate the gospel to the world for the sake of numbers, a presumption that the message must be reduced to a minimum in order to make it possible for all men to want to become Christian. As a matter of fact, easy salvation (what Bonhoeffer calls "cheap grace") is part and parcel of the variety of culture Christianity to which I referred before. My emphasis on repentance naturally raises the question of whether repentance, as I define it, does not ask too much of a new convert. May I ask in response how much is too much? The most that man can give either to the living God or to the false gods of this world is his own life. But is that not precisely what God demands of man? Granted that following conversion there is a process of growth in which one comes to an increasing understanding of the implications of his commitment to Christ. The point, however, is that a conversion without repentance — that is to say, a spurious conversion — can only lead to a Christian life without repentance — that is to say, a spurious Christian life. Birth and growth form an organic unity; the only faith that will *grow* in obedience is the faith that is *born* in obedience to God's command to repent. Becoming a Christian is not a religious change, in which one becomes the adherent of a cult, but a reorientation of the whole man in relation to God, to men, and to creation. It is not the mere addition of new patterns imposed on the old — such as church attendance, Bible reading, and prayer — but a restructuring of one's whole personality, a reorientation of one's whole life in the world. If a person doesn't see that this is what he is in for with Christ, he is not in. The task of the evangelist in communicating the gospel is not to make it easier, so that people will respond positively, but to make it clear. Neither Jesus nor his apostles ever reduced the demands of the gospel in order to make converts. God's kindness, which is meant to lead to repentance, provides the only solid basis for discipleship. Cheap grace simply will not suffice. He who accommodates the gospel to the mood of the day in order to make it more palatable does so because he has forgotten the nature of Christian salvation; it is not man's work but God's. "With men it is impossible, but not with God, for all things are possible with God" (Mark 10:27).

The future of the church does not depend on our ability to persuade people to give intellectual assent to a truncated gospel but on our faithfulness to the full gospel of our Lord Jesus Christ and God's faithfulness to his Word. "Half gospels have no dignity and no future," said P. T. Forsyth. "Like the famous mule, they have neither pride of ancestry nor hope of posterity."

Under the heading "evangelism and other-worldliness" I speak of two extreme positions with regard to the present world. The one is that which conceives of salvation as something that fits within the limits of the present age in terms of social, economic, and political liberation. The personal dimensions of salvation are eliminated or minimized. The individual is lost in society. There is little or no place for forgiveness from guilt and sin or for the resurrection of the body and immortality. This world is all that there is, and the fundamental mission of the church must therefore be conceived in terms of the transformation of this world through politics. At the other end of the scale is the view according to which salvation is reduced to the future salvation of the soul and the present world is nothing more than a preparatory stage for life in the hereafter. The social dimensions of salvation are completely (or almost completely) disregarded, and the church becomes a redeemed ghetto charged with the mission of rescuing souls from the present evil world. Didn't Jesus say, "My kingdom is not of this world"? Why should the church be concerned for the poor and the needy? Didn't he say, "The poor you always have with you"? The only responsibility that the church has toward the world, then, is the preaching of the gospel and the planting of churches: "There are many goods the church *may* do of course, but they do not belong to its essential mission."

I maintain that both of these views are based on incomplete gospels and that the greatest need of the church today is the recovery of the full gospel of our Lord Jesus Christ—the whole gospel for the whole man for the whole world.

On the one hand, the gospel cannot be reduced to social, economic, and political categories, nor the church to an agency for human improvement. Even less can the gospel be confused with a political ideology or the church with a political party. As Christians, we are called to witness to the transcendental, other-worldly Christ, through whose work we have received forgiveness of sins and reconciliation to God. We believe in man's need of a new birth through a personal encounter with God in Jesus Christ, by the action of the Holy Spirit, through the proclamation of the Word of God. And we maintain that nothing can take the place of spiritual regeneration in the making of new men. This is biblical soteriology, and we are fully committed to it. We cannot accept the equation of salvation with the satisfaction of bodily needs, social amelioration, or political liberation.

On the other hand, there is no biblical warrant to view the church as an other-worldly community dedicated to the salvation of souls or to limit its mission to the preaching of man's reconciliation to God through Jesus Christ. As Elton Trueblood has put it, "A genuine gospel will always be concerned with human justice rather than with the mere cultivation of a warm inner glow." The responsibility of defining that relation between the gospel and the concern for human justice falls within the province of another paper—the one by my colleague Samuel Escobar.* I will limit myself to answering a few key questions out of the many that have been sent to me in response to my own paper:

1. *"How involved should we be in justice and economics?"* The fact is that, whether we like it or not, we are already involved. Politics and economics are unavoidable; they are a part of the

*Ed. Note: The reference is to "Evangelism and Man's Search for Freedom, Justice, and Fulfillment," by Samuel Escobar. This paper also appears in *Let the Earth Hear His Voice,* pp. 307-18.

reality that surrounds us while we are in the world. The real question, therefore, is, "Since we are in fact involved, how can we make sure that our involvement is faithful to the gospel of our Lord Jesus Christ?" Even though we may try to avoid taking any notice of politics and economics, *they* always take notice of us.

2. *"Is the change of the structure of society a part of the evangelistic mandate?"* The same question, in essence, is asked in other words: "Are you not confusing the two kingdoms?" Here I can only reiterate that "the imperative of the evangelical ethic forms an indivisible whole with the indicative of the gospel." Another way to put it would be to say that the two tables of the law belong together, or that concern for man's reconciliation with God cannot be separated from concern for social justice, or that the evangelistic mandate has to be fulfilled in the context of obedience to the cultural mandate, or that the Kingdom of God manifests itself in the midst of the kingdoms of men, or simply that the mission of the church cannot be separated from its life. I refuse, therefore, to drive a wedge between a primary task — namely, the proclamation of the gospel — and a secondary (at best) or even optional (at worst) task of the church. In order to be obedient to its Lord, the church should never do anything that is not essential; therefore, nothing that the church does in obedience to its Lord is unessential. Why? Because love for God is inseparable from love for our neighbors; because faith without works is dead; because hope includes the restoration of all things to the Kingdom of God. I am not confusing the two kingdoms; I do not expect the ultimate salvation of man or society through good works or political action. I am merely asking that we take seriously the relevance of the gospel to the totality of man's life in the world. The only possible alternative is to say that God is interested in our calling him "Lord, Lord" but not in our obedience to his will in relation to such crucial issues as social injustice and oppression, famine, war, racism, illiteracy, and the like.

3. *"Is it legitimate to say that Jesus was a political king? Are you not defining politics in your own terms?"* When I say that in describing Jesus as the Christ we are in fact describing him in political terms, I do not mean that he involved himself in what we today

consider political action in a narrow sense, but rather that the title *Messiah* (king) is a political description. He did not come to create a religion but to accomplish God's purpose of placing all things under his government. Those who acknowledge him as Lord are not only reconciled to God but also given in him a model for human life, life in the *polis*. Here and now, in this world, his disciples are called to bring their personal and corporate life into line with the will of God expressed in the ethics of the Kingdom, the central principle of which is love.

4. *"In emphasizing the ethical, how do we avoid moralism and legalism in our teaching?* By teaching the true nature of Christian morality — namely, that morality is not outward subjection to rules and norms but heartfelt obedience in response to God, that the essence of Christian morality is gratitude. The way to avoid the danger of falling into moralism and legalism is not to eliminate the ethical demands of the gospel but to see that obedience is an essential aspect of faith's response to the gospel and is always obedience by the power of God, who works in us through the Spirit.

5. *"What can the church do, when the problems are so staggering?"* The church has not been called to solve all the problems but to be faithful to God with what it has. The greatest contribution that the church can make to the world is to be all that it is supposed to be. Among other things, it should be the following:

First, it should be a community of *reconciliation*. In the midst of a fragmented world, here is a community in which all barriers that divide disappear, in which men learn to welcome one another as Christ has welcomed them, for the glory of God. Second, it should be a community of *personal authenticity*. In the midst of a world in which each man has to fit into the mold imposed on him by his society, here is a community in which everyone is accepted as he is and encouraged to develop fully as individuals made in the image of God. Third, it should be a community of *serving and giving*. In the midst of a world in which man lives to be served and to receive, here is a community in which man lives to serve and to give.

This brings me to a conclusion. Our greatest need is for a more biblical gospel and a more faithful church. We may go away from this Congress with a nice set of papers and statements that will be filed away and forgotten, and with the memories of a big, impressive world meeting. Or we may go away with the conviction that we have magic formulas for the conversion of people. My own hope and prayer is that we go away with a repentant attitude with regard to our enslavement to the world and our arrogant triumphalism, with a sense of our inability to break away from our bonds and yet also with a great confidence in God, the Father of our Lord Jesus Christ, who "by the power at work within us is able to do far more abundantly than all we ask or think. To him be glory in the church and in Christ Jesus, to all generations for ever and ever. Amen."

Spiritual Conflict

We believe that we are engaged in constant spiritual warfare with the principalities and powers of evil, who are seeking to overthrow the church and frustrate its task of world evangelisation. We know our need to equip ourselves with God's armour and to fight this battle with the spiritual weapons of truth and prayer. For we detect the activity of our enemy, not only in false ideologies outside the church but also inside it in false gospels which twist Scripture and put man in the place of God. We need both watchfulness and discernment to safeguard the biblical gospel. We acknowledge that we ourselves are not immune to worldliness of thought and action, that is, to a surrender to secularism. For example, although careful studies of church growth, both numerical and spiritual, are right and valuable, we have sometimes neglected them. At other times, desirous to ensure a response to the gospel, we have compromised our message, manipulated our hearers through pressure techniques, and become unduly preoccupied with statistics or even dishonest in our use of them. All this is worldly. The church must be in the world; the world must not be in the church. (Eph. 6:12; 2 Cor. 4:3, 4; Eph. 6:11, 13-18; 2 Cor. 10:3-5; 1 John 2:18-26; 4:1-3; Gal. 1:6-9; 2 Cor. 2:17; 4:2; John 17:15)

—*Lausanne Covenant, Clause 12*

The Lausanne Congress could have been nothing more than an enormous (and expensive) launching platform for a vast program of worldwide evangelization that avoided the theological problems posed by evangelization for the church today. There is reason to believe that a large percentage of the participants shared the pragmatic viewpoint expressed in the editorial of a well-known evangelical magazine in North America shortly before the Congress. It stated that since the Berlin Congress (1966) had established the theological framework for evangelization (the key word had been *evangelism*), the 1974 Congress would concentrate on the practical aspects of that task (the key word would be *evangelization*). Fortunately, as this vast gathering developed, the theological problems imposed themselves upon the discussions and resulted in the Lausanne Covenant, a document that questions positions traditionally entrenched in the evangelical churches.

The twelfth paragraph of the Covenant warns against worldliness in the church, placing this warning in the context of the spiritual conflict to which the New Testament often refers. It points to the subtle ways in which the world conditions the church, even to the extent of shaping its message and evangelistic methods. It concludes with an echo of John 17: 16: "The church must be in the world; the world must not be in the church." In this essay we will take this paragraph as an invitation to reflect upon the meaning of the world in its negative sense (to which the Covenant refers), the influence the world exerts upon the church, and the role the gospel must play in the church if it is to be faithful to God in its confrontation with the world.

THE WORLD TODAY

The dominant characteristic of the modern world is the rapid growth of a new type of society — the consumer society — as the culmination of the technological revolution that began in the nineteenth century. The phenomenon of internal migration has compounded the effects of the dizzying worldwide growth of an urban civilization that is defined chiefly by its reverance for technological products. Virtually all of humanity today participates in the life of the city. As Jacques Ellul has observed, "We are in the city, even if we live in the country, for today the country (and soon this will be true even of the immense Asian steppe) is only an annex of the city."[1] His as-

1. Ellul, *The Meaning of the City*, trans. Dennis Pardee (Grand Rapids: William B. Eerdmans, 1970), p. 147.

sertion not only underscores a statistically verifiable fact —
namely, the tremendous demographic expansion of the urban
center[2] — but also constitutes a recognition of the global character of the "consumer mentality" that characterizes modern
society in both the developed and underdeveloped countries.[3]

The consumer society is the offspring of technology and
capitalism. Historically it appeared in the West when the
bourgeoisie assumed political power and made technology the
instrument of its own enrichment. Private property, which in
pre-industrial society had given security to the common people,
no longer fulfilled a social function but was transformed into
an absolute right.[4] The great capitalistic industries emerged.
Their goal became an ever-increasing production rate, although
a good portion of the products would be trivialities — "articles
which, though reckoned as part of the income of the nation,
either should not have been produced until other articles had
been produced in sufficient abundance, or should not have been
produced at all."[5] Any activity not directly related to industrial
development was relegated to a lower plane. Labor relations
came to be governed by personal convenience for the industrial
proprietors, for whom property is a means of personal enrichment rather than an instrument of service to society. The mass
media (especially radio and television) came to be used to condition the consumers to a lifestyle in which they work to make
money, make money to buy things, and buy things to find

2. At the beginning the nineteenth century there was no city with
more than a million inhabitants; in 1945 there were already thirty, and by
1955 there were sixty. Some cities are growing at a fantastic rate. Sao Paulo,
for instance, grew by over a half million every year during the mid-1970s.
It is estimated that Mexico City will have a population of thirty million by
the end of this century.

3. To understand the applicability of the expression "consumer society"
to urban centers in even underdeveloped societies, it is helpful to consult
the work by Juan Luis Segundo, *The Hidden Motives of Pastoral Action: Latin
American Reflections*, trans. John Drury (1972; Maryknoll, N.Y.: Orbis Books,
1978). He distinguishes between the "consumer society," which exists in
any urban concentration, and the "abundant society," which is found only
in the countries in which industrialization has reached its greatest
development.

4. This thesis has been elaborated by R. H. Tawney in *The Acquisitive
Society* (New York: Harcourt, Brace and World, 1948), pp. 8-19, 52-83.

5. Tawney, pp. 37-39.

value for themselves. As Ellul has pointed out, lifestyle in the technological society is shaped by advertising.[6] Advertising is controlled by those whose interests are aligned with a constant increase in production, which in turn depends upon a level of consumption possible only in a society that believes that to live is to possess.[7] In this way, technology is placed in the service of capital in order to impose the ideology of consumerism.

Analysts of contemporary society generally hold that the developed countries are making a transition from the first to the second technological revolution. If in the first revolution man's work was replaced by that of the machine, in the second revolution man's very thinking is being replaced by the machine. The era of automation and cybernetics is upon us. Today as never before we have at our disposal the technological resources to put an end to one of the most pressing problems haunting the masses in three-fourths of the globe: hunger. Nevertheless, technology maintains its ties with the economic interests of a minority who remain untouched by the misery of "the disinherited of the earth." The emergence of huge multinational industrial conglomerates has been perhaps the most important factor in the exportation of the consumer ideology to the Third World. The urban centers are not merely the base of operations for these industries; their very existence depends upon their capacity to become a coordinated system and organize all of life as a function of production and consumption. For this reason, the city gradually presses man into a materialistic mold, a mold that gives absolute value to *things* as status

6. Ellul, *The Technological Society*, trans. John Wilkinson (1954; New York: Vintage Books, 1964), pp. 406-7.
7. "If the overriding economic principle is that we produce more and more, the consumer must be prepared to want — that is, to consume — more and more. Industry does not rely on the consumer's spontaneous desires for more and more commodities. By building in obsolescence it often forces him to buy new things when the old ones could last much longer. By changes in styling of products, dresses, durable goods and even food, it forces him psychologically to buy more than he might need or want. But industry, in its need for increased production, does not rely on the consumer's needs and wants but to a considerable extent on advertising, which is the most important offensive against the consumer's right to know what he wants" (Erich Fromm, *The Revolution of Hope: Toward a Humanized Technology* [New York: Bantam Books, 1968], pp. 38-39).

symbols, a mold that leaves no room for questions about the meaning of work or the purpose of life.

The present industrial system serves capital, not man. As a result, it turns man into a one-dimensional being — a cog in the massive machinery that operates by the laws of supply and demand and is the principal cause of global environmental pollution. It creates a yawning, ever-widening chasm between the haves and have-nots on a national level and between the rich countries and the poor countries on an international level. Today, despite technological advances and industrial expansion unprecedented in human history, the underdeveloped nations are further than ever from the solution to their problems. The technological age, which brought in the harnessing of atomic energy and the conquest of outer space, is paradoxically the age of hunger.[8] In general, the rich nations refuse to recognize the relationship between their own economic development and the underdevelopment of the poor nations.[9] International organizations find their hands tied because they have no means of eliciting the cooperation of the great industrial countries.[10] As Josué de Castro has affirmed, "the official doctrine of development of the great western powers is very narrow, and is dominated by selfish concerns derived from an unadulterated colonialist inspiration."[11] Avarice is the very cement of the economic system that has engendered the consumer society.

8. It is estimated that at present sixty-five percent of the world's population suffers from hunger. The hunger zones coincide with the underdeveloped zones which are subject to economic exploitation by the rich nations. For more on this, see Reginald H. Fuller and Brian K. Rice, *Christianity and the Affluent Society* (Grand Rapids: William B. Ecrdmans, 1966) — especially Chapter 9, "Starvation by 1980," pp. 150-66.

9. The remarks of U.S. Senator Mark Hatfield at the Conservative Baptist Association of America convention in 1974 are noteworthy: "As Americans we must no longer assume that our extra abundance can feed the hungry of the world. Our surplus supply is not enough. Rather, the world will be fed only by the sharing of resources which the rich of the world have assumed to be their unquestioned possession, and that sharing involves the changing of values and eating patterns which the affluent have barely even questioned" (*Eternity*, November 1974, p. 38).

10. The difficulty of enlisting the help of the rich countries to combat hunger has been amply indicated by the meetings of the United Nations Conference on Trade and Development, which have yet to produce any concrete measures for solving the problem.

11. Castro, *El libro negro del hambre* (Buenos Aires: EUDEBA, 1971), p. 88.

In the modern world, consumerism has even invaded the areas where poverty reigns. In both the wealthy zones and the poverty belts of the large urban centers, the mass media spread their image of happiness — the image of *homo consumens*. As a result, the whole world is becoming a "global village," united around the principle of consumerism. Although the underdeveloped countries are consumers on a level much lower than that of the developed countries, the mentality that gives a preferred status to consumer goods prevails in both. The obsession of the wealthy is what Josué de Castro has aptly described as "ostentatious consumerism": "the consumerism of imported luxury items with little or no usefulness in the collective social and economic development and which in fact substantially impairs the progress of the economy."[12] On the other hand, the poor desire the upward social mobility that would enable them not only to satisfy their most basic needs (food, clothing, and shelter), but also to acquire all those goods advertised as status symbols (especially a car and electrical appliances). The so-called "revolution of rising expectations" has an ambiguous value; although it clearly entails a search for respect and human dignity on the part of indigenous peoples, it also reflects their conditioning by the mass media with respect to the concept of *homo consumens* as the ideal for mankind.

Behind the materialism that characterizes consumer society lie the powers of destruction to which the New Testament refers. The Apostle Paul perceived that the principalities and powers of evil were entrenched in the ideological structures that oppress men. Although this is not the place to elaborate upon this subject,[13] I believe that the two following observations regarding the Pauline concept of the relation between "the world" (in its negative sense) and demonic powers are relevant:

1. The world is a system in which evil is organized in opposition to good. Nevertheless, it is its connection with Satan and his forces that gives it that character. Satan is "the god of this world" (2 Cor. 4:4; cf. John 12:31; 14:30; 16:11; 1 John

---

12. Castro, p. 69.

13. Various New Testament studies (among them works by Berkhof, Caird, Barth, and Whitely) have dealt with the field of Pauline demonology and shown its relevance to social ethics. See John H. Yoder, *The Politics of Jesus* (Grand Rapids: William B. Eerdmans, 1972), pp. 135-62.

5: 19); his forces are "the powers that rule this world" (1 Cor. 2: 6 TEV), "the cosmic powers . . . the authorities and potentates of this dark world" (Eph. 6: 12 NEB), "the elemental spirits of the universe" (Gal. 4: 3, 9; Col. 2: 8, 20).[14] This apocalyptic vision of the world permeates the Pauline Epistles and points to a cosmic dimension not only of sin but also of Christian redemption. The work of Jesus Christ cannot be understood apart from this background.[15]

2. The demonic powers enslave man in the world through the structures and systems he treats as absolutes. In an important article entitled "The Law and This World According to Paul: Some Thoughts Concerning Gal. 4: 1-11,"[16] Bo Reicke has shown that in Galatians 4: 8ff. the Apostle Paul is warning his readers not only against legalism but also against a return to their slavery to spiritual powers that exercise their dominion over men through organized religion, against a return to gods who in their essential nature are not gods at all (*tois physei mē ousin theois*).[17] This interpretation concurs with the best reading of 1 Corinthians 10: 20, in which the idea is *not* that pagan sacrifices are offered to the demons "and not to God" (RSV) but rather that they are offered to the demons and "that which is not God" (NEB). In the words of C. K. Barrett, Paul held idolatry to be "evil primarily because it robbed the true God of the glory due to him alone . . . but it was evil also because it meant that man, engaged in a spiritual act and directing his worship towards something other than the one true God, was brought into intimate relation with the lower, and evil, spiritual powers."[18] The same relation between the demonic powers and the idolatrous making absolute of a man-made system appears

14. "The elemental spirits of the universe" (RSV) is a better translation of *stoicheia tou cosmou* than "rudiments of the world" (AV). For more on this point, see my article "La demonologia de Colosenses," *Diálogo teológico*, October 1973, pp. 37ff.

15. See George Eldon Ladd, *The Presence of the Future: The Eschatology of Biblical Realism* (1964; Grand Rapids: William B. Eerdmans, 1974), pp. 118-19, 149-54.

16. Reicke, "The Law and This World," *Journal of Biblical Literature* 70 (1951): 259-76.

17. The NEB translation reads "beings which in their nature are no gods."

18. Barrett, *The First Epistle to the Corinthians*, Black's New Testament Commentaries (London: Adam and Charles Black, 1971).

in Colossians 2:16ff. and is not unrelated to the references to the "wisdom of this world" in the first two chapters of 1 Corinthians. To speak of the world is to speak of an oppressive system governed by the powers of evil who enslave men through idolatry.

The relevance of these Pauline concepts today is obvious once we understand the consumer society's idolatrous character and power to condition men. Translated into the language of modern sociology, the apostle's vocabulary describes institutions and ideologies that transcend the individual and condition his thought and lifestyle. Those who limit the workings of the evil powers to the occult, demon possession, and astrology, as well as those who consider the New Testament references to those powers as a sort of mythological shell from which the biblical message must be extracted, reduce the evil in the world to a personal problem and Christian redemption to mere personal experience. A better alternative is to accept the realism of the biblical description and understand man's situation in the world in terms of an enslavement to a spiritual realm from which we must be liberated. As A. M. Hunter affirms, "There is no metaphysical reason why the cosmos should not contain spirits higher than man who have made evil their good, who are ill-disposed to the human race, and whose activities are coordinated by a master-strategist."[19] In his rebellion against God, man is a slave of the idols of the world through which those powers act. Today, the idols that enslave man are those of the consumer society.

Both technology and capital can put themselves at the service of either good or evil. From their union, which recognizes no ethical principle, has emerged the society that worships economic prosperity and the consequent material well-being of *homo consumens*. The consumer society is the very social, political, and economic situation in which the world dominated by the powers of destruction has taken form today: the blind faith in technology, the irreversible reverence for private property as an inalienable right, the cult of increased production through the irresponsible sacking of nature, the disproportionate en-

19. Hunter, *Interpreting Paul's Gospel* (London: SCM Press, 1955), p. 75n. 1.

richment of the multinational corporations that further impoverishes the "disinherited of the earth," the fever of consumerism, ostentatiousness, and fashion. This materialism is the ideology that is destroying the human race. The church of Jesus Christ is engaged in a spiritual conflict with the powers of evil entrenched in ideological structures that dehumanize man, conditioning him to make the absolute relative and the relative absolute.

THE WORLDLINESS OF THE CHURCH

The church is an eschatological reality: it belongs to the era of fulfillment introduced by Jesus Christ, the firstfruits of the new humanity. It is, however, also a historical reality, and as such it is subject, along with the rest of humanity, to the conditioning influence the world exerts on human life in all its dimensions.

In the period between the resurrection and second coming of Christ, the new era supersedes the old, and eschatology operates in the very stream of history. The resulting eschatological tension colors the whole life and mission of the church. The Lausanne Covenant refers to one of the most important aspects of that tension: "We believe that we are engaged in constant spiritual warfare with the principalities and powers of evil, who are seeking to overthrow the church and frustrate its task of world evangelization." Later in the same paragraph, the Covenant points out that the activity of the powers of destruction is perceived not only in terms of "false ideologies outside the church" but also in terms of the church's accommodation to the world in thought and action. This explicit recognition of the church's vulnerability before the world constitutes in itself one of the most praiseworthy notes of the whole document, all the more significant when its contrast to the usual triumphalism of evangelicals is taken into account. In his book *The Hidden Motives of Pastoral Action: Latin American Reflections*, Juan Luis Segundo has pointed out the mechanisms operating in Latin America — a traditionally Roman Catholic continent — that have made the church opt for an accommodation to consumer society rather than for the biblical message with its demands for personal conviction. His thesis can be summarized as follows:

1. *Urban society demands that the basic questions of human life are not discussed.* For this reason its unity depends upon a common participation not in universal values or a common vision of the world (as is the case in traditional societies) but rather in consumerism. Values and worldviews are relegated to the sphere of private life and, ultimately, considered purely relative.

2. *Christianity can no longer count on the help that closed societies provided in the past.* Without this help, an open society maintains a vague attachment to Christianity, related to man's uprootedness in the city, and this rootless attachment makes room for religious rites. The transmission of Christianity from one generation to another, however, no longer can be left to the social milieu.

3. *In a consumer society, being a Christian depends upon personal conviction.* Any profound idea that challenges the "massification" of man is revolutionary, and only a heroic minority holds to it.

4. *Pastoral work, therefore, must choose between a minority that accepts the demands of the gospel and a "consumer majority" that is falsely committed to Christianity.*

5. *Pastoral work has substituted the values of "artificial consumer majorities" for true Christianity and thus has reduced its demands to a minimum.* The main reason for this is a three-fold fear. First, there is a fear of freedom on the part of the priests, since "any major shift from the use of pressure to reliance on people's free will and decision would entail great material and psychological anxiety for most members of the clergy, and similar anxiety for other people engaged in pastoral work."[20] Second, there is a fear for the destiny of the masses, since "if we make the shift from protecting artificial majorities to cultivating heroic minorities, then the *majority* of people will be left without protection and without a minimal level of Christianity."[21] Third, there is a fear for the gospel: it is reasoned that the gospel *alone* cannot achieve what the church, through its alliance with the system, can; in other words, it is assumed that the church is not ready to depend exclusively upon the gospel.

20. Segundo, p. 87.
21. Segundo, p. 88.

This is the incisive analysis of the situation of Christianity within the consumer society as seen by a Latin American theologian. I have considered it useful to summarize it point by point because Segundo clearly delineates the motivation behind *any* kind of Christianity that has stronger ties to the Constantinian mentality than to the gospel of Jesus Christ. What Segundo says about Latin American "culture Christianity" can also be applied to the "culture Christianity" I refer to in "Evangelism and the World" [see pp. 1-44 herein] — the Christianity that is identified with the "American Way of Life," the influence of which has spread to almost all the countries of the world. Like traditional Roman Catholicism, it has accommodated itself to the world in its eagerness to reach the majority so that there may be more Christians. As a result the church, far from being a factor for the transformation of society, becomes merely another reflection of society and (what is worse) another instrument that society uses to condition people to its materialistic values. We can see its accommodation to the world in the two spheres that the Lausanne Covenant points out in referring to the danger of worldliness in the church in "thought and action."

1. In the sphere of thought, the church's accommodation to the world is realized mainly through the reduction of the gospel to a purely spiritual message — a message of reconciliation with God and salvation of the soul. In keeping with this, the mission of the church is defined exclusively in terms of evangelization, which in turn is understood as the proclamation that by virtue of the death of Jesus on the Cross, the only thing a man need do to be saved is to "accept Jesus as his all-sufficient Savior." This separates faith from repentance, the "essential" elements of the gospel from the "nonessential," the *kērygma* from the *didachē*, salvation from sanctification. On its most basic level, it entails distinguishing between Christ as Savior and Christ as Lord. This produces a gospel that permits a man to maintain the values and attitudes prevalent in a consumer society and at the same time enjoy the temporal and eternal security that religion provides. His life will be clearly divided between his "religion" compartment and his "secular activities" compartment. God has something to say with regard to the first but not the second: he will be a God interested in the

worship service but not in social problems, politics, business, or international relations.

This version of the gospel is custom-made for the "artificial consumer majorities." It is another easy product to market in the consumer society. It represents one of those "false gospels which twist Scripture and put man in the place of God" to which the Lausanne Covenant refers. The error of adopting such a gospel can be corrected only through a return to the biblical gospel, to the gospel that centers on Jesus Christ as Lord of the universe and of the whole of life, to the gospel clearly defined in "A Response to Lausanne" in the following terms:

> The Evangel is God's good news in Jesus Christ; it is good news of the reign he proclaimed and embodies; of God's mission of love to restore the world to wholeness through the cross of Christ and him alone; of his victory over the demonic powers of destruction and death; of his Lordship over the entire universe; it is good news of a new creation, a new humanity, a new birth through him by his life-giving Spirit; of the gifts of the messianic reign contained in Jesus and mediated through him by his Spirit; of the charismatic community empowered to embody his reign of shalom here and now before the whole creation and make his good news seen and known. It is good news of liberation, of restoration, of wholeness, and of salvation that is personal, social, global, and cosmic.

2. In the sphere of action, culture Christianity reflects the conditioning of the consumer society. Only this can explain the obsession with numbers mentioned in the Lausanne Covenant: "At other times, desirous to ensure a response to the gospel, we have compromised our message, manipulated our hearers through pressure techniques, and become unduly preoccupied with statistics or even dishonest in our use of them."[22] This expresses one of the most obvious ways in which

22. The affirmation preceding that quoted in the text reads as follows: "For example, although careful studies of church growth, both numerical and spiritual, are right and valuable, we have sometimes neglected them." It is difficult to see in what sense the neglect of church growth studies can be considered an example of the fact that "we ourselves are not immune to worldliness of thought and action, that is, to a surrender to secularism."

the church has accommodated itself to the world. To accompany a truncated gospel, we have an evangelistic methodology that mechanizes the addition of people to the church. If in consumer society the constant increase of production is the only interest, it is quite understandable that consumer religion would give priority to the numerical increase of the church.

Some might object by saying that keeping a numerical count of believers is a legitimate concern for any person whose heart is quickened with the very desire of God "who desires all men to be saved and to come to the knowledge of the truth" (1 Tim. 2:4). Juan Luis Segundo has responded to that objection:

> It is clear . . . that there are two different ways to count Christian heads. One is the statistical approach based on minimal requirements: baptism, some practice of the sacraments, profession of adherence to Christianity in censuses, and the absence of heresies as defined in Denzinger. The second way of counting Christians only considers those who are willing to carry the Christian message to the rest of society, to tolerate contact with other ideas and conceptions of life and win out over them, and to commit themselves personally to a radical transformation of society in line with Christ's message.[23]

In the final analysis, these two methods correspond to two different conceptions of the gospel, the mission of the church, and the Christian life. If our evangelical churches have given primacy to an accounting on the basis of the bare minimum (the only exception being that the denominational manual rather than the Denzinger provides the criteria for defining heresy), this demonstrates that they have not been able to escape the conditioning of their consumer society; in their interest to find more converts, they have accommodated their message to this society. The necessary reform demands a total reconstruction of the local church so that it may embody the demands of the gospel.

Given the context—the references to the worldliness of the church, the manipulation of hearers, and the exaggerated preoccupation with statistics—that defense of the use of "studies of church growth, both numerical and spiritual," evidently corresponds more to the insistence of a pressure group upon the drafting committee than to logic.

23. Segundo, p. 71.

THE GOSPEL, THE WORLD, AND THE CHURCH

The church has only two alternatives in its confrontation with the world: either it adapts itself to the world and betrays the gospel, or it responds to the gospel and enters into conflict with the world.

The world (in the negative sense of the word) is a system in which evil is organized against God. The lifestyle that it imposes on men is a slavery to the principalities and powers of evil. It cannot tolerate the presence of values or criteria that challenge its powerful conditioning influence. Its influence is so subtle that it infiltrates even the one dimension of life in which man would like to believe himself most free: religion. As the Lausanne Covenant clearly indicates, satanic activity can even be present within the church, in the message it preaches and the methodology it uses to spread its message.

The gospel is the good news of the victory of Jesus Christ over the powers of darkness. The Savior whose death was an atonement for sin is also the Lord who "disarmed the principalities and powers and made a public example of them, triumphing over them" (Col. 2:15). His salvation provides not only freedom from the consequences of sin but also freedom from the power of sin. It deals not only with man's reconciliation to God but also with a complete restructuring of life according to the model for the new man provided by God in Jesus Christ. In other words, the gospel offers not only a religious experience but also a new creation, a new lifestyle under the rule of God.

The church is called to incarnate the Kingdom of God in the midst of the kingdoms of this world. The gospel leaves it no other alternative. Committing itself to such a task, however, means entering into conflict with the world. One dare not think that the church can resist the conditioning of the world without that very resistance plunging it into conflict with the powers of destruction. When one takes into account the origin and history of the church, it is not surprising to find that in their confrontation with the world, Christians are caught up in a conflict; rather, it is surprising that Christians would *not* expect this to happen. The church derives its meaning by virtue of its connection with Jesus Christ, the Suffering Servant whose rejection of the establishment of his time brought him to his death. The Apostle Paul affirms that it was "the powers that rule the world" (NEB)—the forces of evil—that crucified the Lord of Glory. From that point on, the way of the church is stamped with the Cross. In the words of Martin Luther King, "If the church of Jesus Christ is to regain once more its power, message, and authentic ring, it must conform only to the demands of the Gospel."[24]

The Epistle to the Galatians illustrates the practical meaning of the Cross of Christ in the church's confrontation of the world. In the very first verses Paul places his ideas in a cosmic context by affirming that Christ "gave himself for our sins, that he might *deliver us from this present evil world*, according to the will of God and our Father" (1:4 AV). In a later passage he uncovers the hidden motives of the false teachers who had infiltrated the church in Galatia to deform the gospel message: they wanted to maintain their good standing before men and avoid the conflict. Paul's very questions suggest that this was indeed the case: "Am I now seeking the favor of men, or of God? Or am I trying to please men?" From the perspective of the gospel, there is only one alternative: "If I were still pleasing men, I should not be a servant of Christ" (1:10). The radical nature of the option reflects the great distance between two lifestyles: that which corresponds to the present evil world, being subject to the powers of destruction, and that which corresponds to the new creation, being under the Lordship of Jesus Christ. The false teachers had wanted to avoid the conflict, and that had led them to adulterate the gospel: they wanted to compel the believers to submit to the rite of circumcision so that they might "make a good showing in the flesh . . . that they may not be persecuted for the cross of Christ" (6:12). For his part, Paul understands that if Christ died to free us from the present evil world, the Cross of Christ stands between him and the world: it is the Cross "by which the world has been crucified to me, and I to the world" (6:14).

Conflict is inevitable when the church takes the gospel seriously. It is just as true today in the consumer society as it

24. King, *Strength to Love* (London: Collins, 1974), p. 22.

was in the first century. From the perspective of the gospel it is not a matter of a man leaving time in a schedule already full of secular activities to give his dues to God, to devote some time to religion and thus make himself worthy of the inner peace and material prosperity that religion provides. What *is* important is that he be liberated from his slavery to the powers of destruction and integrated into the purpose of God to place all things under the Lordship of Jesus Christ, into the new creation which is made visible in the community that models its life on the Second Adam. When, in its desire to avoid the conflict, the church accommodates itself to the spirit of the age, it loses the prophetic dimension of its mission and becomes an agent of the status quo. The salt loses its savor. It becomes a thermometer instead of a thermostat. As a result, it opens itself to the criticism exemplified in the words of Pierre Bunton:

> It has all but been forgotten that Christianity began as a revolutionary religion whose followers embraced an entirely different set of values from those held by other members of society. Those original values are still in conflict with the values of contemporary society; yet religion today has become as conservative a force as the force the original Christians were in conflict with. [25]

Consumer society has imposed a lifestyle that makes property an absolute right and gives priority to money over men and production over nature. This is the form that "the present evil world" has taken, the system in which the powers of destruction have organized human life. The danger of worldliness against which the Lausanne Covenant warns us has a concrete form: it is the danger of accommodating ourselves to the form of this evil world, with all its materialism, its obsession with individual success, its blinding selfishness.

Jesus Christ died for our sins, to free us from the present evil world. His incarnation and his Cross are the norms for the life and mission of the church. His victory is the basis of our hope in the midst of the conflict. His call is "to equip ourselves with God's armour and to fight this battle with the spiritual weapons of truth and prayer."

25. Bunton, *The Comfortable Pew* (Philadelphia: Lippincott, 1965), p. 80.

I appeal to you therefore, brethren, by the mercies of God, to present your bodies as a living sacrifice, holy and acceptable to God, which is your spiritual worship. Do not be conformed to this world but be transformed by the renewal of your mind, that you may prove what is the will of God, what is good and acceptable and perfect. (Rom. 12:1-2)

What is the Gospel?

The most important questions that should be asked with regard to the life and mission of the church today are not related to the relevance of the gospel but to its content. To be sure, there is a place for the consideration of ways in which the gospel meets man's needs in the modern world, but far more basic is the consideration of the *nature* of the gospel that could meet man's needs. The *what* of the gospel determines the *how* of its effects in practical life.

In light of contemporary pragmatism, it can hardly be expected that the primacy of theological questions should be widely recognized. The assumption is often made that we Christians *know* our message and that all we need is a better strategy and more efficient methods to communicate it. Accordingly, the effectiveness of evangelism is measured in terms of *results*, with little or no regard for faithfulness to the gospel. There are three good reasons why we should replace this approach with a new emphasis on the gospel as the basis on which evangelism must stand or fall:

1. The first condition for effective evangelism is *assurance concerning the content of the gospel*. Although such assurance is possible only where there is a personal response to the gospel by faith, the proclamation of the gospel entails much more than a mere description of personal experience; it involves a portrayal of the facts of the gospel as an objective reality breaking into the human situation and transcending man's apprehension of it. No one can claim to be adequately equipped for evangelism before he is able "to tell the old, old story" with full assurance concerning its constituent elements and its overall significance.

2. The only response that biblical evangelism can legiti-

mately look for is *a response to the gospel*. The genuineness of an individual's conversion is directly dependent on the genuineness of the gospel to which he has responded in repentance and faith. A spurious gospel can bring about only spurious conversion. The Christian who fails to concern himself with a clear understanding of the message he is to proclaim is liable to lead men to respond to himself rather than to the gospel.

3. The distinctive mark of a Christian experience is that it is *an experience of the gospel*. Christian experience is always a religious experience, but not every religious experience is Christian.

Without question, in the New Testament the gospel has a well-defined content. For all the variations that may be found in the way it is formulated, it can be referred to as *to euangelion* ("*the* gospel") without qualification.[1] It is a message that can be preached (Matt. 4:23; 9:35; 24:14; 26:13; Mark 1:14; 13:10; 14:9; 16:15; Gal. 2:2; 1 Thess. 2:9), witnessed to (Acts 20:24), proclaimed (1 Cor. 9:18; 2 Cor. 11:7; Gal. 1:11; cf. 1 Cor. 9:14), made known (Eph. 6:19), and chattered (1 Thess. 2:2), as well as heard (Acts 15:7; Eph. 1:13; Col. 1:23) and believed (Mark 1:15) or received (1 Cor. 15:1; 2 Cor. 11:4). So definite is its content that Paul is able to state in unequivocal terms that aside from the gospel preached by him there is no other gospel (Gal. 1:6-9). If that is so, the question we must ask with regard to any of the current formulas that claim to synthesize the gospel is not whether it works but whether it is true to the biblical evangel. My aim in this study is not to present a summary of the gospel as such but to provide biblical criteria to evaluate existing summaries frequently used for contemporary evangelical purposes.

THE HISTORICAL BACKGROUND OF *EUANGELION*

In the Old Testament there are several occurrences of the word *euangelion* ("news," "tidings") that carry no religious con-

---

1. The noun *euangelion* does not occur in Luke or John. It is used four times in Matthew, eight times in Mark, sixty times in the Pauline Epistles, once in 1 Peter, and once in Revelation. The verb *euangelizomai* occurs once in Matthew, ten times in Luke, fifteen times in Acts, twenty-one times in the Pauline Epistles, once in Hebrews, three times in 1 Peter, and twice in Revelation.

notations. The evangel that Ahimaaz the son of Zadok brings to David is the king's victory over Absalom (2 Sam. 18:20, 22, 25)[2]. A gospel of God's deliverance of Israel from the hand of the invading Syrians is brought to King Joram by a group of lepers (2 Kings 7:9). With a similar secular import, the verb *euangelizomai* (Heb. *biśśar* is used to refer to the bringing of news regarding the enthronement of a new king, the victory over an enemy, and the birth of a son (1 Kings 1:42; 1 Sam. 31:9). In Psalm 68 the "good news" the messengers are to announce (v. 11) is given them by the Lord and related to the defeat of Israel's enemies: "The kings of the armies, they flee, they flee!" (v. 12). The evangelists are a great host of singing women, like Miriam and Deborah of old. Quite early in the history of its interpretation, this text was applied to the Messiah.

More significant for the understanding of the Christian gospel is what is said concerning the bringing of good tidings (*euangelizomai*) in the second section of Isaiah (chaps. 40-66) — a section of the Old Testament widely used by Jesus Christ and the early church. In an important passage, the prophet foresees Israel's return from the Babylonian exile, through which God's universal sovereignty is manifest, and exclaims, "How beautiful upon the mountains are the feet of him who brings good tidings, who publishes peace, who brings good tidings of good, who publishes salvation, who says to Zion, 'Your God reigns' " (Isa. 52:7). In New Testament times this restoration of Israel (which is the theme of the "good tidings" also mentioned in Isa. 40:9; 41:27; and 61:1-3) is taken as a promise of the salvation wrought by Jesus and proclaimed by the Christian messengers. Isaiah's gospel is the coming of the messianic era by the power of God. And in it the Christian gospel is anticipated.[3]

2. In the same context the word that is translated in verses 20, 22, and 25 as "tidings" is also translated as "reward for the tidings" in verse 22. Cf. 2 Samuel 4:10.

3. Various passages from Isaiah (especially 40:9; 41:27; 52:7; and 61:1) also played an important role in Rabbinic literature in connection with the messianic hope. The one who brings the good news of liberation is the Messiah, or the prophet Elijah, or an anonymous messenger. His message is not only for Israel but also for the Gentiles, and it has to do with a messianic restoration or salvation.

For the Greeks the news announced by an evangelist is a news of victory. Raising his hand, he shouts "Be glad, we have won!" Whether the evangel has to do with victory in a game or victory in a battle, it is received with joy and he is rewarded with an *euangelion*. But *euangelion* may also have religious connotations in the Gentile world. This happens when the term is used in connection with the imperial cult, as is the case in the inscription on the Priene (Asia Minor) Monument (dated 9 B.C.), which, referring to Augustus, reads, "The birthday of the god was for the world the beginning of the joyful tidings which have gone forth because of him."[4]

AN ESCHATOLOGICAL MESSAGE

It is hard for any reader of the New Testament to avoid noticing the importance that the Old Testament had in the proclamation of the gospel. It is quite clear that for the primitive church the Christian evangel derived all its meaning from the fact that in the story of Jesus Christ (including his life, death, resurrection, and exaltation) the Old Testament prophecies had been fulfilled. Their frequent reference to the Hebrew scriptures is far more than a literary device; it expresses their understanding of Jesus' work as the fulfillment of God's promises contained in those scriptures. They saw the story of Jesus as the culmination of an age-old redemptive process that went back to Abraham, the father of Israel.

The world in which the gospel was first proclaimed was a world burning with messianic expectations. Whatever one may think of the connection between the New Testament and contemporary Jewish apocalyptic writings, the fact remains that they show that a living eschatological hope was a part of the atmosphere in which the gospel events took place. Thus it is not difficult to imagine the impact that the evangel must have made on Israel when it was first sounded forth. What the gospel heralds proclaimed was nothing less than the very fulfillment of God's long-awaited promise to visit his people!

4. Friedrich, "Euangelion," in *Theological Dictionary of the New Testament*, edited by Gerhard Kittel and Gerhard Friedrich, translated by Geoffrey W. Bromiley (Grand Rapids: William B. Eerdmans, 1964-76), 2: 724.

The note of fulfillment is first struck by John the Baptist. His message is "Repent, for the kingdom of heaven is at hand." He himself is a prophet in whom Isaiah's prediction in 40:3 is being fulfilled: he is "the voice of one crying in the wilderness: Prepare the way of the Lord, make his paths straight" (Matt. 3:2-3). He is, in fact, the messianic forerunner, and his ministry is described by Mark as "the beginning of the gospel of Jesus Christ" (Mark 1:1) precisely because John the Baptist is the first one to announce that God is about to act through the Coming One for salvation and judgment (Matt. 3:7-12; Luke 3:16-18). He stands in the period between the age of promise and the age of fulfillment: "the law and the prophets were until John; since then the good news of the kingdom of God is preached" (Luke 16:16).

Mark reports that "after John was arrested, Jesus came into Galilee, preaching the gospel of God and saying, 'The time is fulfilled and the kingdom of God is at hand; repent, and believe in the gospel' " (Mark 1:15). John the Baptist had announced the imminence of God's visitation. Now Jesus proclaimed that the day of eschatological fulfillment had in fact been brought in. Correctly understood, his words are one of the most amazing claims ever made. They throw into relief the following facts with regard to the gospel:

1. The gospel proclamation itself marks the *kairos*, the time assigned by God for the fulfillment of his purpose. The decisive hour in the history of salvation has arrived. The hope of the prophets is being realized.

2. The content of the gospel is not a new theology or a new teaching about God but an event — namely, the coming of the Kingdom. The verbal form (*engiken*) indicates that Jesus' announcement is not just the imminence but the actual arrival of a new reality that is already present among men.

3. The reference to both the Kingdom of God and the gospel points to Isaiah 52:7. In other words, Jesus sees himself as the herald of a new age in which Isaiah's message — "Your God reigns" — is fulfilled.

4. The proclamation of the gospel is inseparable from a call to repentance and faith. Because God is *now* acting, men are summoned to leave their sin and turn to him. Without repen-

tance and faith, there can be no participation in the blessings of the new age.

Fulfillment is also the main theme of Jesus' first sermon at the synagogue in Nazareth, according to Luke. After reading from Isaiah a passage that refers to the proclamation of the good news of messianic salvation (Isa. 61:1-2), Jesus closed the book, gave it back to the attendant, and sat down. To the amazement of his audience he then affirmed, "Today this scripture has been fulfilled in your hearing" (Luke 4:20-21). He is the Anointed One of God who has come "to preach good news to the poor"; he has been sent "to proclaim release to the captives, and recovering of sight to the blind, to set at liberty those who are oppressed, to proclaim the acceptable year of the Lord" (Luke 4:18-19). He is the herald of a new era made present through his own action on behalf of the poor, the captive, the blind, and the oppressed. His evangel is good news about something that is happening by the power of the Spirit acting through him. As Gerhard Friedrich has noted, "When heralds proclaimed the year of jubilee throughout the land with the sound of a trumpet, the year began, the prison doors were opened, the debts were remitted. The preaching of Jesus is such a blast of the trumpet."[5]

The same note of fulfillment is also sounded in various other things that Jesus said in different situations. Speaking on the question of fasting, for instance, he made use of a metaphor — the marriage feast — reserved in Judaism for reference to the messianic consummation: "Can the wedding guests fast while the bridegroom is with them? As long as they have the bridegroom with them, they cannot fast" (Mark 2:19). The implication is that his disciples do not fast because in his coming the time of fulfillment has arrived. Again, addressing his disciples he tells them, "Blessed are the eyes which see what you see! For I tell you that many prophets and kings desired to see what you see, and did not see it, and to hear what you hear, and did not hear it" (Luke 10:23-24). Their blessedness consists in actually seeing the messianic salvation that was the object of hope of former generations. In the same vein, when John

5. Friedrich, 2:706.

the Baptist sent his disciples to Jesus and expressed hesitation as to whether he had correctly identified the Messiah, Jesus replied to them, "Go and tell John what you hear and see: the blind receive their sight and the lame walk, lepers are cleansed and the deaf hear, and the dead are raised up, and the poor have good news preached to them" (Matt. 11:4-5; cf. Luke 7:22). His answer echoes Isaiah 35:5-6. The claim is obvious: the Eschaton has arrived and is manifesting its presence among men now, although not along the lines expected by John. In his own ministry the prophetic expectations are being fulfilled. His miracles as well as his proclamation of good news to the poor are unmistakable signs that the Coming One has come.

The most distinctive characteristic of Jesus' teaching concerning God's Kingdom is the fact that before the end of the age the Kingdom is active among men in his own person and ministry. As G. E. Ladd has stated, this is *the heart of his proclamation and the key to his entire mission.*[6] Jesus' emphasis does not lie simply on the *proximity* of the Kingdom, but on its actual anticipated arrival. Such is the force of the verb in Matthew 12:28, which the Revised Standard Version correctly translates as follows: "But if it is by the Spirit of God that I cast out demons, then the kingdom of God has come [*ephthasen*] upon you." God's dynamic action through the Holy Spirit is delivering men from evil power, and that proves that in Jesus' person and work the Kingdom of God has already come. Yet its presence is not self-evident because the fulfillment of the Old Testament prophecies about it does not take place in the commonly expected terms. That is why the Pharisees, in their rejection of Jesus as the Messiah, are unable to see that the Kingdom is in their midst (Luke 17:21).

The Kingdom as a present reality is the subject not only of Jesus' proclamation (Matt. 4:23; 9:35; Mark 1:14-15; Luke 4:43; 8:1; 16:16) but also of the message that he commits first to the Twelve (Matt. 10:7; Luke 9:2, 6) and later to the Seventy (Luke 10:9, 11). In fact, according to Jesus' own words in his Olivet discourse, the Kingdom is the subject of Christian preaching until the end of the present age (Matt. 24:14; cf.

6. Ladd, *The Presence of the Future: The Eschatology of Biblical Realism* (1964; Grand Rapids: William B. Eerdmans, 1974), p.139. Italics his.

Mark 13:10). In light of this saying, it is not surprising to find that in Acts Luke describes the message preached by Philip in Samaria as "good news about the kingdom of God" (Acts 8:12) and states that Paul argued and pleaded about the Kingdom of God at the synagogue in Ephesus (Acts 19:8) and preached the Kingdom of God in Rome (Acts 28:23, 31). If these references to the content of the message proclaimed after Pentecost prove anything, they prove that the message that spread according to Jesus' promise to the apostles— namely, that they would be his witnesses "in Jerusalem and in all Judea and Samaria and to the end of the earth" (Acts 1:8)—was essentially the same as the message proclaimed by Jesus himself—namely, that in his own person and ministry God had acted decisively to bring in his Kingdom.

This view of the unity of the gospel as news regarding a new eschatological reality made manifest in Jesus Christ is confirmed by the testimony of the whole of the New Testament. On the day of Pentecost Peter announced that Jesus, who was crucified, had been raised up and "exalted at the right hand of God" as "both *Kyrios* and Messiah" (Acts 2:33, 36). It was affirmed that the Old Testament predictions concerning the Holy One who would not see corruption (Ps. 16:8-11) and concerning the King who would sit upon David's throne (Ps. 89:3-4; 132:11) had been fulfilled. Peter's point is quite clear: Jesus was on the throne; the messianic age had arrived. His message echoes the claim with which Jesus himself introduced his Great Commission: "All authority in heaven and on earth has been given to me" (Matt. 28:18). And it anticipates the basic thrust of apostolic preaching, summarized in the most ancient Christian creed— namely, Jesus Christ is *Kyrios*: the Messiah of Israel is Lord of all (Acts 10:36; 11:20; Rom. 10:9, 12). The gospel that God promised beforehand through his prophets in the holy Scriptures has to do with Jesus, "who was descended of David according to the flesh and designated Son of God in power according to the Spirit of holiness by his resurrection from the dead, Jesus Christ our Lord" (Rom. 1:1-4).[7] As Oscar Cullmann

---

7. Other brief Pauline summaries of the gospel (1 Cor. 15:1-3; 2 Tim. 2:8) also show the importance of the Old Testament as the substructure of the New Testament message. Silence regarding Jesus' death in Romans 1:1-4

has emphasized, the confession of Jesus as *Kyrios* sums up the faith of the primitive church, for it points to the fact that he who was crucified in the past and is also to return in the future is *today* exercising sovereignty over the whole universe, sitting at the right hand of God.[8]

From a New Testament perspective, the keynote of the gospel message is the fulfillment of the promises God gave in the Old Testament. Because of Christ Jesus' work, it is possible for men to taste "the powers of the age to come" here and now (Heb. 6:5). Christians are those "upon whom the end of the ages has come" (1 Cor. 10:11). To be sure, they still look forward to a future apocalyptic coming of the Kingdom; the fulfillment of the Old Testament hope that has taken place in the person and work of Jesus Christ is a "fulfillment without consummation."[9] But the decisive eschatological events have already taken place, and, as a result, the Messiah "must reign [*basileuein*] until he has put all his enemies under his feet" (1 Cor. 15:25). The "not yet" of futuristic eschatology is subordinate to the "already" of realized eschatology.

The gospel is in its essence the good news that "when the time had fully come" (Gal. 4:4) God sent his Son, in whom and through whom the Old Testament hope is fulfilled. We cannot dispense with the note of eschatological fulfillment and remain faithful to the gospel.

A CHRISTOLOGICAL MESSAGE

As we have seen, the gospel is clearly centered in the Lord Jesus Christ. In the final analysis, he himself (including his person and his work) *is* the gospel. The New Testament throws into relief such an identification by referring now to Christ (Acts 5:42; 8:5; 9:20 [cf. v. 22]; 19:13; 1 Cor. 1:23; 2 Cor. 2:12; 4:5; 9:13; 10:14; 11:4; Phil. 1:15) and now to the gospel (Acts 8:35; 11:20; 14:7; 16:10; 17:18; Rom. 15:20; 1 Cor.

and regarding the incarnation in 1 Corinthians 15:1-3 should make us wary of any attempt to find the whole gospel in any one summary of it.

8. Cullmann, *The Christology of the New Testament*, rev. ed., translated by Shirley C. Guthrie and Charles A. M. Hall (1955; Philadelphia: Westminster Press, 1963), pp. 203-33.

9. See Ladd, pp. 114-21.

1:17; 2 Cor. 2:12; Gal. 1:8, 11; 2:2; Eph. 3:8; 1 Thess. 2:9; 1 Pet. 1:12) as the subject matter of apostolic preaching.[10] The key to understanding Jesus' evangel lies in the dynamic meaning of the term *kingdom* (*basileia*). The kingdom that Jesus proclaims is the power of God active among men in his own person and ministry. Before the end of the age God has irrupted into history to accomplish his redemptive purpose, and he has done so in Jesus Christ. In announcing that "the kingdom of God is at hand," Jesus does not mean that the end of the world is within sight but that through his own mission God is visiting his people, thus fulfilling the prophetic hope. He is (according to Origen's apt description) the *autobasileia*,[11] through whom God is at work. Consequently, sacrificing for his sake is equivalent to sacrificing for the sake of the Kingdom of God.[12]

Due account should be taken of the flexibility that characterized the presentation of the gospel in the primitive church. Michael Green has correctly pointed out that the disagreement among scholars with regard to the points included in the apostolic proclamation is itself a warning against all efforts to reduce the message to a fixed form.[13] The gospel may be described as "good news of peace by Jesus Christ" (Acts 10:36), "the mystery [or testimony] of God" (1 Cor. 2:1), "the word" (Acts 8:4), "the word of the Lord" (Acts 15:35), "the word of the cross" (1 Cor. 1:18), "the word of truth" (James 1:18; Eph. 1:13), "the word of God" (Heb. 4:12; 1 Pet. 1:23 [cf. v. 25]; Acts 4:31; 6:2; 11:1; 13:44), "the testimony to the resurrection of the Lord Jesus" (Acts 4:33 [cf. 17:18]; 2 Tim. 2:8), "the gospel of God" (Mark 1:14; Rom. 1:1; 2 Cor. 11:7 [cf. 1 Tim. 1:11]), "the gospel of the kingdom" (Matt. 24:14 [cf. Luke 8:1]), "the gospel of Christ" (Rom. 15:19 [cf. 1:3]; 1 Cor. 9:12 [cf. Eph. 3:8]), "the gospel of the grace of God" (Acts 20:24), and "the gospel of your salvation" (Eph. 1:13). The variety of

---

10. Galatians 1 clearly shows that preaching the gospel (vv. 8, 11) is equivalent to preaching Christ (v. 16) and preaching "the faith" (v. 23).
11. Origen, *Commentary on Matthew*, bk. 14, sect. 7.
12. The expression "for my name's sake" (*eneken tou onomatos mou*) in Matthew 19:29 (cf. Mark 8:35; 10:29) is replaced by the expression "for the sake of the kingdom of God" (*eneken tēs basileias tou theou*) in Luke 18:29.
13. Green, *Evangelism in the Early Church* (London: Hodder & Stoughton, 1973), pp. 60-61.

descriptions brings out the many-sidedness of the gospel, but it also reflects the effort that the early heralds of the good news made to adjust their presentation to the situation of their listeners. Underlying all the descriptions and welding them into unity, however, is the figure of Jesus as the Messiah come from God at the climax of the history of salvation to fulfill the Old Testament promises. He was shamefully killed on a cross, but God raised him up from the dead and exalted him as Lord over all things. As the exalted Lord, he has sent the Holy Spirit and is now bestowing upon his church the gifts and blessings of the new age. He will come at the end of history to bring his work to consummation. Those who call upon him as Lord in repentance and faith become partakers of his resurrection life and coworkers with him in his mission in the world.

The central events in which God's redemptive purpose is fulfilled are Jesus' death and resurrection. They are events foretold by the Scriptures (Matt. 26: 54, 56; John 19: 28; 20: 9) and the messianic prophecies (Luke 24: 25-27, 44-46; Acts 13: 27-29; 17: 2-3; 18: 28; 26: 22-23; 28: 23; Rom. 1: 2-4) in general and by various messianic predictions in particular.[14] The emphasis that the New Testament places on them can be explained only on the basis of Jesus' own understanding that his messiahship was being fulfilled in terms of the Servant of the Lord ('ebed Yahveh). The identification of the Messiah with the Suffering Servant is emphasized by Jesus' combination of references to the glorification of the Son of Man with references to suffering and death (Mark 8: 31 and par.; 9: 12 and par.; 9: 31; 10: 32-34 and par.; and 10: 45). As H. N. Ridderbos puts it, "This mysterious duality of being Lord and servant, of the necessity of suffering and, nevertheless, being endowed with divine power, is the most essential element in the description all four gospels give to Jesus' earthly life."[15] Jesus says that it was through his acceptance of humiliation as the Servant of the Lord mentioned

14. The following Old Testament predictions are referred to in the New Testament: Isaiah 53 in Acts 3: 18 (cf. vv. 13, 26); 4: 27; 8: 32-35; Luke 22: 37; and Mark 15: 28. Psalm 2: 7 in Acts 13: 33 (cf. Heb. 1: 5; 5: 5; and Rom. 1: 4). Psalm 16: 10 in Acts 2: 24-31; 13: 34-37. Psalm 69: 9 in Romans 15: 3-4.

15. Ridderbos, *Paul and Jesus: Origin and General Character of Paul's Preaching of Christ,* translated by David H. Freeman (Philadelphia: Presbyterian and Reformed Publishing Co., 1958), p. 31.

in Isaiah 53 that he would receive the power and authority that belonged to him as the Son of Man mentioned in Daniel 7. And this "mysterious duality" became the basis for the apostolic proclamation of Jesus as the "Holy and Righteous One" (Acts 3:14; cf. 7:52), the "Prince of Life" (Acts 3:15), God's "Holy Servant" (Acts 4:27; cf. 8:32ff.), who, having died "for [uper] our sins," (1 Cor. 15:3),[16] had been raised from the dead and exalted as Kyrios over the whole universe (Acts 2:36; 10:36; 11:20). In Paul's words, the one who "humbled himself and became obedient unto death, even the death of the cross" was therefore highly exalted and given "the name which is above every name" (Phil. 2:8-9). At the heart of the gospel is Jesus Christ, who, as the exalted Lord, remains a crucified Messiah (1 Cor. 1:23; cf. 2:2)[17] and as such "the power and wisdom of God."

A SOTERIOLOGICAL MESSAGE

The Gospels present Jesus as the Messiah who brings the fulfillment of the Old Testament hope. The burden of his min-

16. Behind the affirmation that "Christ died for our sins" lies the picture of the Suffering Servant, "who was delivered up for our trespasses" (Isa. 53:12, LXX). Santos Sabergal maintains that "while the Pauline context of the Christological confession underlines the royal function of the Christos, the construction uper tōn amartiōn ēmōn, like the remaining Pauline uper-formulae, relates it, quite probably, to the messianic figure of the suffering Ebed-Yahveh of Deutero-Isaiah" (Christos: Investigación exegética sobre la cristología joanina [Barcelona: Editorial Herder, 1972], p. 146). Isaiah 53 is also behind Jesus' definition (in Mark 10:45) of his mission as that of giving his life "as a ransom for many" (cf. Isa. 53:10) and behind the characterization of Jesus in the early preaching (e.g., Acts 8:32ff.). In other contexts, Jesus' death is described as that of one "hanging on a tree" (Acts 5:30; 10:39; 13:29; Gal. 3:10; cf. Deut. 21:22ff.), as a propitiation (Rom. 3:25), as the means by which he took upon himself the consequences of our sin (2 Cor. 5:21). "The richness of New Testament teaching on this subject centres on Christ," says Leon Morris, "and again and again the key to the understanding of a particular way of viewing the cross is to see that Christ has stood in our place. . . . Was there a price to be paid? He paid it. Was there a victory to be won? He won it. Was there a penalty to be borne? He bore it. Was there a judgment to be faced? He faced it. View man's plight how you will, the witness of the New Testament is that Christ has come where man ought to be and has met in full all the demands that might be made on man" (The Cross in the New Testament [Grand Rapids: William B. Eerdmans, 1965], pp. 405-6).

17. The tense of the verb (estaurōmenos, "crucified") indicates that the purpose of the description is not to emphasize the past historical event of the crucifixion but the present state of the exalted Lord (cf. Rev. 5:6).

istry is not the creation of a new religion or the teaching of a philosophical system but the proclamation of good news about an event — the arrival of a new age, the coming of the Kingdom of God. His announcement is that God is now active in history through the person and mission of his Son. As the Messiah, however, Jesus does not fulfill God's promises in terms of a political-national victory for Israel. He brings a victory of universal dimensions. His exorcism of demons is a sign that prior to the eschatological destruction of Satan and his angels in eternal fire (Matt. 25:41) God has invaded Satan's realm as one who enters a strong man's house and binds him (Matt. 12:29; cf. Luke 11:21-22). The miraculous healings he performs are tokens of the coming end, the *eschaton*, when death will be swallowed up in life.[18] As the Son of Man who brings the Kingdom of God, he has the power to forgive sins (Mark 2:10; cf. Luke 7:48). His message points to God as one who has taken the initiative to seek out the lost and to place them under his rule (Mark 2:15-17; Luke 15) in a new relationship in which he is recognized as the Father (Matt. 6:32-33; Luke 12:30).[19] The Kingdom that Jesus brings is a realm of salvation, in which the blessings of the messianic age are available to the subjects in advance, a realm that men may enter *now*. His gospel is good news concerning a new soteriological order that has irrupted into history in his person and ministry and in which the Old Testament hope is fulfilled in an unexpected way. The content of the gospel was actually foretold by the prophets; what is new is that God himself is now "preaching good news of *Shalom* by Jesus Christ" (Acts 10:36). This peace, *Shalom*, points to a new order created by the Anointed One of God. It is "the

18. See Matthew 11:4-5 and 12:28, in which healings are clearly interpreted as signs of the presence of the Kingdom in Jesus' ministry. They are therefore anticipatory of immortality in the everlasting Kingdom (cf. Matt. 25:34, 46). It is not irrelevant to our theme to notice that the verb *sozein* ("to save") is sometimes used in connection with physical healings (see Mark 5:34 and 10:52; Luke 17:19).

19. The connection made in the Gospels between the Fatherhood of God and the Kingdom shows the importance of a personal relationship to God for participation in the blessings of his reign. "To be in the Kingdom is to receive the gospel of the Kingdom and experience its salvation" (Ladd, p. 203).

acceptable year of the Lord," and its proclamation itself is a sign that a new era has begun (see Luke 4: 18-19, 21).

In Ephesians 2, Paul makes clear that the messianic peace, *Shalom*, wrought by Jesus Christ involves not only a new relationship to God but also a new relationship between man and his neighbor. *Shalom* is not a gift that the Lord gives apart from himself; rather, he himself is *Shalom* (Eph. 2: 14), and through his death he has brought all hostility among men to an end. In fulfillment of Isaiah 52:7, he has come preaching *Shalom* (Eph. 2: 17); in agreement with Isaiah, his proclamation of *Shalom* is "to the far and near," to Jews and Gentiles (Eph. 2: 17). He has thus created a new humanity (the "new man," Eph. 2: 15), marked by unity in Christ and "access in one Spirit to the Father" (Eph. 2: 18). The proclamation of the good news of *Shalom* by Jesus Christ brings about a community that embodies the blessings of the new age — the church.

Significantly enough, in Romans 10:5 Paul applies (in plural) to the apostolic messengers, including himself, the same Isaianic reference to the herald of good news that in Acts 10:36 and Ephesians 2:17 is applied (in singular) to Jesus Christ. Now that Jesus has been exalted as Lord, he bestows the blessing of the new age upon all those who call upon him. Salvation in his name is available to all men. But how can men call upon him unless they hear about him, and how shall they hear about him without a messenger, and how shall a messenger preach without being sent? The answer is provided in men whose mission is patterned on the mission of Jesus Christ, who came preaching good news of *Shalom*. "As it is written, 'How beautiful are the feet of those who preach good news.' "

The apostolic mission is derived from Jesus Christ. He is the content as well the model and the goal for the proclamation of the gospel. The apostolic task therefore involves a concern for a total restoration of man as the image of God. From a New Testament perspective, the salvation (*sōtēria*) that the gospel brings is deliverance from all that interferes with the accomplishment of God's purpose for man.

1. *Salvation is deliverance from the consequences of sin*, whether these are described as condemnation (John 3: 17; Mark 16: 16; cf. 1 Cor. 3: 15), judgment (John 12: 47; Rom. 5: 21), perdition

(Matt. 16:25; Mark 8:35; Luke 9:24; 19:10; 1 Cor. 1:18; 2 Cor. 2:15; 1 Thess. 2:10), death (Rom. 1:32; 6:23; 2 Cor. 7:10; James 5:20), or wrath (Rom. 2:5; 5:9; 1 Thess. 5:9; Eph. 2:3). Seen in connection with the plight of man before a righteous God, the gospel is the proclamation of the fact that through faith in Christ men are "justified" — that is, given God's verdict of acquittal, declared "not guilty" (Rom. 3:20, 24; 4:5; 5:9; Gal. 2:16; 3:11; Titus 3:7);[20] they are "reconciled" to God and therefore are no longer at enmity with him (Rom. 5:10ff.; 2 Cor. 5:18ff.; Col. 1:19-22); they are "forgiven" (Acts 2:38; 10:43). This is salvation as an accomplished fact (Rom. 8:24; Eph. 2:5, 8), and it is vividly portrayed in baptism.

2. *Salvation is deliverance from the power of sin.* Those who acknowledge Jesus Christ as Lord are transferred by God "from the dominion of darkness . . . to the kingdom of his beloved Son" (Col. 1:13). They are given new life "in Christ" (Rom. 5:17, 21; 6:23; 8:2; Col. 3:3-4; Phil. 1:21; 1 Thess. 5:10), which involves three things:

a. *Membership in the people of God* with a lineage that goes back to Abraham (Gal. 3:27-29). In view of all that the New Testament has to say with regard to the connection between salvation and the church, there is no exaggeration in Michael Green's statement that "the church is in a very real sense a part of the gospel."[21] The church is not the Kingdom, but it is the realm in which the blessings of the new age, including salvation from the powers of destruction, are experienced.

b. *Moral transformation.* Breaking with every evil thing and cleaving to what is good are actions intrinsic to identification and union with Jesus Christ. Christians were buried into his death and raised with him so that they may live "in newness of life" (Rom. 6:4). They have died with Christ and are therefore to "put off" all kinds of evil practices; they have been raised with Christ and are therefore to "put on" Christ, the New

---

20. On the importance of the forensic meaning of justification in Paul's teaching, see Morris, pp. 240-47.

21. Green, "Methods and Strategy in the Evangelism of the Early Church" (a paper presented at the International Congress on World Evangelization in Lausanne, Switzerland, July 1974), p. 3.

Man.[22] The gospel is "the power of God for salvation" (Rom. 1:16) not only because it delivers man from the guilt of sin but also because it brings forth fruit in terms of faith, love, and hope, which are shown in the way he lives (Col. 1:6). In contrast to the dichotomy between religion and ethics that characterized most of the ancient religions, the New Testament knows nothing of a faith that is not expressed in practical conduct. "Faith by itself, if it has no works, is dead" (James 2:17). The gospel is not only to be believed but also to be obeyed (1 Pet. 4:18. Cf. Rom. 2:8; Gal. 3:1; 5:7; 2 Cor. 9:13; 1 Pet. 1:22). Indeed, faith is genuine only in the degree to which it obeys. Good works done in love are not a mere addendum to salvation but part and parcel of the new creation realized in Jesus Christ (Eph. 2:10; cf. Titus 2:14).

c. *The gift of the Holy Spirit.* If the gospel comes to men not as an empty word but "in power," it does so because of the presence of the Holy Spirit in its proclamation (1 Thess. 1:5. Cf. 1 Cor. 2:4-5; 1 Pet. 1:12). It is the Spirit who communicates eternal life (John 3:5-8)—the life of the new age—with all the ethical virtues that characterize it: "love, joy, peace, patience, kindness, goodness, faithfulness, gentleness, self-control" (Gal. 5:22). Given the fulfillment of God's promises of old (Acts 1:4; 2:33, 39; cf. Joel 2:28), he is called "the Holy Spirit of promise (Eph. 1:13; 4:30), because in him God has given a pledge that his saving purpose will one day be fully accomplished (Eph. 1:14. Cf. 1 Cor. 2:9; 1 Pet. 1:4). But the gift of the Spirit is an essential element of the Christian life here and now as well: "Anyone who does not have the Spirit of Christ does not belong to him" (Rom. 8:9; cf. 8:14). Like forgiveness, from which it is inseparable, the gift of the Spirit is received "by hearing with faith" (Gal. 3:2, 5; cf. Luke 11:13). The salvation that the gospel proclaims is not restricted to deliverance from the consequences of sin; it involves deliverance from the dominion of sin so that man may live an upright life by the power of the Spirit. The Kingdom of God, the resources

---

22. Jesus himself offered his life as a pattern for the life of his disciples, as is brought out by such important sayings as those recorded in Mark 10:45 and John 13:15. Cf. 2 Corinthians 8:9, Philippians 2:5, and Galatians 6:2.

of which have been placed at man's disposal through Jesus Christ, takes shape in the present in terms of righteous action (*dikaiosunē*), harmony with one another (*eirēnē*), and joy (*chara*) in the Holy Spirit (Rom. 14:17).[23] The salvation that the Christian gospel proclaims implies a present participation in the blessings of the messianic age that have been brought back from the end of time by the Agent of "realized eschatology"— the Spirit of God. Thus conceived, salvation is a *process* that advances from the act in which the believers were given the Spirit as a mark of ownership—a "seal" (*sphragis*)—toward their full redemption as God's possession in the coming age (Eph. 1:13-14; cf. 2 Cor. 1:22).

3. *Salvation includes a complete restoration of man as the image of God, made for communion with God, for fellowship with his fellow man, and for ruling over God's creation.* In all its dimensions it will be realized only in the future, when creation itself will be set free from its bondage of decay and obtain the glorious liberty of the children of God" (Rom. 8:21). The New Testament is unanimous in expressing the hope of God's final victory in Jesus Christ. Never does it become preoccupied with futuristic eschatology. Yet it does provide a firm basis for the assurance that God's redemptive work will be brought to completion "at the day of Jesus Christ" (Phil 1:6), which is also "the day of wrath when God's righteous judgment will be revealed," when "he will render to every man according to his works: to those who by patience in well-doing seek for glory and honor and immortality, he will give eternal life; but for those who are factious and do not obey the truth, but obey wickedness, there will be wrath and fury" (Rom. 2:6-8; cf. v. 16). The consummation of redemption and its obverse—judgment—is a constituent part of the gospel. And the hope that comes to man

23. As William Sanday and Arthur C. Headlam have pointed out, "This passage [Rom. 14:17] describes man's life in the kingdom, and these words denote not the relation of the Christian to God, but his life in relation to others. *Dikaiosunē* therefore is not used in its technical sense of the relation between God and man, but means righteousness or just dealing; *eirēnē* is the state of peace with one another which should characterize Christians; *chara* is the joy which comes from the indwelling of the Holy Ghost in the community" (*The Epistle to the Romans*, 5th ed., International Critical Commentary series [Edinburgh: T. & T. Clark, 1902], p. 392.

through the gospel is a powerful incentive to faith in God and love for fellow Christians here and now (Col. 1:4-5). It looks forward to "a new heaven and a new earth" (Rev. 21:1; cf. 2 Pet. 3:13), to the universal recognition of Jesus Christ as Lord (Phil. 2:10-11; Eph. 1:10), to the transformation of "our lowly body" into a body resembling Christ's "glorious body" (Phil. 3:21; cf. Rom. 8:23 and 1 Cor. 15:35-50). At the same time, it projects the final events back into history and fills the ethical actions of the present with eschatological significance.

Salvation as justification can be distinguished from salvation as sanctification and salvation as glorification. This distinction reflects the New Testament presentation of salvation as an accomplished fact (Eph. 2:5, 8; Rom. 8:24; Titus 3:5), as a present process (1 Cor. 1:18; 2 Cor. 2:15), and as a future event (Rom. 5:9; 1 Pet. 1:5). The three tenses of salvation — past, present, and future — are united into an organic whole; they may be distinguished but must not be separated. The salvation that the gospel proclaims is not limited to man's reconciliation to God. It involves the remaking of man in all the dimensions of his existence. It has to do with the recovery of the whole man according to God's original purpose for his creation.

A CALL TO REPENTANCE AND FAITH

The gospel contains a call that runs throughout the New Testament — a call to repentance and faith. If our evangelism is to be faithful to the gospel it must then include that note also. As James Packer has pointed out well, "Evangelizing includes the endeavour to elicit a response to the truth taught. It is communication with a view to conversion. It is a matter, not merely of informing, but also of inviting."[24] Without such an invitation, the presentation of the gospel is not complete; the call throws into relief the fact that in order to be effective for salvation, the gospel requires a positive response.

The Synoptic Gospels are unanimous in summarizing the message of John the Baptist as a message of the "baptism of

24. Packer, *Evangelism and the Sovereignty of God* (London: InterVarsity Press, 1963), p. 50.

repentance for the forgiveness of sins" (Mark 1: 4; Luke 3: 3; cf. Matt. 3: 6, 11), and Matthew and Mark show that Jesus summoned men to repent in view of the fact that the Kingdom of God was being offered them as a gift, in anticipation of the end of the age (Mark 1: 15; Matt. 4: 17).[25] According to the Lucan version of the Great Commission, the message that the Lord commanded his disciples to proclaim to all nations was "repentance and forgiveness of sins . . . in his name" (Luke 24: 47). On the day of Pentecost, Peter was faithful to that charge when he exhorted the people to "Repent, and be baptized every one of you in the name of Jesus Christ for the forgiveness of your sins" (Acts 2: 38; cf. 3: 19). And so was Paul when he told his audience on the Aereopagus that "the times of ignorance God overlooked but now he commands all men everywhere to repent" (Acts 17: 30) and when, according to his witness to the elders of the Ephesian church, he testified "both to Jews and to Greeks of the repentance to God and of faith in our Lord Jesus Christ" (Acts 20: 21). In fact, Paul's statement before King Agrippa, which he had declared "first to those at Damascus, then at Jerusalem and throughout all the country of Judea and also to the Gentiles, that they should repent and turn to God and perform deeds worthy of their repentance" (Acts 26: 20), makes it obvious that repentance was a regular element of Paul's message. Moreover, the repentance he sought was a radical reorientation of one's life, involving a breaking away from sin and the adoption of a new lifestyle — a repentance evidenced by specific deeds (*erga*).

Repentance is inseparable from faith. There is no basis for the claim that has sometimes been made — namely, that the call to repentance was addressed to the Jews and had connection with the old dispensation — "salvation by works" — whereas the only requirement for the Gentiles under the new dispensation — "salvation by grace" — is faith. In support of that thesis it has been pointed out that Paul, the apostle to the Gentiles, hardly

25. Says Ladd, "This summons to repentance is not laid upon men because God is about to do something in the future, whether near or remote; it is conditioned by the fact that God *is now* acting. . . . In fact we may say that the very summons to repentance is itself the action of God's kingdom" (p. 178).

ever made use of the word *repentance* (*metanoia*) in his Epistles. No full discussion of this view is here possible; a few brief comments will have to suffice.

1. No sharp distinction between the old dispensation and the new can be maintained in light of the New Testament insistence on the unity of the history of salvation. Already with the patriarch Abraham, faith was shown to be the basic principle determining man's relationship to God (Rom. 4; Gal. 3). Abraham is, in fact, the father of all the faithful (Rom. 4:11, 16).

2. As we have seen, repentance was a constituent element of the message that Jesus charged his disciples to preach in all the nations, and Luke's history of the expansion of Christianity leaves no doubt that the apostles (including Paul) were faithful to that commission.

3. The whole New Testament shows that separation from sin and obedience to the truth are essential to salvation. In contrast to "worldly grief"—a sorrow that is void of any determination to put away sin—"godly grief produces a repentance that leads to salvation" (2 Cor. 7:10). As Leon Morris has put it, "The repentant sinner is not only sorry about his sin but by the grace of God he does something about it. He makes a clean break with it."[26] Where there is no concrete repentance, as where there is no genuine faith, there will be no salvation. Mental assent to the Lordship of Christ is insufficient for participation in the blessings of the Kingdom made available through him. Jesus said "Not every one who says to me, 'Lord, Lord,' shall enter the kingdom of heaven, but he who does the will of my Father who is in heaven" (Matt. 7:21).

4. The genuineness of both repentance and faith is revealed by their fruits: good works. Yet there is no question that salvation is by grace alone. Apart from divine intervention, the gospel remains "veiled" and cannot be perceived by the natural man (2 Cor. 4:3; cf. 1 Cor. 2:14). Repentance is commanded (Acts 17:30), but it is possible only when God himself grants it (Acts 11:18). It is God's goodness that leads man to repentance (Rom. 2:4). Were it not for God's grace, man would nat-

---

26. Morris, p. 261.

urally prefer to avoid the uncomfortable experience of breaking away from sin in order to follow a new way of life. It is God's gift of himself in Jesus Christ that enables man to respond in repentance and faith. The gospel is "the power of God for salvation to every one who has faith" (Rom. 1:16), yet it is the gospel itself that creates the power to believe.

The gospel is God's gift, and as such it demands the "obedience of faith" (Rom. 1:6). "God is for us and our release only that we may be for Him and His service," P. T. Forsyth has declared. "He is for us, to help, save and bless, only that we may be for Him, to worship Him in the communion of the Spirit and serve Him in the majesty of His purpose forever. First we glorify Him, then we enjoy Him forever."[27]

---

27. Forsyth, *The Principle of Authority in Relation to Certainty, Sanctity and Society* (London: Independent Press, 1952), p. 13.

The Contextualization of the Gospel

The gospel is the good news that God has put himself within man's reach. To accomplish this, he has broken into human history through the breach made by Jesus Christ in the time-space reality. Though God had made himself known in many ways in the past, in these last days he has visited us in the person of his own Son — the Word made man — at a particular time and in a definite place. It may be said that God has contextualized himself in Jesus Christ.

The incarnation makes clear God's approach to the revelation of himself and of his purposes: God does not shout his message from the heavens; God becomes present as a man among men. The climax of God's revelation is Emmanuel. And Emmanuel is Jesus, a first-century Jew! The incarnation unmistakably demonstrates God's intention to make himself known from within the human situation. Because of the very nature of the gospel, we know it only as a message contextualized in culture.

The consideration of the relationship between the gospel and the cultural context that surrounds it touches a wide variety of subjects, from the field of biblical hermeneutics (which deals with the reading of the gospel as it is revealed in Scripture) to the field that we might call "universal theology" (which considers the incarnation of the gospel in the varied cultures of the world). Without attempting to be exhaustive, I would like in this essay to try to bring into focus the problem of the contextualization of the gospel with a view to demonstrating the need for theological reflection in the Third World and the importance of such reflection for a full understanding of the gospel. In the first section I will address the issue of hermeneutics and its significance for the communication of the gospel from one culture to another. In the second section I will attempt to describe the theological situation in the Third World, the result of Western missionary efforts. In the third section I will argue for the contextualization of the gospel in terms of churches that incarnate the gospel in their own individual cultures and thereby collectively generate an evangelical theology that overcomes cultural barriers and reflects the many-sided wisdom of God.

To avoid any misunderstanding, I must state before beginning to consider the subject at hand that it is not my intention to detract from the work done by Western missionary societies or to deny the benefits the Third World has received from their efforts. I approach the subject as one whose own Christian roots spring from the missionary movement that has its center in the West. If I refer to weaknesses in missionary work, it is because I believe that to the extent to which we understand the factors that conspire against the contextualization of the gospel in each culture we will be in a better position to do our part so that all Christians, without regard to race or nationality, may come "to the unity of the faith and of the knowledge of the Son of God, to mature manhood, to the measure of the stature of the fullness of Christ" (Eph. 4:13). My purpose is to make a positive contribution to the consideration of matters that have profound significance for the life and mission of the church around the world.

THE GOSPEL AND CULTURE

The Word became man. It was acculturized, since man is a cultural being. It was thus that God put himself within man's reach, and consequently it is impossible either to understand or to communicate the gospel without referring to culture.

The Interpretation of the Gospel

The ordinary Christian usually assumes that in his Bible reading he can get along quite well without hermeneutics. He approaches the Bible as if it had been written by only one human and in historical circumstances much like his own. He believes he has direct access to the message revealed in Scripture, and he even distrusts any effort that may be made to understand this message in the light of its original historical context. In addition to adopting this simplistic approach to the reading of the Bible, he often completely neglects the history of biblical interpretation, setting out to understand the written Word as if he were the first to do so.

Implicit in this approach to Bible reading is the assumption that revelation consists basically of doctrinal statements that can be easily translated from the original languages (Hebrew and Greek) to the reader's own language. It is assumed that on the basis of the translated Bible, and with no historical study, an individual can easily understand the meaning of what he is reading and even arrive at a systematization of the biblical message, a systematization that for him is equal to Christianity itself. It is assumed that knowledge is basically rational and that it is communicated directly from the mind of God to the human mind through the sacred writings. Reality is perceived by means of concepts that are expressed in words. If any room is left for theology, it is for a type of theology that has as its basic task the systematization of the biblical statements regarding God, man, and the relation between the two.

When a person attempts to go beyond the mere reading of the Bible, he must immediately take into account the problem of hermeneutics. If the central theme of the Bible is God's action in history, which reached its culmination in the person and work of Jesus Christ, then clearly it will be impossible to understand the biblical message apart from its original historical context. Even the most elementary books on hermeneutics point out the importance of the historical background of the Bible for the understanding of its significance. The raw material of theology is not abstract concepts but rather a message concerning historical events the narration and interpretation of which are colored by the Semitic and Greco-Roman cultures in which the biblical authors lived. The initial task of theology is exegetical, and exegesis demands the construction of a bridge between the interpreter and the biblical authors by means of the historical method, the basic presupposition of which is that the Word of God cannot be understood apart from the cultural and linguistic situations in which it was originally given.

Nevertheless, hermeneutics is not merely a matter of analyzing texts in the light of their historical context. There is a basic error in the thinking of those who hold that interpretation is a purely scientific process the success of which is guaranteed by the correct use of exegetical tools. The fact is that there are at least three factors that condition one's understanding of the Word of God: the interpreter's attitude toward God, his ecclesiastical tradition, and his own cultural background.

1. *The interpreter's attitude toward God is decisive in his understanding of the Word.* Biblical revelation has to do with historical events and the interpretation of these events by the biblical authors, and the study of this revelation must therefore include historical investigation. But revelation is also intended to convince men of their sin and of the grace of God so that they will enter into a relationship of personal communion with him. It is not enough that the interpreter be familiar with the original historical context in which this revelation was delivered; in order to truly comprehend it, he must appropriate for himself the perspective of the biblical authors, the perspective of man in communion with God. As Paul Minear has pointed out, if there is an original *Sitz im Leben* (a life situation) there is also a *Sitz im Glauben* (a faith situation) that the interpreter must fully take into account.[1] By its very nature, religious knowledge includes the historical, the metaphysical, the ethical, and the personal: "It includes cognitive elements that are objectively true as well as the subjective and emotive aspects of personal involvement."[2] There is no knowledge of God that is not accompanied by the recognition that one has been known by God.

2. *It is very difficult for the interpreter to shake himself free from the influence of his own ecclesiastical tradition in his understanding of the Word.* If the purpose of God's revelation was not the production of a book but the formation of a people that should be the bearer of the Word, it follows that we must not neglect the history of biblical interpretation, which is the history of the ways in

1. See Minear, *Eyes of Faith* (London: Lutterworth Press, 1948), p. 181.
2. Arthur F. Holmes, *Faith Seeks Understanding: A Christian Approach to Knowledge* (Grand Rapids: William B. Eerdmans, 1971), p. 135.

which God's people, the church, has understood the written revelation down through the centuries. It must be recognized, however, that too often tradition becomes (even for those who profess the principle of *sola scriptura*) a factor of exegetical control that keeps the interpreter from hearing the message of Scripture. This is the origin of many of the doctrinal characteristics that divide Christians into "denominations," each of which considers itself superior to the rest.[3]

3. *The interpreter's understanding of the Word is conditioned by his culture.* He does not live in a vacuum but in a concrete historical situation, in a culture from which he derives not only his language but also his patterns of thought and conduct, his methods of learning, his emotional reactions, his values, interests, and goals. God's Word reaches him in terms of his own culture or it does not reach him at all. The knowledge of God is possible only when the Word becomes incarnate, so to speak, in the situation of the interpreter. In the words of James D. Smart,

> The interpretation does not begin when we sit down with the text and a number of commentaries to weigh the validity of a variety of suggested meanings. It begins before we are conscious of doing anything other than read the words. We hear them in a context, a highly complex context, the total context of our present historical existence. We hear them as the persons that we are, and their meaning for us is determined not only by the words but the character of the context in which we receive them. No man has direct access to the content of Scripture either by the perfection of his scholarship or the power of his inspiration. Every apprehension of the text and every statement of its meaning is an interpretation and, however adequately it expresses the content of the text, it dare not ever be equated with the text itself.[4]

3. On the problem of tradition as a form of "worldliness in the Church," see F. F. Bruce, *Traditions Old and New* (Exeter: Paternoster Press, 1970), pp. 163-74. We should also keep in mind, however, Richard Niebuhr's argument that in the development of denominationalism, theological factors are secondary to ethnic, social, economic, and cultural factors (See *The Social Sources of Denominationalism* [Hamden, Conn.: Shoe String Press, 1954]).

4. Smart, *The Strange Silence of the Bible in the Church: A Study in Hermeneutics* (London: SCM Press, 1970), pp. 53-54.

The recognition of the subjective element in the interpretation of Scripture is disturbing to those who would like to equate their own theology with the Word of God. A rationalistic mentality would prefer to conceive of the gospel as a system of truth at which one may arrive directly by means of the "scientific," "objective" method, apart from the element of personal commitment. The fact is that absolute objectivity is impossible. The interpreter is always present in his interpretation, present as a fallible being. Naturally interpretations can be subjected to controls that will ensure a closer approximation to the revealed message. This is the function of hermeneutics as a scientific discipline. But we must not ignore the distance that separates the revealed gospel from every interpretation of it. Every interpretation takes the shape given by the interpreter and therefore reflects, to a greater or lesser degree, the cultural context by which he is conditioned.[5] In summary, the knowledge of God derived from Scripture through exegesis is true but not complete, and thus no theology can be absolute. God always transcends our image of him.

Because the understanding of the Word of God is always relative to the culture of the interpreter, theology in any culture always runs the risk of being, to some extent, a reduction of the gospel. No culture completely fulfills the purpose of God; in all cultures there are some elements unfavorable to the understanding of the gospel. For this reason, the gospel never becomes completely incarnate in any given culture. It always transcends cultures, even cultures that it has deeply affected. I do not have the space here to elaborate on this point, but suffice it to say as an example that the individualism that characterizes Western culture has clouded the social dimension of the gospel in the eyes of the majority of Christians in the Western World.

If an interpreter allows the content of his interpretation to be affected by any of the values or premises of his culture that are incongruent with the gospel, the result is syncretism. In every syncretism there is an accommodation of the gospel to

5. Even the use of "scientific" tools in exegesis is conditioned by the cultural context of the interpreter. For example, the middle voice of the Greek can be translated directly into Spanish but not into English.

some value prevalent in the culture, an accommodation that usually stems from the desire to make the gospel "relevant." As early as the second century, the Gnostics attempted to accommodate the Christian faith to certain emphases in Greek philosophy. The history of theology since then is full of similar attempts. In our day, the adaptation of Christianity to Marxist premises has created a syncretism that claims to restore to the gospel its social and political dimension — some forms of "liberation theology." That these forms should be coming out of Latin America — a continent characterized by revolutionary ferment — eloquently demonstrates the extent to which theology is a reflection of the historical situation.

On the other hand, every culture also possesses elements favorable to the understanding of the gospel. By this I do not mean to say that the central themes of theology are derived from culture or that theology is absolutely determined by theological culture. My thesis is rather that every culture makes possible a certain approach to the gospel that brings to light certain of its aspects that in other cultures may remain less visible or even hidden. Seen from this perspective, the same cultural differences that hinder intercultural communications turn out to be an asset to the understanding of the many-sided wisdom of God; they serve as channels for the expression of aspects of the truth of the gospel that a theology tied down to one particular culture can easily overlook. As Eugene Rubingh has pointed out, the "primal vision" characteristic of African culture places the African in a privileged position to understand that "each is part of all, and the kingdom embraces every facet, every moment, every act."[6]

To date, textbooks on biblical hermeneutics (practically all written in the West) have had very little to say about the relationship between the interpretation of the Word of God and the cultural context of the interpreter. Frequently they give the impression that the only culture that need be taken into account

6. Rubingh, "The African Shape of the Gospel," *HIS* 33 (October 1972): 9ff. The phrase "primal vision" is taken from John V. Taylor; see his book *The Primal Vision: Christian Presence amid African Religion* (Philadelphia: Fortress Press, 1963), in which he shows that the African holds that the universe and human life form a whole the harmony of which must be preserved at any price.

is that of the biblical authors, that in some sense the interpreter can withdraw from his own historical situation in order to make an "objective" analysis of the text. It may be said that hermeneutics itself, as it is generally conceived of in these textbooks, is conditioned by the Cartesian divorce between subject and object that characterizes Western epistemology and that has resulted in "secular Christianity."[7] What is urgently needed is a recovery of the epistemology of biblical realism, a recovery that will give proper emphasis to the following facts[8] involved in the knowledge of God revealed in the gospel:

1. *The knowledge of God is personal and therefore inseparable from life in community.* No one knows God in isolation from his neighbor. "He who does not love does not know God; for God is love" (1 John 4: 8). The gospel includes God's purpose to wipe out the division between men — the curse invoked at Babel — and to create a new man characterized by "the unity of the faith and of the knowledge of the Son of God" (Eph. 4: 13) — the new humanity prefigured in the church at Pentecost, composed of representatives "from every nation under heaven" (Acts 2: 5). The fullness of the knowledge of Jesus Christ is not the private property of any one segment of the church in any one given culture; it belongs to the totality of the church. As Eugene Ahner puts it, "our understanding of the Gospel will not be complete until people from every nation and every culture give expression to that faith."[9]

2. *The knowledge of God is personal and therefore it takes place in the context of our bodily existence in the world.* The God whom the gospel proclaims is a God who has entered into human history in order to put himself within man's reach and to participate in all the contingencies of everyday life. The incarnation is a negation of every attempt to reach God by means of mysticism, asceticism, or rationalistic speculation; we know God through the Word who takes on concrete form in our own culture.

7. On this point, see Robert J. Blaikie, *Secular Christianity and the God Who Acts* (London: Hodder & Stoughton, 1970).

8. These theses are taken from Arthur Holmes's discussion of the nature of personal knowledge in *Faith Seeks Understanding*, pp. 125-31.

9. Ahner, response to Pierce Beaver's paper "The Missionary Image Today," in *Mission in the 70's*, ed. John T. Boberg and James A. Scherer (Chicago: Chicago Cluster of Theological Schools, 1972), p. 47.

3. *The knowledge of God is personal and therefore involves the emotions as well as reason.* Emotion is also an essential part of man made in the image of God. Therefore, if there is a place for a warning against "the escape from reason," there should also be room for a warning against the escape from passion. Too often Western theology is reduced to a cold, scientific, impersonal analysis of the truth of God; it lacks the emotional note that shows that man's love for God must be with his whole heart. The theological contribution from other cultures in which the dispassionate scientist has not been so idealized may provide the necessary corrective.

When we take into account the influence that the cultural context of the contemporary interpreter exerts on his interpretation of the gospel, it becomes obvious that even in the best of cases this interpretation is only an approximation, more or less accurate, of the revealed message. The interpreter does not have direct access to the gospel; nor can he penetrate into the world of the biblical writers, freeing himself of his own historical situation. Nevertheless, the knowledge of God revealed in the gospel is not withheld from him as a personal knowledge in the terms we have described thanks to the Holy Spirit, by whose action the gospel is contextualized in culture.

The Communication of the Gospel

Neither the interpretation nor the communication of the gospel can be carried out in a vacuum; they are realized in, and conditioned by, a given cultural context.

Anyone accustomed to public speaking is aware of the difficulties of communication, even when the speaker and the audience share the same culture. The fact is that the same words do not transmit the same message to all listeners. Each listener understands the message according to his own definitions, prejudices, concepts, and previous experiences. It is not surprising that there are so many misunderstandings in communication!

The problem is further complicated in intercultural communication. In addition to the difficulties involved in the simple verbal translation of a message from one language to another, there are the complexities of the transmission of the message from one culture (with its own thought patterns and standards of conduct, its own cognitive process and manner of learning) to another culture in which all, or almost all, is different. Obviously, if there is to be real communication, it is not enough simply to translate the terms from one language to more or less equivalent terms in the other language. As Eugene A. Nida has pointed out, in order for communication to take place it is necessary for the communicator to establish an effective relationship between the message and the total cultural context.[10] If the elements of communication — circumstances, techniques and methods, and the role of the participants — facilitate or obstruct communication, how much more will the content of the communication be affected by the epistemological approach and the symbols employed to transmit a message in a concrete situation. Where there is no common conceptual basis between the communicator and the receiver, at best the message given by the first will be reinterpreted by the second and integrated into his own ideological structure.[11]

A consciousness of the critical role that culture plays in communication is of special importance for the intercultural communication of the gospel. There are at least three reasons for this:

1. *The incarnation is a basic element in the gospel.* Since the Word became man, the only possible communication of the gospel is that in which the gospel becomes incarnate in culture in order to put itself within the reach of man as a cultural being. Any attempt to communicate the gospel without an initial profound identification of the communicator with the receiving culture is sub-Christian. The whole Bible is an eloquent witness to God's purpose to meet man and to converse with him in his specific historical situation. This is indicated by the anthropo-

10. See Nida, *Message and Mission: The Communication of the Christian Faith* (New York: Harper, 1960), pp. 171-88. David J. Hesselgrave has pointed out seven aspects of culture in the context of which every message is "codified" and interpreted: the concept of the world, the cognitive process, linguistic form, behavior patterns, means of communication, social structure, and motivations (Dimensions of Crosscultural Communication," *Practical Anthropology*, January-February 1972, pp. 1ff.).

11. On this point, see Charles Kraft, "Ideological Factors in Intercultural Communication," *Missiology: An International Review*, 2 (July 1974): 295-312.

morphic language of the Bible: God walks in the garden in the cool of the day; God has eyes, hands, feet; God repents. It is indicated by the action of the Logos, who pitched his tent at a definite spot in time and space, as a member of the Jewish nation. It is further indicated by the diversity of emphasis in the presentation of the apostolic message to be noted, for example, in a comparative study of Peter's sermon at Pentecost and Paul's address to the Areopagus in Athens, or of the Gospels and the Epistles. All authentic communication of the gospel is patterned on biblical communication and seeks to find a point of contact with man within his own culture.

2. *Without a translation that goes beyond the words to break into the raw material of life in the receiving culture, the gospel is a fantasy.* The gospel involves the proclamation of Jesus Christ as Lord of the totality of the universe and of human existence. If this proclamation is not directed to specific needs and problems of the hearers, how can they experience the Lordship of Christ in their concrete situation? To contextualize the gospel is so to translate it that the Lordship of Jesus Christ is not an abstract principle or a mere doctrine but the determining factor of life in all its dimensions and the basic criterion in relation to which all the cultural values that form the very substance of human life are evaluated. Without contextualization, the gospel will become tangential or even entirely irrelevant.[12]

3. *In order for the gospel to receive an intelligent response, either positive or negative, there must be effective communication, communication that takes into consideration the point of contact between the message and the culture of the hearers.* There can be no true evangelization unless the gospel confronts cultural values and thought patterns. As David Hesselgrave puts it, "Intercultural communication is as complex as the sum total of human differences."[13] If such is the case, evangelization cannot be reduced to the repetition of literally

---

12. Jacob A. Loewen agrees that in order for the message to be relevant it must speak to specific needs in the culture, but he correctly observes that "the truly relevant message speaks not only to an immediate need, but to a range of basic problems. As a true message from God it will provide a new and renewed reason to be for both individual and society" ("The Church: Indigenous and Ecumenical," *Practical Anthropology*, November-December 1964, p. 244).

13. Hesselgrave, p. 1.

translated doctrinal formulas that may have proved successful in other latitudes. If evangelization is to go beyond the conscious level and if its claims are to provide more than just an invitation to intellectual assent, it must include contextualization of the gospel as one of its essential elements. Otherwise, it will produce false conversions or negative responses that reflect faulty communication rather than a rejection of Jesus Christ.

In conclusion, without the contextualization of the gospel there can be no real communication of the Word of God. Communication of the gospel can be carried out only with reference to the complexity of cultural factors involved in communication. This is not a question of a simple literal translation, but of an interpretation that requires the guidance of the Holy Spirit.

THE GOSPEL IN THE THIRD WORLD

One of the most outstanding events of our day is that the gospel of Jesus Christ is being preached in practically all the nations of the Earth. The missionary movement based in the West has written some of the most glorious pages in the history of Christianity. And it is largely due to the efforts of this missionary movement that the church is a worldwide community today.

The question must be raised, however, about the extent to which the geographic expansion of the gospel has been accompanied by an incarnation of the gospel in the many varied human cultures. Can it be honestly said that Christians around the world are demonstrating that the gospel is a universal message, the relevance of which is not limited to the Western world? What is the contribution of the church in the Third World to the task of elaborating a theology that reflects God's purpose "that all come to the unity of the faith and of the knowledge of the Son of God"? In the paragraphs that follow I will attempt to answer these questions briefly, with special reference to the situation in Latin America.

A Church without Theology

It happened during an international congress on the communication of the gospel in Latin America. The plenary session brought together several hundred Christian leaders, all active in the proclamation of the gospel. The relationship between theology and evangelism was one of the topics under discussion. Someone made the observation that without theology, evangelism becomes proselytism and faith becomes an ideology. A response was not long in coming. A well-known evangelist spoke up to make what he undoubtedly regarded as a "defense" of evangelism against theology. "What sense is there in spending time and energy on theology, when the pressing need today is to preach the gospel?" That, for him, was the question.

That unforgettable episode throws into relief a fact that cannot be denied: the church in Latin America is a church without a theology. This is a categorical statement, and it is not to be expected that it will be accepted without discussion. After all, someone will say, is not the gospel being preached, and is not the preaching of the gospel in itself a theological discourse? Yes, it is. In a sense, wherever the good news of salvation in Jesus Christ is preached, there is theology. A theology is always implicit in the communication of the gospel even on the most elementary level. Without theology, the gospel cannot exist: if the gospel is not theological, then it is not the gospel. In this sense we must accept the observation that "there is theology without the church, but there cannot be a church without theology."[14] Furthermore, it must not be assumed that the only theology that deserves the name is speculative theology, written by a theologian enclosed in his ivory tower. Whoever is tempted to make this assumption should observe that the only theology known in the Bible is what may be called "functional theology," a theology hammered out in the heat of the battle and for the battle. No biblical writer was a professional theologian!

In stating that the church in Latin America is a church without theology, however, I am not denying the existence of an implicit theology nor am I lamenting the absence of a speculative theology. The statement has meaning only within the

14. Lamberto Schuurman, *El cristiano, la Iglesia y la revolucion* (Buenos Aires: Editorial La Aurora, 1970), p. 87.

framework of a deeper analysis of the function of theological reflection in relation to the life and mission of the church. It is the recognition that, as José Míguez Bonino has written, "the Christian Church owes a great debt to Latin America: four and a half centuries of Roman Catholicism and one century of Protestantism have produced a minimum of the creative thinking that these peoples have the right to expect from those who hold that they have received the mission of announcing the Word of God to men."[15] In this sense, our statement points out one failure of the church regarding its responsibility in relation to the gospel — the responsibility of thinking from the perspective of God's revelation, on the significance of that revelation here and now, and on its implications for the mission of the church in a concrete situation.

To be more exact, we might say that the church in Latin America is a church with no theological reflection of its own. Does anyone doubt the truth of this statement? Let him notice the quantity of Christian literature translated from English (and how poor many of these translations are!) and the scarcity of literature we ourselves have produced. Let him notice how much of our preaching is limited to a mere repetition of poorly assimilated doctrinal formulas with no application to our own historical reality. Let him observe the extent to which our churches, without thinking, maintain the theological coloring of the missions that established them and hold theological study to consist basically in the study of the doctrinal distinctives of the churches to which they trace their origins. Let him examine the faculty and the curriculum of the majority of our seminaries and Bible schools. Let him review our hymnology and "chorusology." An examination of all these aspects of our church situation will show him that our "theological dependence" is just as real and as serious as the economic dependence that characterizes the countries of the Third World.

It is true that the last few years have seen in Latin America the growth of a theological movement that has gone far beyond the boundaries of this continent. Gustavo Gutiérrez, Hugo

15. Míguez Bonino, intro. in Rubem Alves, *A Theology of Human Hope* (Washington, D.C.: Corpus Books, 1969), p. 1.

Assmann, Juan Luis Segundo, and José Miranda (all Roman Catholic writers) are names familiar to many readers in Europe and North America. Without meaning to belittle their contributions, however, I think it is important to note the following pertinent points: (1) the volume of their production is still very small and their impact too limited to make any significant change in the picture of the church painted above; and (2) although a number of Protestant churches have appropriated this theology for want of a theology of their own with which to face the task of contextualizing the gospel, it is highly doubtful that this theology will have any wide effect outside the small circle of its Roman Catholic adherents.[16]

If the church in Latin America — a continent traditionally "Christian" — suffers from an endemic theological anemia, it is not surprising that the same picture is repeated in Asia and Africa. Without ignoring the work that a few thinkers are undertaking in an effort to give expression to the Christian faith in the context of their own culture, it must be admitted that on the whole the church in the Third World continues to be a church without a theology. Wilbert R. Shenk does not exaggerate when he says that "in spite of some surface signs of success, the modern missionary movement has failed at a profound level until today. The church which is the product of this historic movement suffers seriously from spiritual and intellectual rootlessness."[17]

There is no hope that this situation will change as long as we conceive of the theological responsibility of missions as the exportation of theologies elaborated in the West. Especially in the fields of theological education and Christian literature, there

16. Since I first wrote this essay there has been an amazing theological explosion in Roman Catholic Circles in Latin America, especially in Brazil. The influence of Latin American liberation theologians has been strongly felt among common people in the *comunidades de base* (Christian grassroots communities), the multiplication of which is one of the most significant developments within the Roman Catholic Church today. By contrast, conservative evangelicals in this region of the world continue to be largely dependent on "imported theology." I would estimate that less than three percent of the books printed in Spanish or Portuguese by evangelical publishers are being written by Latin American authors.

17. Shenk, "Theology and the Missionary Task," *Missiology: An International Review* 1 (July 1973): 296.

is urgent need for a realization of the damage caused to the church in the Third World by the continual bombardment it receives of the doctrinal formulations and predigested "Christian answers" of the West. This imposition of Western cultural models, often supported by economic power, cannot but retard indefinitely the growth of indigenous churches, rooted in their own culture and capable of making their own theological contribution. [18] And as long as the gospel does not attain a profound contextualization in the local culture, in the eyes of people in that culture it will continue to be a "foreign religion."

If the Western-based missionary movement is evaluated not from the perspective of its express intentions but from the perspective of its results, the obvious conclusion is that as far as the formation of indigenous churches in the Third World goes, missionary practice lags far behind theory. Without taking into consideration the important role of culture in both the interpretation and the communication of the gospel, missionaries have generally assumed that their task is to extract the message directly from the biblical text and to transmit it directly to their hearers in "the mission field." Such an attitude is simplistic; it does not fit reality.

It is this simplistic attitude that accounts for the objection, common in missionary circles, to any suggestion that there is a need to formulate an evangelical theology in Latin America, Asia, or Africa. "What's wrong with biblical theology?" they ask. "There is no need for a lot of theologies. One theology is

18. The tie between the missionary movement and Western "power" goes beyond the limits of this study. Suffice it to say here that too frequently missions have used their economic power to dictate programs of theological education and literature and, consequently, to dictate their theology. As long as the power of decision is in the hands of missionaries or (what is worse) mission executives, there is no chance that the churches of the Third World will develop as truly indigenous churches. Their needs will continue to be defined from outside their own situation, and missionary work will continue to be conducted by big-business companies. Obviously, the theological problem is inseparable from the question of power.

On the relationship between missions and Western colonial domination, see Jacob Loewen's essay "Evangelism and Culture," in *The New Face of Evangelicalism*, ed. C. René Padilla (London: Hodder & Stoughton, 1976). See also Orlando E. Costas, "Captivity and Liberation in the Modern Missionary Movement," in *Christ Outside the Gate: Mission Beyond Christendom* (Maryknoll, N.Y.: Orbis Books, 1982), pp. 58-70.

sufficient for the whole world." This is the approach to theology that has kept the church in the Third World completely dependent on Western thought patterns. It is the approach that in the name of orthodoxy has time and again imposed on the young church the doctrinal emphases characteristic of the founders of the missions and has cut off at the roots any creative reflection that goes deep into native cultures. It is, finally, the approach that is inadvertently extending a "culture Christianity" in which biblical elements are combined with elements of Greek philosophy and of the European-American heritage.[19]

The church in the Third World needs a theology that answers to its own needs. From Western missions it has received the gospel reduced and wrapped in cultural clothing that robs it of much of its transforming power. This is its greatest tragedy and its greatest challenge.

The Causes of This Situation

It would be presumptuous to try to explain all the reasons behind the theological deficit that the church in the Third World is suffering. I will limit myself to suggesting two causes that are immediately evident.

1. *The divorce between evangelism and theology.* A quarter of a century has passed since the first Latin American Evangelical Conference, when Dr. Manuel Gutiérrez Marín and Dr. Marc Boegner, outstanding representatives of the evangelical churches of Latin Europe, pointed out the absence of theology in the declarations made by the assembly. More than a decade later, recalling this incident, Adam F. Sosa, an Argentine evangelical writer, spoke out in defense of "the theological position of Latin

19. The theological methodology that Western missionaries have taken to the rest of the world quite clearly reflects the cultural influence of Greek philosophy and not simply the structure of the Christian faith itself, which is closely tied to the Hebrew tradition. Elements of Greek philosophy entered Western Christian theology early in the church's history, as, for example, in the question of the immortality of the soul (on which, see Oscar Cullmann, *Immortality of the Soul or Resurrection of the Dead? The Witness of the New Testament* [London: Epworth Press, 1958]) and in the related issue of spirit/matter dualism.

Influences that have crept into theology and mission work from the modern Western philosophical tradition include rationalistic epistemology, individualism, materialism, and a general atomization of reality.

American evangelicals."[20] To do this, he presented a series of arguments intended to show that in our continent the most important thing for the church is to win men and women to the gospel, and that this tradition is at least as valid as the European Protestant tradition. We are the children, he said, not of the Reformation but of the evangelical revival of the eighteenth century and its daughter movements. Our trademark, consequently, is evangelism, not theology or liturgy. Our origin explains our legitimate emphasis on experience rather than creed, on lay involvement in evangelism as opposed to the indifference of the historic churches to mission, on the "segregated churches" rather than the "national churches." The same argument could well have been used in Asia or Africa.

Since that day a lot of water has gone under the bridge. Changes have taken place in every aspect of life. The numerical growth of Protestant churches in the Third World has drawn the attention of the Church Growth experts. Nevertheless, Sosa's defense of "our tradition" is for many Third World evangelical leaders still as valid today as when it was first written. According to them, we are still in the "stage of faith and evangelistic passion." It is their desire that we continue in this stage for a long time.

It is fitting to ask here if this one-sided emphasis on evangelism does justice either to the Word of God or to the situation of the church of Christ in the Third World. It may well be that maintaining the tradition of our "revivalist" origins is precisely the biggest obstacle to our fulfilling the mission of the church in this critical period of history! In the final analysis, we have to ask what gospel it is that we are preaching if our preaching

20. Sosa, "Some Considerations on the Theological Positions of Evangelicals in Latin America," *Pensamiento Cristiano* 8 (March 1961): 232-41. The same divorce between evangelization and theology that can be detected in this article underlies the observation that "the crucial issues" confronting the church in Latin America are related to "the effective communication of the Gospel" and not to "European and North American theological emphases concerning secularized Christianity" in *Latin American Church Growth*, by William R. Read, Victor M. Monterroso, and Harmon A. Johnson (Grand Rapids: William B. Eerdmans, 1969), p. 351. It is paradoxical that such an observation should appear not in a theological study of the communication of the gospel written from the Latin American perspective but in a pragmatic study representative of North American missiology.

is not fed by a conscientious study of the Word of God and by serious reflection on its significance in our concrete situation. Can we claim to have made the Christian faith really *ours* if we limit ourselves to repeating doctrinal formulas worked out in other latitudes? Can there be evangelism that is really biblical — that really presents the whole counsel of God — without theological reflection that seeks to understand the relevance of the gospel to the totality of human life in a given historical context?

2. *The concentration of evangelical work on numerical growth.* In theory, no one denies that the qualitative growth of the church is important. An analysis of the situation, however, shows an undeniable concentration of evangelical work on the multiplication of the number of churches and church members as the ultimate criterion by which the growth of the church is measured. The harm that this emphasis has caused in the Third World is incalculable. In addition to creating a regrettable spirit of competition that is more related to the capitalistic system than to the Word of God, it has caused almost the whole evangelistic thrust in the "mission field" to be thrown into the spread of a simplistic version of the gospel, a message that perennially excludes the deeper dimensions of faith, a "culture Christianity" that refuses to acknowledge the need to let the Word of God speak from within the human situation. What matters is multiplying the number of "believers," even though in order to do this it may be necessary to leave out everything that cannot be made to fit into a completely individualistic, other-worldly system. Evangelism becomes a technique to "win souls," and for this, theological reflection is unnecessary; it is enough to use canned methods and imported formulas of salvation.

Furthermore, if numerical growth is what matters most, missionary strategy will have to give priority to the classes of people that are most "productive" in terms of conversions. There will not be time for the people who demand answers that are well thought out and relevant to the historical situation — the type of answers that presuppose theological reflection. Can this be one of the reasons why relatively little has been done among university students and intellectuals in the Third World?

Consequences of the Theological Deficit in the Third World

As we have already noted, the existence of an "implicit theology" in the Third World cannot be denied. Nor can it be denied that even on the most elementary level the theology that dominates the scene on the "mission field" is one that has been elaborated in other latitudes—a collection of concepts that have little to do with the problems that the "underdeveloped lands" put before the Christian faith. We would do well to note three consequences of this situation:

1. *The lack of contextualization of the gospel in the cultures of the Third World.* In Asia as well as in Africa, Christianity is an ethnic religion—the white man's religion. In Latin America, on the other hand, it serves as a cultural decoration that could easily be left out. As José Míguez Bonino has said, "Neither Roman Catholicism nor Protestantism . . . has rooted deeply enough in Latin American human reality to produce creative thinking. In other words, both churches have remained on the fringe of the history of our peoples."[21]

Obviously, this is not to say that the message of the gospel should be one thing here and another one there. It has been given "once and for all," and its proclamation is faithful in the degree to which it manifests the permanence of the revealed data, either here or there. Nor am I suggesting that there is a need for an "indigenous theology" characterized by local folklore and completely conditioned by the historical situation. Even less would we wish a theology that, in an effort to "contextualize" the gospel, superciliously ignores the results of long years of work in the field of biblical research carried on by theologians in Europe or North America. It would be ridiculous to think that we in the Third World must start at the beginning, ignoring the contributions that others have made to our thinking. What is necessary, however, is a theology that will take advantage of that which is of value in any study, whatever its source, and on that basis show the revelance of biblical reve-

21. Míguez Bonino, pp. i-ii. On the foreign nature of Christianity in Africa after many years of missionary labor, see Dean S. Gilliland, "The Indigenous Concept in Africa," *Missiology: An International Review* 1 (July 1973): 343-56.

lation to our culture, the relation between the gospel and the problems that the church is facing in our society.

If the gospel is not contextualized, the Word of God will remain a *logos asarkos* (unincarnate word), a message that touches our lives only tangentially. This is precisely one of the most tragic consequences of the lack of theological reflection among us — that the gospel still has a foreign sound or no sound at all in relation to many of the dreams and anxieties, problems and questions, values and customs in the Third World. This is why the middle-class Latin American Protestant (and we suspect that the same is true in Asia and Africa), in the midst of the pressing material needs of the majority of the population, can adopt without any problem a lifestyle completely out of tune with the situation.[22] This is why the African, underneath all the doctrinal structure that he accepts at the conscious level, can maintain intact his traditions and customs, whether or not they are congruent with biblical faith.

Those who object to the contextualization of the gospel out of fear of syncretism must take into account the fact that precisely when there is no conscious reflection on the form that obedience to the Lordship of Jesus Christ must take in a given situation, conduct can quite easily be determined by the culture rather than by the gospel.[23] When the attention is centered on verbal formulations or on exterior aspects of the Christian life with a view to shutting the front door to syncretism, it is most probable that syncretism will enter through the back door and produce a "culture Christianity" that simply assimilates the values of the surrounding society. In every effort to communicate the gospel while doing justice to the cultural context, there is the danger of syncretism. The alternative, however, is not what

22. On this point, see Charles Denton, "The Protestant Mentality: A Sociological Approach," *Practical Anthropology*, May-June 1964, pp. 105ff. The same phenomenon is found among Latin American Indians, as Samuel Ruiz García has pointed out in "The Incarnation of the Church in Indigenous Cultures," *Missiology: An International Review* 1 (July 1973): 21-27. Ruiz García states that "sandwich religion, with its pagan filling and Christian form, results from missionary work which has failed to present the Gospel message in terms that speak to the real anxieties and questions of a people in their cultural milieu" (p. 21).

23. On the distinction between contextualization and syncretism, see Nida, pp. 185-86.

Charles Kraft has termed "extractionism," in which the missionary tries to communicate the message in terms of his own frame of reference,[24] but a new reading of the gospel from within the historical situation under the guidance of the Holy Spirit. After all, it must not be forgotten that the "extractionist" approach, which has accompanied the Western missionary movement, has not been able to prevent pagan elements from persisting in the church in the Third World. There is no way to avoid the dangers in intercultural communication when teaching is reduced to indoctrination and the teachers are unaware that such dangers exist.

2. *The inability of the church to withstand the ideologies of the day.* The church that does not feed its faith through reflective thinking easily falls victim to prevailing ideologies. It lacks the criteria to evaluate the answers given by society. The result is that the church conforms to contemporary circumstances and becomes a guardian of the status quo; or, on the other hand, it may let itself be conditioned by ideological propaganda calling for change and, unconsciously, let itself be used to that end. I believe it is in this area that there lies the greatest danger for a "church of the masses" with no theological orientation — which is what the church in Latin America is at this moment in history, faced with the danger of being carried away by whatever winds happen to blow, with no criteria to discern what the gospel demands in this situation. This is true especially in countries such as Chile and Brazil, in which politicians see in the church, with its large number of members, a force to be exploited for their own interests. Without theology, without a fixed point of reference from which to evaluate the ideologies, the church becomes absorbed by the world. Is this not what we so often see in the case of young people reared in Christian homes and churches, for example, who, when they begin to consider the application of Christian discipleship in concrete situations, find that they are unable to speak to the interpretation of reality propounded by their Marxist friends? (I refer to Marxism here because presently it is the ideology

24. See Kraft, "Ideological Factors in Intercultural Communication," *Missiology: An International Review* 2 (July 1974): 304.

with the widest "missionary" outreach in the majority of Latin American countries.) There is an urgent need for a theological framework that will help us evaluate the different interpretations of our present situation (or change it) without falling into the sanctification of either a rightist or a leftist ideology.

3. *The loss of second- and third-generation "Christians."* This is a common phenomenon. I have seen it all over Latin America. It happens particularly with university students, people who were brought up in Christian homes but today will have nothing to do with the gospel or with the church. Why? To say that "they have gone into the world because they loved darkness rather than light" is not enough. One of the many "sociologists" who are studying the "fabulous growth of the church in the Third World" could render an invaluable service to the study of missions by conducting a survey not only of those who enter the church but also of those who leave. I suspect on the basis of mere observation that the study would show at least two things: first, that the number of second- and third-generation "Christians" who have left the church in the last ten or fifteen years is well up in the hundreds; and second, that in very many cases (it would be foolish to risk an estimate of the percentage) the reason for leaving was a crisis of faith stemming from the absence of a sound theological basis and of an understanding of the wider dimensions of the Christian faith. The young person whose biblical knowledge never gets beyond Sunday School level sooner or later finds that his Christian system breaks down, that his faith does not have an adequate basis on which to sustain the weight of the objections raised by life in contemporary society. It is not really surprising that many of the young guerrilla leaders in some countries are from Christian homes! What the church was unable to give them in terms of a purpose in life and an adequate perspective from which to understand history, they have found in a secular ideal that in the end destroys their "inherited faith."

TOWARD A CONTEXTUALIZED GOSPEL

A photocopy of a theological document written in Europe or North America can never satisfy the theological needs of the church in the Third World. Now that the church has become a world community, the time has come for it to manifest the universality of the gospel in a theology that is not bound by a particular culture but shows the many-sided wisdom of God. If it is widely recognized that the European and North American cultural appendages of the gospel have become an increasingly heavy burden on those who feel called to carry Christ's message to peoples of non-European traditions, the moment has come to do something about it. The theological task can no longer be regarded as the task of one sector of the church; it must be viewed as the task of the whole church in search of "the unity of faith and the knowledge of the Son of God."

Guidelines for an Evangelical Theology

This moment in history makes a demand on Christians everywhere—to delve deeply into Scripture under the guidance of the Holy Spirit in order to find whatever light it will throw on today's problems. If the gospel is to be not just intellectually accepted but also lived, it must necessarily take shape within our cultural context. The role of theology is to interpret and clarify God's Word for the sake of obedience to Christ in the concrete historical situation. In other words, theology is an instrument for the contextualization of the gospel. And for it to fulfill its purpose it must be based on biblical revelation, in the context of real life and for obedience to Christ today. It must therefore take into account the following guidelines:

1. *The basis of theology is the Word of God.* God has spoken in Jesus Christ and what he has said in him (including his person and work) is the central theme of Scripture. The Word of God has been "inscripturated" and as such plays an absolutely essential normative role in theological thinking by the action of the Holy Spirit. Without this control exercised by the Word and by the Spirit who works through the Word, theology becomes mere human wisdom—a mere projection of man, an anthropology.

The normative character of the Word, if it is to be more than just theory, demands serious exegesis. And it is absurd to think that in order to be "indigenous," exegesis must somehow get along without the basic tools that have been provided by European and North American biblical scholarship.

2. *The context of theology is the concrete historical situation.* "Pure theology" produced in an ivory tower bears a closer relationship to scholasticism than to the Bible. Theological thinking is not basically an intellectual exercise, but rather a discovery of the will of God regarding the practice of truth. The study of the Bible is not so much a matter of assimilating information as of discerning the will of God in the context of specific commitment. Jesus said, "If any man's will is to do His will, he shall know whether the teaching is from God or whether I am speaking on my own authority" (John 7: 17).

3. *The purpose of theology is obedience to Christ.* It may well be repeated that the only theology known to the Bible is a "functional theology," a theology elaborated for the purpose of carrying out God's plan through his people. For this reason evangelical theology must never lack the pastoral touch. In a sense, it is a pastoral homily in which God makes himself known to us as the God who uses us as the light of the world and the salt of the earth. This implies that theology cannot focus solely on the individual and his needs but must go one step further to discern the will of God in relation to the world in which the church is called to live out the gospel.

The Church and the Contextualization of the Gospel

In the final analysis, the contextualization of the gospel is not man's work but God's. It is only as the Word of God becomes flesh in the people of God that the gospel takes shape within culture. It is not God's purpose that the gospel be merely a message in words; it must be a message incarnate in his church and, through it, in history. The God who has always spoken to men from within the historical situation has appointed the church as his instrument for the manifestation of Christ's presence in the midst of men. The contextualization of the gospel can never take place apart from the contextualization of the church.

If the church is to reveal Christ within culture, it must first experience the reality of Christ's death with regard to culture. As Hans Bürki has put it, "The first decisive operation of the gospel in confronting culture-man with God is to cut him free from his cultural umbilical cord."[25] In practical terms this means that the totality of life (including patterns of thinking and conduct, values, habits, and roles) must be judged by the standard of the Word of God, so that only what is honoring to Christ remains and is fulfilled. Dying with Christ, we die to our own culture and are thereby enabled to recognize with greater objectivity the ways in which we are conditioned by it as well as to appreciate the values in any culture other than our own. We thus catch a glimpse of the relevance of the gospel to Jews and Gentiles and consequently of the glory of the risen Christ who transforms culture.

The truly indigenous church is the one that through death and resurrection with Christ embodies the gospel within its own culture. It adopts a way of being, thinking, and acting in which its own cultural patterns are transformed and fulfilled by the gospel. In a sense, it is the cultural embodiment of Christ, the means through which Christ is formed within a given culture. The task of the church is not the extension of a culture Christianity throughout the world but the incarnation of the gospel in each culture. Missionary work must therefore be oriented toward the formation of what Charles H. Kraft calls "dynamic equivalence churches," which he compares with dynamic translations of the Bible.[26] Those churches in the Third World that remain tied to the Western mother church are "literal translations," alienated from their own culture. They reduce the Christian faith to outward conformity to words that have been transliterated from another culture. The indigenous churches are "dynamic translations" that produce in their own society the same kind of impact as that which was produced by the early church in the Greco-Roman world. They use the forms of the local culture, but they transform them into tools for the expression of the Christian faith. It is only through "dynamic equivalence churches" that the gospel will be contextualized. These churches alone will be able to generate a gen-

25. Bürki, "The Gospel and Human Culture," in *The Gospel Today* (London: IFES, 1975).
26. See Kraft, "Dynamic Equivalence Churches," *Missiology: An International Review* 1 (July 1973): 39-57.

uine evangelical theology in which the many-sided wisdom of God will be reflected.

The contextualization of the gospel will not consist in an adaptation of an existing theology to a given culture. It will not merely be the result of an intellectual process. It will not be aided by a benevolent missionary paternalism intended to help the young church to select those cultural elements that can be regarded as positive. The contextualization of the gospel can only be a gift of grace granted by God to a church that is seeking to place the totality of life under the Lordship of Christ in its historical situation. More than a wonder of nature, the incarnation is a wonder of grace.

Christ and Antichrist in the Proclamation of the Gospel

Simply to mention the Antichrist places us face to face with a difficult problem of biblical interpretation. Who (or what) is the Antichrist? Since the first centuries in the history of the church many have conceived of him as an apocalyptic personage whose appearance in history will precede the second coming of Christ. At present in Latin America various modern versions of this interpretation are being circulated, each one claiming to be the only one possible. The time in which the Antichrist was identified with the Pope, following Luther and other Reformers, has already passed (or at least is passing).[1] Today, in certain systems of literal interpretation, the Antichrist is variously identified with a future universal dictator who with his armies will oppose Christ in the battle of Armageddon, and also with a mythological figure representative of a completely outdated Jewish apocalyptic.

I do not claim to have the key to the interpretation of all the affirmations the New Testament makes concerning the Antichrist. For the purposes of this essay I prefer to leave in suspense

1. In *The Smalkald Articles* Luther says, "just as we may not worship the devil himself as a lord and a god, neither can we accept his apostle, the Pope or the Antichrist, as head or lord of the government, because his papal government consists in lies and murders, in eternal perversion of souls and bodies, as I have already shown in several books" (*Obras de Martin Lutero* [Buenos Aires: Editorial Paidós, 1971], 5: 176). In the opinion of George Milligan, "with a few honourable exceptions, the equation 'the Pope, or the Papacy, is Antichrist' may be said to have been the prevailing view of Protestant exegetes for a period of about two hundred years" (*St. Paul's Epistles to the Thessalonians* [1908; reprint, Grand Rapids: William B. Eerdmans, 1952], p. 169).

the answer to the questions raised by futuristic eschatology — not because I believe they are not important but because (in addition to doubting my competence to answer them) I consider them to be outside the limits of the topic we are considering. Leaving aside these questions, we can concentrate our attention on the significance of the proclamation of the gospel in relation to the conflict represented by the Christ-Antichrist antithesis. In the first part of this essay I will summarize New Testament teaching concerning the Antichrist, emphasizing what to my understanding is clear on the basis of the study of the texts. In the second part I will attempt to discern the signs of the times in the Latin American situation. In the third part, finally, I will suggest some consequences for the work of evangelization in our context.

I. THE ANTICHRIST IN THE NEW TESTAMENT

In order to explain the origin of the figure of the Antichrist, scholars often make reference to the apocalyptic and pseudepigraphical literature of the intertestamental period and the first century of the Christian era. We cannot take the time here to analyze this question of special interest to students of the origins of religion; we will limit ourselves to observing that the points of coincidence between the Antichrist of the New Testament and certain mythical figures that appear in such books as 4 *Esdras*, the *Testament of the Twelve Patriarchs*, the *Book of Jubilees*, *The Assumption of Isaiah*, and the *Sibylline Oracles* show that the New Testament figure developed in an atmosphere in which the expectation of the end of the world, rooted in the Old Testament prophecies, was mixed with a negative understanding of contemporary historical events.

Much more obvious, however, is the connection of the Antichrist of the New Testament with Daniel's prophecy, as we will see when we examine the various New Testament passages on the subject — Mark 13; 2 Thessalonians 2:1-12; Revelation 13; 1 John 2:18-29 and 4:1-6; and 2 John 7.[2]

---

2. The term *Antichrist* is used only in the letters of John (five times), but it is evident that the concept is present as well in the other passages mentioned.

Mark 13

The "Little Revelation" of Mark 13 (par. Matt. 24 and Luke 21) refers to "the desolating sacrilege" (v. 14, RSV) the appearance of which will coincide with a period of intense suffering unparalleled in human history. This is the description of a person who incarnates the most horrifying idolatry ("The Awful Horror", as Today's English Version translates it). The terminology is derived directly from Daniel 9:27; 11:31; and 12:11 — passages that have as background the desecration of the Temple in Jerusalem committed by Antiochus Epiphanes to convert it into a center for the worship of Zeus, chief of the Olympian gods, of whom the tyrant claimed to be the earthly manifestation (167 B.C.). In the context of Mark 13, the reference to the desolating sacrilege may be related to the fall of Jerusalem (70 A.D.), when the Roman legions surrounded the city with their standards adorned with the imperial eagle detested by the Jewish nationalists.[3] But a strange grammatical phenomenon suggests that the sacrilege is a person, of whom it is said that he occupies the place where he ought not be (*estēkota opou ou dei*), that is, the place that belongs to God.[4] This last description coincides with that ascribed to the Antichrist in 2 Thessalonians 2:4: "he takes his seat in the temple of God, proclaiming himself to be God."

Another important element in relation to the coming of the Antichrist in Mark 13 is the reference to the false prophets (*pseudoprophētai*) and the false christs (*pseudochristoi*) who will perform signs and miracles "to lead astray, if possible, the elect" (v. 22; cf. v. 6). The extent to which the action of these masters of deceit is directly inspired by the Antichrist is not stated explicitly in the passage, but it is clear that it is part of a complex picture of rebellion against God and general apostasy that will precede the coming of Christ and that will find its fullest expression in the Antichrist.

3. See R. A. Cole, *The Gospel according to St. Mark: An Introduction and Commentary* (London: Tyndale Press, 1961), p. 202. The reference to the Roman armies in Luke 21:20 is clear.
4. The noun *abomination* (*to bdelugma*), neuter in gender, is modified by a masculine participle (*estēkota*).

2 Thessalonians 2:1-12

It is not difficult to demonstrate that Paul's image of the Antichrist derives its outlines from the apocalyptic visions of the prophet Daniel. The following parallel concepts may be noted:

2 Thessalonians 2	Daniel
"the rebellion" (v. 3); "with all wicked deception for those who are to perish" (v. 10)	"By his cunning he shall make deceit prosper under his hand" (8:25); "He shall seduce with flattery those who violate the covenant" (11:32); "those who acknowledge him he shall magnify with honor" (11:39)
"the man of lawlessness" (*anomias*, "without law") (v. 3)	"he . . . shall think to change the times and the law" (7:25)
"who opposes and exalts himself against every so-called god or object of worship, so that he takes his seat in the temple of God, proclaiming himself to be God" (v. 4)	"the horn which had eyes and a mouth that spoke great things" (7:20); "he shall speak words against the Most High" (7:25); "the he-goat magnified himself exceedingly" (8:8); "and the king shall do according to his will; he shall exalt himself and magnify himself above every god" (11:36)
"the son of perdition" (v. 3); "and the Lord Jesus will slay him with the breath of his mouth and destroy him by his appearing and his coming" (v. 8)	"by no human hand, he shall be broken" (8:25)

In the context of 2 Thessalonians 2 the Antichrist is an eschatological figure whose manifestation (*apocalypsis*, vv. 3, 6) will precede the second coming of Christ. His coming (*parousia*, v. 9) is a sign of the Parousia (the coming of Christ). It has not yet taken place, according to the apostle, and consequently his readers must not allow themselves to be deceived by the idea that "the day of the Lord" is going to take place immediately or even perhaps that it has already taken place (v. 3). But "the mystery of lawlessness is already at work" (v. 7); there are already signs that presage the revelation of the anti-Messiah. It is obvious that the end is drawing near.

The various descriptions of the Antichrist in this passage compose the portrait of a sinister personage. The picture is not that of an incarnation of Satan, but rather one of a man invested with satanic powers that enable him to execute supernatural acts. His signs and wonders are "pretended" (RSV; "lying," AV), not because they lack reality but rather because they deceive (vv. 10-11). Thus they are the antithesis of the miracles that are carried out by the power of Jesus Christ; they are, we might say, the anti-miracles that accompany the diffusion of error just as the miracles of Christ accompany the diffusion of the gospel. All the work of the Antichrist is a parody of the work of Jesus Christ, by means of which the "man of lawlessness" (the "without-law") propagates the lie. But the intention of the Antichrist goes further than being a pseudo-Messiah, supplanting Christ; his intention is to occupy the place that belongs to God, "proclaiming himself to be God" (v. 4). His action thus projects the most abominable presumption imaginable — the claim to universal worship. For this reason he "opposes and exalts himself against every so-called god or object of worship" (v. 4). As Geerhardus Vos has put it, "The plagiarisms adopted are in their very complexion but tools toward the setting up of an openly professed un-Messianic program, a program not only void objectively, but *meant* to be void of all Christian religious acknowledgments and aspirations. The Man-of-Sin is the irreligious and anti-religious and anti-Messianic subject *par excellence.*"[5] The Antichrist is thus the supreme manifestation of human rebellion against God, the manifestation that marks the culmination of the history of sin that began in Eden.

Certain data concerning the Antichrist contained in this passage suggest that his opposition to Christ takes place basically on the moral and religious level: he proclaims himself to be God and he seduces his followers with pretended signs and wonders. His coming is the cause of "apostasy" (v. 3, AV margin; "the rebellion," RSV; "a falling away," AV), a massive for-

5. Geerhardus Vos, *The Pauline Eschatology* (Grand Rapids: William B. Eerdmans, 1961), p. 118.

saking of the Christian faith which in turn culminates with the acceptance of "the lie" (v. 11, AV; "what is false," RSV) by those who are to perish (v. 10). But it is clear that the stage on which the transgressor (the "man without law") acts is so broad and his presumption so absolute that no aspect of human life can remain exempt from his demands. His is a totalitarian power determined to organize the world and all of life under a government that is the very negation of the Kingdom of God. It has to do with a false god who establishes a political order, an empire, on the foundation of falsehood.

There are a number of questions concerning the Antichrist that no exegesis of 2 Thessalonians is capable of answering. Nothing is said, for example, about where this dramatic personage will make his appearance. And it is evident that before receiving the letter, the original readers had already received from Paul certain information that would have helped them to understand what the apostle was saying, and of which we are ignorant. "Do you not remember that when I was still with you I told you this?" he asks (v. 5). And he adds, "you know what is restraining him [*to katechon*]" (v. 6); "only he who now restrains it [*ho katechōn*]" (v. 7). Because of our chronological and geographical distance, we do not know *what* or *who* restrains the Antichrist. The only thing we do know is that Paul maintains that there is something and someone holding back the advent of the Man of Sin, someone who will have to be taken "out of the way" so that later, immediately (*tote*), the Antichrist might be revealed and destroyed by Jesus Christ "with the breath of his mouth" (v. 8). With the judgment of God executed on "the son of perdition" (v. 3) and all "those who are to perish, because they refused to love the truth and so be saved" (v. 10), the drama of history will have come to the last act.

1 John 2:18, 22; 4:3; 2 John 7

In contrast to Paul's readers, John's readers were not facing the problem of discerning the fulfillment of their expectations concerning the coming of Christ. Instead, they were facing the problem of heretics in the church who were attacking the gospel. The focus of the teaching moves from the future to the present, from an apocalyptic personage to the false teaching. The context, nevertheless, continues to be eschatological, since John understands that "it is the last hour," as is evidenced by the appearance of many antichrists (2:18), forerunners of the Antichrist.

The antichrists that have appeared are neither persons who want to take the place of Christ nor the pseudochrists of Jesus' prediction (see Mark 13:22); rather, they are adversaries of Christ who deny the Father and the Son (2:22). They are human teachers who have left the church to which the apostle is writing (2:19), and they are spreading the lie that is described as a denial that "Jesus is the Christ" (2:22), a denial of the Son (and consequently of the Father) (2:23), and a denial that "Jesus Christ has come in the flesh" (or that "Jesus is the Christ come in the flesh") (4:2-3; 2 John 7). The one who denies that the man Jesus is the eternal Son of God, says the apostle, is "the liar" (2:22), "the deceiver and the antichrist" (2 John 7). The truth of the incarnation is the central truth of the Christian faith; to deny this is, therefore, the supreme lie, and anyone who holds and propagates this lie is indisputably possessed by the spirit of the Antichrist (4:3).

It is evident that John wrote his letters after the heretics had left the church, thus demonstrating that they had not belonged to the people of God (2:19). Nevertheless, the danger of being seduced by this heresy was still present (2:26). For this reason he warns his readers in the first place that they should abide in what they had heard "from the beginning" — that is, in the apostolic teaching (2:24) — which is the same thing as abiding in God (2:24). In the second place, he admonishes them to abide in the Spirit, the anointing that they had received (2:27-28). And in the third place, he warns them not to believe every spirit, but to test the spirits on the basis of their confession that Jesus is the Christ come in the flesh (4:1-3).

Like Paul, John maintains that "the mystery of lawlessness" which precedes the final manifestation of the Antichrist is already in action (1 John 4:3; cf. 2 Thess. 2:7). He suggests that the future coming of the Antichrist will not be a unique, isolated, sudden event, but will instead be the culmination of a whole process in which evil will increase until all its powers are released in the great apostasy and then concentrated in the awful figure of the Antichrist. The Antichrist will be the paradigm of the opposition that the gospel must confront throughout history in the period between the resurrection and the second coming. He will be the final revelation of the rebellion against God that characterizes human life apart from redemption in Christ. He will be the culmination of the denial of Christ with which the world confronts the proclamation of the Good News. He will be the antithesis of Christ, the prototype of all the antitheses that the gospel meets wherever and whenever it is proclaimed with integrity.

Revelation 13

The beast that rises out of the sea and the beast that rises from the earth, according to Revelation 13 (vv. 1-10 and 11-18, respectively), complete the picture of the Antichrist given by the New Testament. Again, the apocalyptic note predominates; the seventh trumpet has sounded, the trumpet that announces the final act of the drama of history.

The beast rising out of the sea is conceived of in terms of the vision of Daniel 7, in which there appear four beasts that rise out of the sea. The fourth one, "terrible and dreadful and exceedingly strong" (v. 7), has ten horns, among which another comes up, a smaller horn. The first beast mentioned in Revelation 13 has these same features. Moreover, in both Daniel and Revelation this beast is described as coming up out of the sea (Dan. 7:1, 7; cf. Rev. 13:1). The parallelism is carried through in the following points:

Revelation 13	Daniel 7
"the beast was given a mouth uttering haughty and blasphemous words" (v. 5)	"in this horn . . . [was] a mouth speaking great things" (v. 8; cf. 11, 20)
"it was allowed to exercise authority for forty-two months" (v. 5)	"and they [the saints] shall be given into his hand for a time, two times, and half a time" (v. 25)

"it opened its mouth to utter blasphemies against God, blaspheming his name and his dwelling" (v. 6)

"He shall speak words against the Most High" (v. 25)

"it was allowed to make war on the saints and to conquer them" (v. 7)

"this horn made war with the saints, and prevailed over them." (v. 21)

This is a description of a totalitarian power that acts under the authority of the dragon (Rev. 13:2) in the same way that the "man of lawlessness" in the Pauline picture comes "by the activity of Satan" (2 Thess. 2:9). He is, in effect, a demonic being and bears upon his seven heads — the symbol of absolute power — a blasphemous name (v. 1). This blasphemous name is not stated explicitly, but it is obvious that it reflects the most audacious presumption that can be imagined — the claim to be God and as such to deserve universal worship (vv. 3, 4). The only ones who refuse to worship him are the Christians, against whom the monster lets loose unrelenting persecution (vv. 7, 8). This beast rising out of the sea is the very incarnation of the "horrible sacrilege" predicted by Jesus Christ for the end of time (Mark 13:14). His features of leopard, bear, and lion (v. 2) combine those of the four beasts of Daniel's vision (ch. 7), which are representative of four successive world empires (Babylonia, Medo-Persia, Greece, and Rome). This combination clearly shows that the beast is not to be identified with any particular government, but rather that it symbolizes the state that demands of its subjects the loyalty due only to God and that is set against Jesus Christ and his church.

The beast that rises from the earth, on the other hand, has the appearance of a lamb but speaks like a dragon (v. 11). It is, therefore, a parody of the Lamb of God. It derives its authority from the first beast, whom it serves by forcing the inhabitants of the earth to render to it the worship that it demands (v. 12). In order to achieve this, it works miracles that remind us of the "signs and lying wonders" of the Lawless One (v. 13; cf. 2 Thess. 2:9). His action against those who refuse to worship the first beast is decisive: they are condemned to death (v. 15) and excluded from all economic activity, regardless of their social position (vv. 16, 17). This second beast, also called "the false prophet" (Rev. 19:20; 20:10), is the symbol of a religion that serves the interests of the state. The two beasts represent any system of government that attempts to exercise complete control over the life of its citizens and makes of religion an instrument of subjection to its totalitarian regime.

Conclusions

Although the picture of the Antichrist in the passages that we have briefly analyzed is not clear in all its details, the following conclusions can be drawn on the basis of the exegesis:

1. The topic of the Antichrist was a part of the oral teaching of the apostles in the first-century church (2 Thess. 2:5; 1 John 2:18).

2. The New Testament writers conceive of the Antichrist as an apocalyptic figure whose final manifestation will precede the Parousia, but they in no way limit his action to the future; rather, they see his activity in contemporary events and personages that affect the life and mission of the church and that point to a future incarnation of evil. Neither the futurist interpretation nor the preterist interpretation of the Antichrist does justice to the biblical data, according to which there is, in the present, an eschatological tension between the "already" and the "not yet" that conditions human history in the period between the resurrection and the second coming of Christ. The appearance of the Antichrist belongs to the end times, but already "it is the last hour" (1 John 2:18), and the Antichrist is present in antichrists that are a foretaste of his final rebellion. No tyrant of the past, not even the Roman emperors who imposed emperor worship and demanded that they be called *Dominus et Deus* (Lord and God) or *Dominus et Soter* (Lord and Savior), exhausts the horrible sacrilege of the anti-king of the final act of history. No false teacher of the past — not even the heretics who deny the incarnation — exhausts the lie of the False Prophet, the author of the Great Rebellion. But "the mystery of lawlessness is already at work," and this prefigures the final opposition to the gospel and makes its presence felt here and now in every totalitarian government and every religion that denies Jesus Christ.

3. The central claim of the Antichrist is to occupy the place

that belongs exclusively to God and to accept the worship that only God deserves. His demand is absolute and therefore places all humanity and each individual face to face with the alternatives of worshiping God and worshiping the Denial of God — and, consequently, of Life and Death.

4. The Antichrist is building up his kingdom on the foundation of error, deceit, and lying. He has the power to work signs and wonders that are a parody of Jesus' miracles and that succeed in persuading those who have not received the love of the truth and been saved.

5. The purpose of the Antichrist is to destroy the church either by means of persecution from outside on the part of an anti-Christian government or by means of enticement into error from within on the part of an anti-Christian religion. The reality of his present activity does not allow us to hold that there exists a road by which humanity can travel directly from history into the Kingdom of God. The pilgrimage toward the Kingdom takes place in the midst of a conflict in which the powers of darkness are constantly opposed to the fulfillment of God's purpose in Jesus Christ. Thus, there cannot be mission without suffering.

6. The action of the Antichrist cannot go beyond the limits fixed by God, the source of all power, the one who holds the final judgment in his hand (Rev. 20:10). He can never frustrate the final fulfillment of God's purpose. In the meantime, the church is called to be faithful to the truth of Jesus Christ both in what it does and in the message it proclaims, even to martyrdom. "This calls for endurance and faith on the part of God's people" (Rev. 13:10, TEV).

II. SIGNS OF THE TIMES IN LATIN AMERICA TODAY

The history of the interpretation of the Antichrist from Justin Martyr and Irenaeus to Hal Lindsey and Tim La Haye constitutes a warning against the danger of dogmatism in any attempt to relate the biblical teaching on this apocalyptic figure with contemporary events. On the other hand, we cannot ignore the apocalypticism of the New Testament without losing an important element of the New Testament message. The apocalyptic symbols used by the New Testament writers, including the figure of the Antichrist, express a vision of the action of God in history, of the cosmic dimensions of the work of Jesus Christ, and of the transcendent significance of the mission of the church without which the Christian faith would suffer irreparable loss.[6] We must, therefore, run the risk of making a mistake and attempt to read the signs of the times in our historic context.

In 1969, in the *Evangelical Declaration of Bogota*, we recognized that "the process of evangelization takes place in concrete human situations," and we spoke of the necessity of incarnating the example of Jesus Christ "in the critical Latin American reality of underdevelopment, injustice, hunger, violence, and hopelessness" (par. 6). Since that time our reality has become much more complex, and each of the characteristics we noted has assumed tragic dimensions. Any observer can prove further that as the population has increased from 200 million to 300 million during this past decade, our continent has been moving toward governments that are attempting to impose a definite model of economic growth regardless of the cost. These are governments that consider themselves to be promoters of the modernization to which "underdeveloped" and "developing" nations aspire.[7] They take for granted the myth of progress — a secularized version of biblical eschatology — and take the model of economic growth exemplified principally by the United States as their model for social change. To do this, they take advantage of an elite among whom the very phenomena of modernization (e.g., technological production and bureaucracy) are creating a new consciousness characterized by, among other things, the

6. Leon Morris is right when he states that "It is much better to see apocalyptic as but one strand in the church's message. It expresses some things well, particularly the eager looking forward to the end" (*Apocalyptic* [Grand Rapids: William B. Eerdmans, 1972], p. 86). After admitting the truth of his statement, however, it is necessary to recover the value of the apocalyptic in relation to the *present implications* of the work of Jesus Christ, which looks simultaneously to the past and to the future.

7. For our purpose, we accept the definition of *modernization* as consisting of "the growth and diffusion of a set of institutions rooted in the transformation of the economy by means of technology" (Peter Berger, Brigitte Berger, Hanifried Kellner, *The Homeless Mind* [New York: Vintage Books, 1973], p. 9).

"rational attitude," the separation of ends from means, the segregation of private life from public life, and anonymity in social
relationships. [8] And these governments make use of the mass
media to spread a view of reality that agrees with their economic
plans.

Government plans that must be carried out at any cost
create a society that progressively adopts the typical values of
"advanced societies" — unlimited increase of production, comfort, efficiency, success. If we recognize, however, that "on the
social and economic level, all countries of all latitudes and racial
origins express the same fundamental aspirations in basically
the same values," [9] it is obvious that the society that is taking
shape in Latin America today (and that is at different stages of
development in the different countries of the continent) is only
one version of the modern industrialized society that little by
little is imposing itself on the whole planet without respect for
ideological boundaries. [10] "The industrialized society," says Raymond Aron, ". . . is far from being universal, but it is poten-
tially so, in the sense that already today it has become a
condition *sine qua non* of power and prosperity." [11]

In 1974, at the International Congress on World Evangelization, I pointed out the importance of recovering the biblical
concept of sin and recognizing that man is the victim of a
transcendent order that imposes on him a lifestyle that is self-
defeating. I pointed out, too, that in the modern world this
order is characterized by *materialism* — that is, "the absolutization

8. See *The Homeless Mind*, p. 9.
9. Raymond Aron, *La Era Tecnológica* (Montevideo: Editorial Alfa, 1968),
p. 59.
10. What has taken place in China since Mao's death illustrates very
well the "convergence of systems" that is taking place in our day. This is
not to deny the radical difference between the capitalist model and the
socialist model on the *ideological* level. But in practice both systems nevertheless pursue material values and define the standard of living basically in
economic terms. What Octavio Paz says about the situation in Mexico is
equally applicable to many other Latin American countries: "In Mexico
today, with the exception of some of us eccentrics who have no confidence
in 'progress' and who would like to see a change in the orientation of our
society, both the rightist and the leftist factions, though unreconcilable,
agree in the same suicidal worship of progress" (*El Ogro Filantrópico* [Tobasco,
Mexico: Joaquín Mortiz, 1979], p. 65).
11. Aron, *La Era Tecnológica*, p. 65.

of the present age in all that it offers — consumer goods, money, political power, philosophy, science, social class, race, nation, sex, religion, tradition . . . ; the 'collective egoism' (to use Niebuhr's expression) that conditions man to seek his realization in 'the desirable things of life'; the Great Lie that man derives his meaning from 'being like God,' in independence from God."[12] Elsewhere, in an essay on the twelfth paragraph of the Lausanne Covenant, I return to the same topic and say that the whole world is becoming a "global village" united by the consumer ideology.[13] Today I would add that the "mystery of lawlessness" seems to me to be at work in our day in that gigantic effort on the part of all nations to become "advanced societies" in accordance with the image presented in the consumer society and by means of scientific, technological, and administrative reasoning. In making this affirmation I am not advocating a utopian "back to nature" movement or the identification of Christian faith with rural society. I am simply pointing out that the model of society that predominates in the modern world is that of a society dedicated to the conquest of physical comfort as if life consisted in the abundance of goods that one possesses, and I am proposing that behind the materialism of this consumer society is the spirit of the Antichrist. To integrate this thesis with the exegesis of the preceding section, I would like to make a few observations.

The period between the resurrection and the second coming is characterized by opposition to the Good News, opposition that is the foretaste of the final manifestation of the Antichrist. But opposition does not always come in terms of persecution. It can also take the form of seduction. Here lies the importance of this warning included in the Lausanne Covenant: "We need both watchfulness and discernment to safeguard the biblical gospel. We acknowledge that we ourselves are not immune to worldliness of thought and action, that is, to a surrender to secularism" (par. 12). The spirit of the Antichrist makes itself felt today in any effort that the church makes to fulfill its commitment following the rules of the game and the

12. See "Evangelism and the World," pp. 1-44 herein.
13. See "Spiritual Conflict," pp. 45-61 herein.

values of the surrounding society. This takes place in evangelization, for example, when the biblical gospel, centered in Jesus Christ, the Lord and Savior, is replaced by a message without the demands of Christian discipleship, geared for mass consumption. It was to this danger that I referred in the Lausanne Congress when I spoke of culture Christianity. The warning stands, all the more necessary as we are more conditioned by the rationalistic approach to human life characteristic of the secularism of modern society.[14]

At times it would appear that *1984*, the novel by George Orwell, has in fact become reality, especially the totalitarian nature of society. Here too the Antichrist can be seen, even more distinctly when we observe the role played by the state, with its overwhelming concentration of political and economic power, in almost all the countries of Latin America. Octavio Paz states this clearly, referring to the state: "Its reality is enormous, so much so that it does not seem real — it is everywhere and it has no face. We do not know who or what it is. Like the Buddhists of the early centuries, who could only represent the Enlightened One by his attributes, we know the State only by the immensity of its devastations. It is the Fleshless One; it is not a presence but a domination. It is the Non-person."[15]

Contemporary materialism, with its one-dimensional view of reality, imposes its values and offers a salvation that is a denial of the salvation in Christ, an anti-salvation. It is in essence the lie that man can be like God in independence from God. For this reason it presents itself not directly as a denial of Christian faith but as a plan of individual and social salvation. It is a secular religion that dominates every aspect of the life

14. One of the principal characteristics of the society dominated by secularism is its faith in reason. From this viewpoint, it may be stated that modern society is not irreligious, but rather that it is dedicated to faith in reason. In the words of Eduard Heimann, "The fundamental concept of modern white society is that of reason. By making reason and the sciences created by reason the guides in the building of society, the modern age is distinguished from preceding ages as well as from contemporary non-Western society. And it is the recognition of scientific reason as the guide in social life which fundamentally unites West and East, the libertarian and equalitarian wings of modern society" (*Reason and Faith in Modern Society* [Middletown, Conn.: Wesleyan University Press, 1961], p. 19).

15. Paz, *El Ogro Filantrópico*, p. 10.

of its adherents and constantly makes use of the means of mass communication to publish its message and to offer hope either in terms of economic growth or in terms of revolution. And it is accompanied by the signs and wonders of modern technology and supported by governments that take advantage of it as the glue that holds society together. As Jacques Ellul says, "A state is insecure unless there is a state religion. Politics demands religion as an ally."[16] For the governments of our countries, whether or not they call themselves Christian, materialism plays the role of religion.

The last few years provide eloquent illustrations in our own historical context of the way in which the state sets itself up as God and enslaves its citizens without the least respect for the most basic human rights. Political murders, torture, disappearances, imprisonment without trial, concentration camps — all this in the name of national security — are also signs of the Antichrist in Latin America.[17]

III. PROCLAMATION IN THE LATIN AMERICAN CONTEXT

We have paused in our reflection on the New Testament teaching about the Antichrist and on the signs of the times in our situation because we want to see more clearly what it means to proclaim Jesus Christ in the Latin American context. The eschatological teaching of the New Testament is not intended to satisfy our curiosity concerning the future or to provide us with material for the elaboration of an imaginative futurology.

16. Ellul, *The Politics of God and the Politics of Man* (Grand Rapids: William B. Eerdmans, 1972), p. 126.
17. The same ideology has gained force in other countries of the world. Referring to the United States, for example, Richard J. Barnet writes, "National security is a modern charm. Like any other charm, its words are full of power and mystery. In the name of national security anything may be attacked, any risk may be taken, any sacrifice may be demanded. Breaking into meetings, tapping telephone lines, deceit in Congress . . . anything goes in the name of national security" ("Challenge to the Myths of National Security," *New York Times Magazine*, 1 April 1979). Military expenditures are linked to the doctrine of national security. In 1977, military expenditures worldwide reached the record level of $433 billion. This was true in spite of the fact that the United States already had enough atomic bombs to destroy the world twelve times over.

Its purpose is rather to invite us to discern the nature of the times in order to be faithful to Jesus Christ in the life and mission of the church in the present situation.

A recognition of the activity of the Antichrist underscores the importance of maintaining a vigilant attitude in order not to be deceived by the Enemy. The Bogota Declaration points out that "social structures have an influence on the Church and on those who receive the gospel. If this reality is ignored, the gospel is disfigured and the Christian life impoverished" (par. 6). The Lausanne Covenant goes even further and warns, as we have already noted, that "we ourselves are not immune to worldliness of thought and action, that is, to a surrender to secularism"; it detects this compromise in the fact that, "desirous to insure a response to the gospel, we have compromised our message, manipulated our hearers through pressure techniques, and become unduly preoccupied with statistics or even dishonest in our use of them" (par. 12). Behind all these forms of worldliness, which take on the values of the secular society, lies the spirit of the Antichrist. In contrast, faithfulness to the gospel demands the proclamation of Christ as Lord of the totality of life. As the Lausanne Covenant states it, "in issuing the gospel invitation we have no liberty to conceal the cost of discipleship" (par. 4).

In the interim between the resurrection and the second coming of Christ the proclamation is carried out in a context of spiritual conflict in which the power of the Antichrist organizes itself to thwart the realization of God's purposes. As Lesslie Newbigin says, "From the point of view of the revelation of the end and meaning of history in Jesus Christ, we can understand that precisely because it is only in Christ that human history can have a meaning, the last and greatest efforts of the powers of this world must be to organize human history as a whole apart from obedience to Christ, that is to say in terms of the reign of anti-Christ."[18]

If the kingdom of Antichrist in Latin America takes the form of a society that places absolute value on material goods,

18. Newbigin, *A Faith for This One World?* (London: SCM Press, 1961), pp. 112-13.

with governments that are willing to pay a high social cost in order to achieve their plans of economic development, the proclamation of the gospel must include the announcement of the good news of salvation in Jesus Christ as well as the denunciation of everything in this society that opposes the fullness of human life. The challenge of the moment is not to criticize the governments in religious language but rather to confront the values and attitudes that make it possible for our people to be domesticated by advertising; it is not to oppose the official myths with other secular myths but rather to point to the judgment of God on every attempt to build the Kingdom of God without God. Since the coming of Christ, the key to history is to be found in his death and resurrection, and the proclamation of the gospel places humanity face to face with only one alternative — Christ or Antichrist.

The recognition of the activity of the Antichrist in the present stage of the history of salvation prevents us from adopting a triumphalistic attitude in regard to the Christian mission. The coming of Christ released the powers of darkness in an effort to counteract the effects of his presence and his redemptive work. The conflict resulted in the crucifixion of the King of glory. That was not the end; it only set the standard for the mission of the church through the centuries. From then on, the mission would inevitably be marked by suffering. For this reason Peter writes, "Beloved, do not be surprised at the fiery ordeal which comes upon you to prove you, as though something strange were happening to you. But rejoice in so far as you share Christ's sufferings, that you may also rejoice and be glad when his glory is revealed" (1 Pet. 4: 12-13). As the Lausanne Covenant points out, according to Christ's warning the persecution is inevitable.

As followers of the crucified Christ, we must not be surprised at the frequently hostile reaction of the world to the proclamation of the gospel. Nevertheless, our faith rests on the resurrection of Jesus Christ and thus we know that God has the last word in the confrontation between Christ and the Antichrist. The final victory belongs to the One who conquered the world by the power of his sacrifice. Consequently we can live awaiting the fulfillment of God's purpose to place all things, both in heaven and on the earth, under the power of Christ (Eph. 1:10). The day and the hour of this final triumph no one knows except the Father (Matt. 24:36). But while we are waiting, we do not sit with our hands folded; we are busy living and announcing the gospel, in faithfulness to Jesus Christ.

There are signs that the end is approaching. We cannot avoid the feeling that the forces of evil are gathering for the final revolt against God and his Anointed. Nevertheless, because Christ was raised from the dead, we dare to believe that the cause of the gospel is the only cause that has a future. Jesus Christ says, "Surely I am coming soon." And we answer "Amen. Come, Lord Jesus!" (Rev. 22:20).

The Fullness of Mission

The expansion of Christianity in the Third World since World War II is indeed impressive. Never before in history has a religion spread so vastly and so rapidly as Christianity has in the last few decades. As a result, the church has now become a worldwide movement. And if it is true, as Emil Brunner has put it, that the church exists for mission as fire exists for burning, it follows that there is no longer any room for the traditional distinction between "sending churches" and "receiving churches." As Stephen Neill has said, "the age of missions is at an end; the age of mission has begun."[1]

The statistics of church growth can easily be used to project a glowing picture of the church in the last quarter of the twentieth century. This has in fact been done in circles where quantitative church growth is regarded as "the chief task" of mission. For a more balanced picture, however, the numerical gains must be set over against the problems that beset the church and place the future of Christianity in some regions of the world under a question mark. From that perspective, the greatest challenge that the church faces today is the challenge to fullness in mission.

THE CHALLENGE OF EVANGELISM AND DISCIPLESHIP

An honest evaluation of the numerical gains that the church has made since World War II must not overlook the fact that

---

1. Neill, *A History of Christian Missions* (Harmondsworth, Middlesex: Penguin Books, 1964), p. 572.

the greatest gains have taken place among animistic peoples and among the deprived classes in the cities. How can one discard the suspicion that they are but a part of the revival of religion that is taking place all over the world? The flourishing of occultism and Asian religions in the West; the resurgence of Islam in some areas of Africa and Malaysia and Pakistan, of Buddhism in Thailand, Vietnam, Cambodia, Burma, and Sri Lanka, of Hinduism in India, and of Shintoism in Japan; the vitality of Spiritism (and especially of *Umbanda*) in Brazil and of the *Sokka Gakkai* in Japan—these phenomena are not unrelated to the emergence of "people's movements" on whose multiplication in a Christian context some overoptimistic North American missionary "strategists" base their theories regarding church growth. The general picture of religious upsurge at a time when the world is becoming unified under the impact of Western technology shows that there is in the human being a "metaphysical void" that modern technology cannot fill. The mass movements to Christianity, like other religious movements that are growing at a fantastic rate in the Third World, seem to be both the result of the impact of Western civilization and a reaction against it.

Once it is realized that the amazing church growth seen in some areas of the world today is parallel to a religious revival outside a Christian context, it becomes obvious that this type of church growth has to be evaluated in the light of God's purpose for the life and mission of the church. Sooner or later, the question of *what* it is that grows has to be raised, in order to see whether the churches that multiply are genuine expressions of the gospel. When this is done, it is clear that numerical church growth in the Third World is only the bright side of a picture that also has a dark side of problems that pose a real challenge to the church.

In the first place, some of the mass movements with a high growth rate may be no more than "baptized heathenism." In the sixteenth century the Roman Catholic Church attempted to Christianize a whole continent (Latin America) on the basis of massive approach. The result of that venture is now seen in its true light by those within Roman Catholicism. As a writer identified with that tradition puts it, "In reality, Latin America is a continent of people who have been baptized but not evangelized."[2] The possibility that the same kind of problem will recur in connection with contemporary mass movements to Christianity is a real one. It is obvious that for many people in the Third World Christianity has become a symbol of modernity, alongside which totally non-Christian views and customs are allowed to survive. This attitude is illustrated by the so-called "cargo cults" associated with Papua New Guinea and other areas, where the new Christians constructed installations on the shore in the hope that God—the "higher power" who they supposed had sent the whites with the many material objects by sea and air—would make them rich. In Africa the practice of polygamy and witchcraft and the use of charms and fetishes often coexist with outward acceptance of the Christian faith. In some areas of Latin America, adherence to Christianity does not necessarily imply a complete move away from Spiritism. Syncretism is thus a real threat that often accompanies mass movements and poses a question regarding the extent to which Christianity has in fact been received by people participating in them. Perhaps the most urgent need in relation to rapid church growth is for a new stress on Christian discipleship as involving the placing of the totality of life under the Lordship of Jesus Christ.

In the second place, even after due account is taken of the expansion of Christianity in the last few decades, the fact remains that there are still many largely unevangelized areas, particularly the Muslim countries and China, the most populous nation of the world, where the church has been reduced to an "underground" cell-type movement.[3] (The new Chinese

2. David Auletta et al., *Misión nueva en un mundo nuevo* (Buenos Aires: Editorial Guadalupe, 1974), p. 34.

3. It is estimated that in 1947 the Roman Catholic Church alone had three million members in China. There were also 5,441 foreign missionaries, 2,798 Chinese priests, 5,112 Chinese sisters, 257 orphanages, 29 publishing houses, 20 bishops, and 1 cardinal. Since 1966, however, there has been no visible Roman Catholic presence in that country (see Auletta, p. 27). According to Leslie T. Lyall, "China has the unenviable distinction of being the only Communist nation in the world, with Albania, to have driven the entire Christian Church underground" (*New Spring in China* [Grand Rapids: Zondervan, 1980], p. 178). The fact remains, however, that despite all the persecution, Christianity has survived in both urban and rural China.

constitution, approved in June 1975, granted religious freedom, but defined it as "freedom not to believe in religion and freedom to propagate atheism.") In Asia—a continent with well over two billion people—there are not more than fifty million Christians, which seems to ratify K. M. Panikkar's claim in his book *Asia and Western Dominance* (1953) that the attempt to convert Asia to Christianity has completely failed. But while Asia is the least evangelized continent, the fact remains that in almost every country of the world Christians are still a small minority.

Finally, we must not forget that Europe—the continent that served as the first base of the modern missionary movement—has become a new "mission field." In his assessment of the present situation and prospects of the Christian faith in the world, Stephen Neill claims that "it is on Europe that the glance of the observer falls with gravest anxiety. We seem to be watching a steady diminution of the spiritual capital of Europe, the disappearance of the old European synthesis of religion and culture, and a desiccation of the human spirit, as a result of which men not merely are not religious, but can see no reason why they should concern themselves with anything beyond the world of the senses."[4] The challenge of evangelism and discipleship is thus one that the church has to face everywhere today, and face over against a secularistic outlook that is part and parcel of Western civilization. The impressive church growth in some areas of the world is indeed small in comparison with the expansion of modern materialism, which has erected *Homo consumens* as the model of the ideal life.[5] One of the most urgent needs in the church today is faith in the power of the gospel as a message of liberation from the world as a system dominated by the gods of the consumer society brought into existence by Western technology. There is no greater contribution that the church can make to humanity than the gospel of Jesus Christ and its liberating power.

A rather romantic view of missionary work has led some missions to concentrate on small tribes in the jungles, to the

4. Neill, pp. 564-65.
5. On this issue, see "Spiritual Conflict," pp. 45-61 herein.

neglect of the cities. [6] As David Sheppard has said, "Urban mission is one of the priorities today in mission work. If we fail here, if we ignore the city and its pressures, there is no gospel which we can preach anywhere else with integrity."[7] Sheppard's statement is as valid in Latin America, Asia, and Africa as it is in England. The "urban explosion" is a worldwide phenomenon; urban mission, therefore, is a priority everywhere. [8] It is there, in the city with all its dehumanizing power, that the need for a gospel with power to transform the totality of life comes into sharp focus. In a world that is becoming increasingly urbanized, the city is beyond doubt the symbol of the challenge that the church faces today with regard to evangelism and discipleship.

THE CHALLENGE OF PARTNERSHIP AND UNITY

At the enlarged meeting of the International Missionary Council held at Whitby (Ontario) in 1947, the church was uniquely confronted with the need to break down the distinction between "older and younger churches" and face its global responsibility. Whitby's emphasis on missionaries as "agents of the church universal," whose responsibility was to be regarded on a par with that of their national colleagues, was a hallmark in missionary thinking.

Today not many would openly argue with A. J. Boyd's statement that "older churches and younger churches are no longer to be thought of as patrons and beneficiaries respectively, or even as senders and receivers, but as partners not merely in a contractual sense, but set by God in that relationship. They come together by God's will, for the doing of God's will, they are partners *in obedience*."[9] In actual fact, however,

---

6. This statement should not be taken as suggesting that it is not important to reach people in the jungles. The point is that there is an imbalance when missionaries concentrate on small isolated tribes and forget the millions in the cities, as seems to be the case in Brazil. See *Latin American Church Growth*, ed. William R. Read, Victor M. Monterroso, and Harmon A. Johnson (Grand Rapids: William B. Eerdmans, 1969), p. 303.

7. Sheppard, *Built as a City: God and the Urban World Today* (London: Hodder & Stoughton, 1974), p. 16.

8. On the growth of cities, see p. 47n.2 herein.

9. Boyd, *Christian Encounter* (Edinburgh: Saint Andrews Press, 1961), p. 19.

Whitby's call to partnership in obedience is still as relevant today as when it was first issued. Many of its recommendations have not yet been implemented by a number of agencies involved in missionary work. Witness the growing numerical strength of North American Protestant missions (almost wholly dependent on North American personnel, leadership, and finances) after World War II,[10] and the persistent separation of "foreign missions" and "local churches" around the world. Witness the prevalence of policies and patterns of missionary work that assume that the leadership of the Christian mission lies in the hands of Western strategists and specialists. Witness the schools of "world mission" based in the West, with no participation of faculty members from the Third World. Witness, finally, the frequency with which an older church (or, more often, a missionary board) in the West maintains a one-way relationship with a younger church (which may or may not be regarded as independent). As long as this situation endures, partnership is no more than a myth.

In many cases missionary work continues to be done from a position of political and economic power and with the assumption of Western superiority in matters of culture and race. Many Christian churches, institutions, and movements in the Third World continue to operate in a "colonial" situation, heavily dependent on foreign personnel and subject to foreign control. Despite the progress made toward genuine independence, Christians in the "developing countries" are caught in a situation in which economic and cultural imperialism has hardly been broken, even though its outward appearance has changed. On the other hand, the mentality of colonial dependence lingers in many "younger churches" to such an extent that an African observer (John Mbiti) feels entitled to say, "The church in Africa has been very missionary minded, but only in terms of receiving missionaries and depending on them." The missionary

10. As of 1 January 1976 there were 37,221 Protestant missionaries from North America (35,969 from the United States and 1,252 from Canada) serving overseas. The increase in the number of missionaries after 1920 was largely due to the increase in the number of missionaries from North America (see *Mission Handbook: North American Protestant Ministries Overseas*, ed. E. Dayton [Monrovia, Calif.: MARC, 1976], p. 24).

movement has been extremely slow to recognize the importance of real partnership in obedience and has fostered among
the "younger churches" an attitude that will prove very difficult
to change. As a result, even after the "Retreat of the West" from
the Third World, Christianity is still commonly regarded as a
Western religion, and the Christian mission is still generally
identified with a white face.

The great reluctance by missionary societies to heed the
call to partnership even in the postcolonial situation is sufficient
to explain the "Call for a Moratorium" issued by the Commission on World Mission and Evangelism of the World Council
of Churches at its assembly held at Bangkok in January 1973.
The recommendation was that mission agencies consider stop-
ping their delivery of funds and personnel to particular churches
for a period of time, as "a possible strategy of mission in certain
situations." The debate that followed was characterized by more
heat than light. The All Africa Conference of Churches added
heat by adopting the Moratorium at its meeting at Lusaka in
May 1974, with the observation, "Should the moratorium cause
the missionary agencies to crumble, the African church could
have performed a service in redeeming God's people in the
Northern Hemisphere from a distorted view of the mission of
the church in the world."

On the other hand, the International Congress on World
Evangelization, held at Lausanne in July 1974, added light by
recognizing that "a reduction of foreign missionaries may sometimes be necessary to facilitate the national church's growth in
self-reliance and to release resources for unevangelized areas,"
as is stated in the Lausanne Covenant. After the Lausanne Congress, at which a number of critical issues were brought up
mainly by Third World speakers, it became increasingly clear
that even the most traditional missionary agencies can no longer
avoid the issue of world partnership in mission. The conviction
expressed in the Lausanne Covenant that "a new missionary era
has dawned" and that "a growing partnership of churches will
develop and the universal character of Christ's church will be
more clearly exhibited" is slowly gaining ground.

The end of Western colonialism has brought the church to
a stage at which the real issues of the Christian mission can be

seen in their true light. It can no longer be assumed that people in the Third World will accept Christianity because of its association with the political, economic, and cultural power of the West. On the contrary, many will find in this association a big stumbling block. Consequently, the Christian mission today has to be carried on from a position of weakness. A new possibility is thus created for the gospel to be presented as a message centered on Jesus Christ rather than as the ideology of the West. Free from its entanglements with Europe and North America, the Christian mission can now be seen as motivated by the desire that Jesus Christ be acknowledged as the Lord of the whole universe and the Savior of all people.

A universal gospel calls for a universal church, in which all Christians are effectively involved in the world mission as equal members in the body of Christ. Partnership in mission is not merely a question of practical convenience but the necessary consequence of God's purpose for the church and for the whole of humanity revealed in Jesus Christ. When Christians fail to work as partners in mission, they also fail to manifest concretely the new reality that they proclaim in the gospel. Because there is one world, one church, and one gospel, the Christian mission cannot be anything other than mission in partnership. The fulfillment of Jesus' prayer that his followers may all be one so that the world may believe in him requires today a supranational Christian community bringing to a world unified by technology a gospel centered in Jesus Christ, the Lord of all. Mission is inseparable from unity, and unity is far more than a question of structures. It has to do with willingness to rejoice with those who rejoice and to weep with those who weep; it has to do (in Tillich's words) with "listening, giving, and forgiving."

How can Christians be united in mission as long as many of them (especially in the West) adopt an ostentatious lifestyle while the large majority of them (especially in the underdeveloped countries) are unable to satisfy essential human needs? The poverty of the Third World places a question mark over the lifestyle of people — and particularly of Christians — in the West. And the proper response to it, to begin with, is a simple lifestyle and a radical restructuring of the economic relationships among Christians everywhere, based on the biblical concept of stewardship. As Ronald Sider has noted, "If a mere fraction of North American and European Christians would begin to apply biblical principles on economic sharing among the worldwide people of God, the world would be utterly astounded."[11] It is high time for rich Christians to take seriously "evangelical poverty" — the poverty inspired by the grace of our Lord Jesus Christ, who though he was rich became poor for us (2 Cor. 8:9).

Yet life in community cannot be conceived in terms of a situation in which one section of the church is always on the giving end while another is always on the receiving end. Rather, it must be understood as a situation in which Christians everywhere are willing to share with one another *out of what they have*, able to see that the aim of giving is not that some may be eased and others burdened but that "as a matter of equality" the abundance of those who have should supply the want of those who do not have, so that the abundance of the latter may supply the want of the former, "that there may be equality" (2 Cor. 8:12-13). The possibility of reciprocal giving between churches is a basic premise without which no healthy relationship between rich and poor churches is attainable. As David Auletta says, "All the churches are poor in one way or another. All of them are involved in mission and are responsible for mission. All of them should be concerned for one another, help each other, share with one another their resources. All the churches should give and receive."[12]

Giving and receiving cannot be maintained unless there is between the churches a mature relationship based on the gospel. If the church ceases to be a community in which people share a common meaning derived from the gospel, sooner or later there will be a return to the old ways of paternalism and dependence. The corrective for paternalism is not independence but interdependence; interdependence comes with a deeper understanding of the nature of unity in Christ and of the situation in which other members of the body of Christ live. If Christians are to take interdependence seriously, they will have to realize that they share a common life — the resurrection life — but they will also have to create channels of

11. Sider, *Rich Christians in an Age of Hunger: A Biblical Study* (1977; Downers Grove, Ill.: InterVarsity Press, 1984), p. 99.
12. Auletta, p. 87.

communication that allow them to see people of other cultures in a different light.

In the effort to foster mutual giving and receiving among the churches, nothing can take the place of Christians coming from other nations and interpreting to fellow Christians across the world the needs and struggles of their own churches. All too often the knowledge that the churches in the West have of the situation of the churches in the non-Western world is limited to the reports sent by missionaries. Missionaries may also be the only source of information that the younger churches have regarding the situation of the churches in the West. The time has come to develop ways of closing the gap between older and younger churches. There are already useful experiments that are being carried out for this purpose, but much more needs to be done to shape patterns of solidarity across political, economic, social, and cultural barriers, and to stimulate the mutual sharing of gifts among the churches.

Of particular importance in connection with this aim are those projects making it possible for young people from the West to live in a foreign country in close contact with human needs, at least for a limited period. Perhaps nothing will do more to awaken the younger generation to the inequalities in the modern world and the urgency of partnership in mission than a firsthand experience of life among the least privileged. It is not surprising that the best suggestion that a North American professor of philosophy was able to give to his Christian friends with regard to what could be done in the face of the problems he had seen in Latin America was that

> Maybe the best thing the young could do is just go there. Not to teach them what we think they must know, but to be taught by them what must be done and then just simply be the manpower, musclepower, brainpower that is needed to do it. And do it without pay; just for shelter, water and some cornmeal. And if there is energy left, to listen, to comfort, to encourage, to lift up and to love in many more ways. And on the basis of that finally to say that true shalom comes from the Lord Jesus Christ.[13]

13. Hendrik Hart, in a mimeographed letter dated 20 July 1975 and entitled "Latin America: Report of a Visit."

Over twenty years ago Max Warren claimed that "partnership is an idea whose time has not yet fully come."[14] The question today is whether partnership will have to survive again for twenty years as an idea, or whether the church is ready to put it into practice for the sake of the gospel *now* — at last.

THE CHALLENGE OF DEVELOPMENT AND JUSTICE

According to a 1974 United Nations report, more than 460 million people in the world are chronically hungry. The UN Food and Agriculture Organization has estimated that if the definition of hunger is broadened to include those who do not get enough proteins and therefore cannot function at full capacity, the number of hungry people in the world would be anywhere between one and two billion.

The hunger crisis has become worse since 1971, when food production dropped by one percent in the poor countries. On the other hand, in the 1970s the wealthy countries (especially the United States, Canada, the European countries, the Soviet Union, and Japan) have seen an "affluence explosion" that has increased the rates of consumption to an unprecedented level. If the hunger crisis has made anything clear, it is that the poor can hardly expect the rich to do their part toward solving the problem — unless the attitude and values of the rich are radically changed. As Senator Mark Hatfield said at the 1974 Conservative Baptist Convention, "As Americans we must no longer assume that our extra abundance can feed the hungry of the world. Our surplus supply is not enough. Rather, the world will be fed only by the sharing of resources which the rich of the world have assumed to be their unquestioned possession, and that sharing involves a changing of values and eating patterns which the affluent have barely even questioned."[15]

The challenge of the Third World is a challenge to the affluent — to their values and ideals, their ambitions and standards, their assumptions and lifestyle. And the response to that

14. Warren, *Partnership: The Study of an Idea* (London: SCM Press, 1956), p. 11.
15. Hatfield, in *Eternity* 25 (November 1974): 38.

challenge cannot come merely in terms of charitable activities and aid programs; it has to come in terms of a redistribution of wealth that will meet the demands of social justice. The poor countries of Asia, Africa, and Latin America have in common an economic system based on the exchange of industrial goods for farming products that was imposed on them by Europe during the eighteenth and the nineteenth centuries, creating a gap that they are now unable to bridge. There is no way out for them unless the affluent nations come to see that economic growth is not an end in itself, that economic life has meaning only in the context of human solidarity and stewardship and responsibility.

Such a change could take place only if the church were willing to follow the way of "Repentance and Self-Limitation." As Aleksandr Solzhenitsyn has eloquently argued in his essay under that title,[16] it is doubtful that without repentance the world will survive. His call to Russia to repent lest it "perish and . . . drag the whole world with it,"[17] is more applicable to the United States than to any other nation of the world. And so is his call to self-limitation through prudent self-restriction. "Such a change," says he, "will not be easy for the free economy of the West. It is a revolutionary demolition and total reconstruction of all our ideas and aims. We must go over from uninterrupted progress to a *stable economy*, with *nil growth* in territory, parameters and tempo, developing only through improved technology."[18]

Genuine repentance must be expressed in actions, and the main action required of the church in the wealthy world is to give priority to inward rather than outward growth. Then and only then will it be able to contribute creatively to the solution of the problems of underdevelopment without falling into the trap of "aggressive benevolence."

The development needed in the Third World is not one patterned on the affluent West, as if the road to development were identical with the imposition of a consumer society on all

16. Solzhenitsyn, in "Repentance and Self-Limitation in the Life of the Nations," in *From under the Rubble* (Boston: Little, Brown, 1975), pp. 105-43.
17. Solzhenitsyn, p. 121.
18. Solzhenitsyn, p. 138. Italics his.

the peoples of the earth. No economic resources are sufficient to meet a world market demand at the level of consumption to which the West has become accustomed. Furthermore, no development is true development if it concentrates on economics but fails to give adequate attention to the deeper questions concerning humanity and the ultimate meaning of human life. The Christian mission is concerned with the development of the whole person and of all people. It includes, therefore, the shaping of a new lifestyle — "a lifestyle designed for permanence"[19] — based on new methods of production and new patterns of consumption. It includes also the creation of a new technology subordinated to humanity and respectful of nature. The time has come to give heed to Ernesto Sabato's words: "It will be necessary to recover the human meaning of technology and science, to set their limits, to finish with their religion."[20]

The challenge facing the church in the field of development today is fundamentally the challenge of *human* development, in a context of justice. The need is for models of mission fully adapted to a situation characterized by a yawning chasm between rich and poor. The models of mission built on the affluence of the West condone this situation of injustice and condemn the indigenous churches to permanent dependence. In the long run, therefore, they are inimical to mission. The challenge both to Christians in the West and to Christians in the underdeveloped world is to create models of mission centered in a prophetic lifestyle, models that will point to Jesus Christ as the Lord over the totality of life, to the universality of the church, and to the interdependence of human beings in the world.

19. E. F. Schumacher, *Small Is Beautiful* (London: Abacus, 1975), p. 16.
20. Sabato, *Hombres y engranajes, Obras y Ensayos* (Buenos Aires: Editorial Sudamericana, 1974), p. 269.

The Unity of the Church and the Homogeneous Unit Principle

Throughout the entire New Testament it is taken for granted that the oneness of the people of God is a oneness that transcends all outward distinctions. The idea is that with the coming of Jesus Christ all barriers that divide humankind have been broken down and a new humanity is now taking shape *in* and *through* the church. God's purpose in Jesus Christ includes the oneness of the human race, and that oneness becomes visible in the church.

In the first part of this essay we shall examine the New Testament teaching on the oneness of the church that expresses God's purpose to unite all things in Jesus Christ. In the second part we shall examine the historical unfolding of God's purpose of unity in apostolic times. Finally, in the last part we shall evaluate Donald McGavran's "homogeneous unit principle" (according to which "men like to become Christians without crossing racial, linguistic or class barriers")[1] in the light of our preceding analysis of scriptural teaching and apostolic practice.

GOD'S PURPOSE OF UNITY IN JESUS CHRIST

The Bible knows nothing of the human being as an individual in isolation; it knows only of a person as a *related* being, a person in relation to other people. Much of its teaching is colored by the Hebrew concept of human solidarity, for which

1. McGavran, *Understanding Church Growth* (Grand Rapids: William B. Eerdmans, 1970), p. 198.

H. Wheeler Robinson coined a label that has since become well worn: "corporate personality." Accordingly, the church is viewed in the New Testament as the solidarity that has been created in Jesus Christ and that stands in contrast to the old humanity represented by Adam. The Adam solidarity involves humankind under the judgment of God. Its oneness is a oneness of sin and death. But where sin has abounded, grace has abounded all the more. As a result, the Adam solidarity can no longer be viewed in isolation from Christ's world, in which God has justified sinners. Over against the darkness of death that fell upon humanity through the first Adam, the light of life has broken into the world through the last Adam (Rom. 5: 12-21). By means of the first Adam, the kingdom of death was established among humankind; humanity as a whole slipped into the void of meaningless existence, out of fellowship with God and under his judgment. By means of the last Adam, a new humanity comes into existence in which the results of the fall are undone and God's original purpose for humanity is fulfilled.

The letter to the Ephesians assembles a number of insights regarding the new humanity brought into being by Jesus Christ. It opens with a doxology (1: 3-14) in which the unity of Jew and Gentile in the church is viewed in the light of God's eternal purpose, which includes the creation of a new order with Christ as the head. Paul writes that God intends the whole universe to be "summed up" or "recapitulated" in Christ, moving toward an *anakephalaiōsis* — a harmony in which "all the parts shall find their centre and bond of union in Christ."[2] In that context, the unity of Jew and Gentile (Eph. 1: 13-14) can be understood only as a prophetic fulfillment of that which God is to accomplish in "the fullness of time" (v. 10).

Both Jews and Gentiles may now receive the seal of the Spirit by faith. Circumcision, which in former days was the sign of participation in the Abrahamic covenant, becomes irrelevant in the new order; it is merely an outward sign, and it has been superseded by the "circumcision made without hands" (Col. 2: 11). With the coming of Christ, "neither circumcision

---

2. J. B. Lightfoot, quoted by F. F. Bruce in *The Epistle to the Ephesians* (London: Pickering & Inglis, 1961), p. 33.

counts for anything, nor uncircumcision, but a new creation (Gal. 6:15; 5:6). God has brought into being a new humanity in which the barriers that separated the Gentiles from the Jews are broken down (Eph. 2:11-22). Out of the two large homogeneous units whose enmity was proverbial in the ancient world God has made one; two enemies have been reconciled in "one body" (v. 16). In his death, Jesus Christ removed the wall that stood between the two systems under which "the people" ('am) and "the nations" (gôyim) had lived in former days. Now both Jews and Gentiles stand as equals in the presence of God (v. 18), as members of a new fellowship that may be described as a city, a family, and a building (vv. 19-20). Thus the unity that God wills for the entire universe according to the first chapter of Ephesians becomes historically visible in a community in which reconciliation both to God and to one another is possible on the basis of Christ's work.

Further on, in chapter 3, Paul claims that God's purpose of unity in Jesus Christ has been made known to him "by revelation" (v. 3). He is a steward of a "mystery" that was hitherto faintly perceived but that has now been revealed—namely, that in Jesus Christ "the nations" have a share in the blessings of the gospel, together with "the people," on the common ground of God's grace. Unmistakably, the unity of Jew and Gentile is here said to be *the gospel* — not simply a result that should take place as the church is "perfected," but an essential aspect of the kerygma that the apostle proclaimed on the basis of Scripture (vv. 8-9). Furthermore, it is conceived as an object lesson of God's manifold wisdom, displayed for the instruction of the inhabitants of the celestial realms, both good and evil (v. 10).

The unity resulting from Christ's work is not an abstract unity but a new community in which life in Christ becomes the decisive factor. The only peoplehood that has validity in the new order is that related to the church as "a chosen race, a royal priesthood, a holy nation, God's own people" (1 Pet. 2:9). Although made up of Jews and Gentiles, the church is placed together with Jews and Greeks (non-Jews) as a third group (1 Cor. 10:32). It is viewed as "the seed of Abraham" in which, since one is incorporated without any conditions apart from faith in Jesus Christ, "there is neither Jew nor Greek, there is neither slave nor free, there is neither male nor female; for you are all one [heis] in Christ Jesus" (Gal. 3:28). No one would, on the basis of this passage, suggest that Gentiles have to become Jews, females have to become males, or slaves have to become free in order to share in the blessings of the gospel. But no justice is done to the text unless it is taken to mean that in Jesus Christ a new reality has come into being—a unity based on faith in him, in which membership is in no way dependent upon race, social status, or sex. No mere "spiritual" unity, but a concrete community made up of Jews and Gentiles, slaves and free, men and women, all of them as equal members of the Christ solidarity—that is the thrust of the passage. And, as Donald Guthrie has put it, "Paul is not expressing a hope, but a fact."[3]

A similar idea is conveyed again in Colossians 3:11, in which Paul states that for those who have been incorporated into the new humanity created in Jesus Christ, the divisions that affect the old humanity have become irrelevant: "Here there cannot be Greek and Jew, circumcised and uncircumcised, barbarian, Scythian, slave, free man, but Christ is all, and in all." Race loses its importance because all believers, whether Jews or Gentiles, belong to the "Israel of God" (Gal. 6:16). Religious background is neither here nor there because "the true circumcision" (Phil. 3:3) is made up of Jews who are Jews inwardly, whose circumcision is "real circumcision . . . a matter of the heart, spiritual and not literal" (Rom. 2:28-29). Social stratifications are beside the point because in the new humanity the slave becomes his own master's "beloved brother" (Philem. 16); the slave is called to serve the Lord rather than man (Col. 3:22); and the free person is to live as one who has a Master in heaven (Col. 4:11). Here—in the corporate new humanity, in the homogeneous unit that has been brought into being in Jesus Christ—the only thing that matters is that "Christ is all and in all." Those who have been baptized "into one body" (1 Cor. 12:13) are members of a community in which the differences that separate people in the world have become ob-

3. Guthrie, *Galatians*, New Century Bible Commentary (Grand Rapids: William B. Eerdmans, 1973), p. 110.

solete. It may be true that "men like to become Christians without crossing racial, linguistic or class barriers," but that is irrelevant. Membership in the body of Christ is not a question of likes or dislikes but of incorporation into a new humanity under the Lordship of Christ. Whether a person likes it or not, the act that reconciles one to God *simultaneously* introduces one into a community in which people find their identity in Jesus Christ rather than in their race, culture, social class, or sex, and are consequently reconciled to one another. "The unifier is Jesus Christ and the unifying principle is the 'Gospel.' "[4]

God's purpose is to bring the universe "into a unity in Christ" (Eph. 1:10, NEB). That purpose has yet to be consummated. But already, in anticipation of the end, a new humanity has been created in Jesus Christ, and those who are incorporated in him form a unity wherein all the divisions that separate people in the old humanity are done away with. The original unity of the human race is thus restored; God's purpose of unity in Jesus Christ is thus made historically visible.

THE UNITY OF THE CHURCH AND THE APOSTOLIC PRACTICE

A cursory examination of the New Testament shows the way in which the teaching on the new unity of the church that we have been discussing was implemented by the apostles. Furthermore, it brings into focus the difficulties that the early church faced as it sought to live in the light of God's purpose of unity in Jesus Christ. The breaking down of the barriers between Jew and Gentile, slave and free, male and female could no more be taken for granted in the first century than could the breaking down of the barriers between black and white, rich and poor, or male and female today. Nevertheless, all the New Testament evidence points to an apostolic practice consistent with the aim of forming churches in which God's purpose would become a concrete reality.

4. Mackay, *God's Order: The Ephesian Letter and the Present Time* (London: Nisbet, 1953), p. 84.

Jesus' Example

The apostles had no need to speculate about what a community in which loyalty to Jesus Christ relativized all the differences would look like; they could look back to the community that Jesus had gathered around himself during his earthly ministry. True, he had not demanded a rigidly structured uniformity, but he had managed to create a community that was held together by a common commitment to him, a community that was able to overcome all the differences that could have separated them. Members of the revolutionary party, such as "Simon who was called the Zealot" (Luke 6:15), had become one with "publicans" — private businessmen in charge of collecting taxes for the government of the occupying power, such as Matthew (Matt. 9:9-13; Luke 19:1-10). Humble women of dubious reputation (Luke 7:36-39) had mixed with women whose considerable wealth made the traveling ministry of Jesus and his followers possible (Luke 8:1-3). Women had been accepted on the same basis as men, despite the common view, expressed by Josephus, that a woman was "in every respect of less worth than a man."[5]

To be sure, Jesus had limited his mission to the Jews and had imposed the same limitation on his apostles before his resurrection. Yet, as Joachim Jeremias has demonstrated, he had anticipated that the Gentiles would share in the revelation given to Israel and would join the body of God's people.[6] Accordingly, he had commanded his disciples to proclaim the gospel to "all nations"; the Gentile mission was to be the means through which the Gentiles would be accepted as guests at God's table (Matt. 8:11; Isa. 25:6-8).

The Jerusalem Church

On the day of Pentecost, the gospel was proclaimed to a large multitude of pilgrims who had come to Jerusalem for the great Jewish Feast of the Weeks (Acts 2:1-13). The heteroge-

---

5. For a brief overview of the place of women in the early church, see Joachim Jeremias, *New Testament Theology: The Proclamation of Jesus* (London: SCM Press, 1971), pp. 223-27.

6. See Jeremias, *Jesus' Promise to the Nations* (London: SCM Press, 1958).

neous nature of the multitude is stressed in the narrative by reference to the variety of languages (vv. 6-8) and lands and cultures (vv. 9-11) represented among them. Granted that the "devout men" (*andres eulabeis*) mentioned in verse 5 should be taken as Jews rather than as Gentile God-fearers, the fact that Luke wants to press home upon us is that "every nation under heaven" was represented and that the mighty works of God were proclaimed in the indigenous languages and dialects of many lands. The worldwide proclamation of the gospel — the proclamation referred to in the succeeding chapters of Acts — was thus anticipated in one single event in which even the linguistic barriers were miraculously broken down for the sake of the spread of the gospel "to the end of the earth" (1:8). The point here is that at Pentecost people became Christians along with other people from "every nation under heaven" (2:5), including "visitors from Rome, both Jews and proselytes" (v. 10). Accordingly, Peter understood Pentecost — the gift of the Spirit — as the means whereby the promise of the gospel that "all the nations of the earth shall be blessed" (Gen. 12:3) was extended not only to those present but also to their descendants, as well as to "all that are far off" (v. 39).

The Christian community that resulted from Pentecost was, of course, made up mainly of Jewish Christians. What else could be expected before the Gentile mission? Yet it would be a great mistake to conclude that it was in their Jewishness that they found their identity. Not racial homogeneity but Pentecost was the basis of their unity. Only in the light of the outpouring of the Spirit are we able to understand how it was possible for the early Jerusalem church to include in its constituency both "unlearned and ignorant men" on the one hand (*agrammatoi ... kai idiotai* in Acts 4:13; *'amme hā'āretz*, "people of the land" in rabbinical terminology) and educated priests (6:7) on the other hand — and, at a later stage, Pharisees (15:5; 11:2); both poor people in need of help and wealthy landlords (2:44-45; 4:32-37), possibly members of a well-to-do foreign community;[7] both Jews — Aramaic-speaking Jews, mostly from Palestine, as well

7. See E. A. Judge, *The Social Patterns of Christian Groups in the First Century* (London: Tyndale Press, 1960), p. 55.

as "Hellenists," Greek-speaking Jews from the Dispersion (6:1ff.)—and at least one Gentile, from Syrian Antioch (v. 5). Luke's record shows that the basic ecclesiastical unit for both preaching and teaching was the house church (Acts 2:46; 5:42; 12:12, 17; 21:18). But there is nothing in Acts to support C. Peter Wagner's view that "the mixed church at Jerusalem divided along homogeneous unit lines"[8] or to lead us even to imagine that there were different house churches for the educated and the uneducated, the rich and the poor, the Jews of Palestine and the Jews of the Dispersion. In fact all the evidence points in the opposite direction. One of Luke's main emphases as he describes the church growing out of Pentecost is that the believers were "together" (*epi to auto* in Acts 2:44), that they had "all things in common" (2:44, 4:32), and that they were "of one heart and soul" (4:32). The burden of proof lies with anyone who, despite Luke's description, continues to hold that the early church in Jerusalem was organized according to homogeneous units.

A problem that soon arose in the early Jerusalem church was in fact the result of the *heterogeneous* nature of the community: the "Hellenists" complained against the "Hebrews" because their widows were not receiving a fair share from the common pool that had been formed (Acts 6:1). No clearer illustration of the way in which the apostles faced the problems of division in the church can be found than the one recorded here. A modern Church Growth expert might have suggested the creation of two distinct denominations, one for Palestinian Jews and another for Greek Jews. That would certainly have been a *practical* solution to the tensions existing between the two conflicting homogeneous units! We are told, however, that the apostles called the community together and asked them to choose seven men who would be responsible for the daily distribution (vv. 2-6). The unity of the church across cultural barriers was thus preserved.

8. Wagner, *Our Kind of People: The Ethical Dimensions of Church Growth in America* (Atlanta: John Knox Press, 1979), pp. 122-23. Indeed, if both Jews and Gentiles were divided into "numerous important homogeneous units" as Wagner maintains (p. 114), why does he argue that the Jerusalem church was divided into only two groups, the Hellenists and the Hebrews?

The Church in Syrian Antioch

Following Stephen's martyrdom, a great persecution arose against the Jerusalem church, apparently directed principally against the Hellenist believers with whom Stephen had been identified (Acts 8:1). One result of the persecution, however, was that the first large-scale evangelization outside Palestine was launched by exiles who traveled as far as Phoenicia, Cyprus, and Syrian Antioch (11:19).

According to Luke's report, for the most part these exiles shared the gospel with "none except Jews" (v. 19). The narrative itself gives no explicit reason why this should be so. Donald McGavran argues that in the years following Pentecost the church made "early adjustments" that favored the spread of the gospel and resulted in "one-race congregations" that "arose by the dozens; perhaps by the hundreds."[9] Luke's record, however, does not substantiate the thesis that the apostles deliberately promoted the formation of "one-race congregations" and tolerated Jewish prejudices against the Gentiles for the sake of numerical church growth. In order to claim that it does, one needs to come to Scripture with the preconceived ideas that the apostles shared the modern theory that race prejudice "can be understood and should be made an aid to Christianization"[10] and that the multiplication of the church invariably requires an adjustment to the homogeneous unit principle. Without these unwarranted assumptions, one can hardly miss the point made by Acts that the extension of the gospel to the Gentiles was such a difficult step for the Jerusalem church that it took place only with the aid of visions and commands (Acts 8:26ff.; 10:1-16) or under the pressure of persecution (8:1ff.; 11:19-20).

No suggestion is ever given that Jewish Christians preached the gospel to "none except Jews" because of strategic considerations. All the evidence points to the fact that restrictions placed on the proclamation of the gospel even by Greek-speaking Jews were due to scruples that would have to be overcome (as in Peter's case when he was sent to Cornelius) if the Gentiles were

9. McGavran, *The Clash between Christianity and Culture* (Washington, D.C.: Canon Press, 1974), p. 23.

10. McGavran, *The Bridges of God: A Study in the Strategy of Missions* (London: World Dominion Press, 1955), p. 10.

to receive the Word of God and if the Jews were to see that "God shows no partiality" (as in the case of those in Judea who heard that Cornelius and his kinsmen and friends had believed). As long as Jewish Christians allowed inherited prejudices to persist, probably because of their fear that this contact with Gentiles might be interpreted by fellow Jews as an act whereby they were "traitorously joining a strange people" (to borrow McGavran's expression), they could preach "to none except Jews." Who would have thought that their approach, based on such a limited outlook, would be used as a pattern for evangelism in the twentieth century?

The evangelists who took the new step of preaching the gospel to Gentiles in Syrian Antioch were unnamed "men of Cyprus and Cyrene" (11.20). The importance of this step can hardly be overestimated. Antioch was the third largest city in the world, "almost a microcosm of Roman antiquity in the first century, a city which encompassed most of the advantages, the problems, and the human interests, with which the new faith would have to grapple."[11] Soon the church there would become the base for the Gentile mission.

There is no evidence that those who received the gospel in Antioch were relatives of the exiles coming from Jerusalem. Perhaps they were, but this is merely a conjecture and lends no solid support to the argument that "in Antioch for both the Jerusalem refugees and the resident Christians we have bridges of relationship into the Greek people."[12] Furthermore, nothing Luke says leads us to the conclusion that the evangelization of Gentiles in this city took place in the synagogue. That might have been the case, but if the correct reading in verse 20 is *Hellēnas* rather than *Hellēnistas*, Gentiles of Greek culture would be meant; Floyd Filson may be right in believing that the evangelized were "Gentiles who had had no previous contact with the synagogue."[13] The message that was preached to them was centered in Jesus as Lord (*Kyrios*) and was thus cast in terms not entirely unfamiliar to people living in a cosmopolitan city

11. Michael Green, *Evangelism in the Early Church* (Grand Rapids: William B. Eerdmans, 1970), p. 114.
12. McGavran, *The Bridges of God*, p. 24.
13. Filson, *A New Testament History* (London: SCM Press, 1965), p. 191.

MISSION BETWEEN THE TIMES

where salvation was being offered by many cults and mystery religions in the name of other lords. God's power was with the evangelists, and as a result many believed.

Unless we are to assume that for the sake of numerical growth the "great number" of those who believed were immediately separated into homogeneous unit house churches,[14] the clear implication is that the church that came into being embraced both Jewish and Gentile believers *on an equal basis* and that there was no thought that the latter had to accept Jewish practices as a prerequisite. At a later stage, as we shall see, the question of the place of Jewish ceremonial law in the church was to become a matter of debate. But there is no evidence that at the start of the Antioch church the evangelists resorted to the homogeneous unit principle in order to accomplish their task. How was unity preserved when there were many members who did not keep the Jewish ceremonial laws and there were others who did? We are not told. We can imagine that difficulties would arise, but, as Adolf Schlatter has noted, "the early Church never shirked difficulties: it attacked bravely. So nothing more is said about these difficulties, and we do not hear how intercourse in the mixed communities was secured."[15]

An insight into the degree to which people from a variety of backgrounds worked together in the Antioch church is found in the list of leaders provided by Luke in Acts 13:1: "Barnabas, Simeon who was called Niger, Lucius of Cyrene, Manaen a member of the court of Herod the tetrarch, and Saul." A more heterogeneous group could hardly be suggested! Barnabas was a Levite, a native of Cyprus (4:36). Simeon, as his nickname Niger ("Black") suggests, was a Jew (or proselyte?) apparently of dark complexion, perhaps to be identified with Simon of Cyrene, who carried Jesus' cross. Lucius was a Gentile (or a Jew with a Roman name?), a native of the African city of Cyrene, perhaps one of the men who had first preached the gospel in Antioch. Manaen was a "foster brother" (*syntrophos*) to Herod Antipas, the tetrarch of Galilee, with whom he had been reared. Saul was an ex-Pharisee, a "Hebrew of Hebrews" and, as a

14. Wagner, p. 124.
15. Schlatter, *The Church in the New Testament Period*, trans. Paul P. Levertoff (London: SPCK, 1961), p. 59.

Roman citizen, a member of a small, privileged minority in the eastern Mediterranean region.[16] What other than a common experience could have glued these men together?

The Early Gentile Churches and the "Circumcision Party"

As long as the church was made up mainly of Jews, apparently it was not a great problem for Jewish Christians to accept Gentile converts as full members of the church without demanding that they become Jews. Peter's report on the way Cornelius and his household had received the Word of God was enough to silence the criticism that the circumcision party in Jerusalem had raised against the apostle (Acts 11:1-18). Later on, the news concerning the numerical growth of the church in Syrian Antioch was welcomed in the mother church, which then sent one of its most outstanding leaders with the commission to instruct the new believers (11:22ff.). When the leaders of the Gentile mission (Barnabas and Saul) visited Jerusalem in connection with the relief sent from Antioch for the brethren in Judea (11:27-30), they had a meeting with James (Jesus' brother), Peter, and John, as a result of which they were given "the right hand of fellowship"; according to Paul, the understanding was reached that "we should go to the Gentiles and they to the circumcised" (Gal. 2:9). The presence of a young Greek convert named Titus with the delegation from Antioch at that time could be taken as a further confirmation that the Jewish Christians did not expect Gentile converts to be circumcised (Gal. 2:1-3).

The increase in the number of Gentile converts that resulted from the spread of the gospel throughout south Galatia following the travels of Paul and Barnabas finally raised the whole issue of the basis on which the Gentiles could participate as full members in the people of God. Was faith to be regarded as sufficient, as the missionaries were preaching? Granted that the gospel was meant to be preached to all men and women, both Jews and Gentiles, should not the Gentile converts be circumcised? Should they not be required to conform to Jewish ceremonial laws and food regulations? Should they not be ex-

16. Judge, pp. 52, 58.

pected to "take upon themselves the yoke of the command-ments" like the proselytes to Judaism? The issue was pressed by a circumcision party within the Jerusalem church made up of people who had previously been associated with the Pharisees (Acts 15: 1, 5).

It is likely that the episode Paul refers to in Galatians 2: 11-14 should be viewed in connection with the visit that according to Acts 15: 1 these members of the circumcision party made to Antioch. Before their coming, Peter had felt free to share a common table with Gentile Christians, for he had learned in Joppa not to call anything "common" (or "unclean") if God had purified it. When they came, however, "he drew back and separated himself, fearing the circumcision party" (Gal. 2: 12). His attitude can best be understood when it is viewed in light of the fact that Jews who sat at a table where food was not kosher thereby opened themselves to the accusation of "trai-torously joining a strange people." According to Paul, those who induced Peter to withdraw from his Gentile brethren had been sent by James. Paul's words need not mean that they had been personally commissioned by James to spy out the Jewish-Gentile relations, but from all we know the conservative party may have forced James to take action against a practice that went against conservative taboos. T. W. Manson may well be correct in suggesting that Peter received a message from James couched more or less in the following terms: "News has come to Jerusalem that you are eating Gentile food at Gentile tables, and this is causing great scandal to many devout brethren be-sides laying us open to serious criticism from the Scribes and Pharisees. Pray discontinue this practice, which will surely do great harm to our work among our fellow-countrymen."[17]

Be that as it may, Peter's action, however justified it may have been in his own opinion, was strongly opposed by Paul, who saw in it a "play-acting" (hypokrisis) that compromised the truth of the gospel (Gal. 2: 13). To be sure, Peter had not agreed with the conservative party on the question of keeping the law as a Christian requirement. His failure had been to give

17. Manson, "The Problem of the Epistle to the Galatians," in *Studies in the Gospels and Epistles*, ed. Matthew Black (Philadelphia: Westminster Press, 1962), p. 181.

up table fellowship with his Gentile brethren not because of his own convictions but because of a fierce pragmatism in the face of the danger of being regarded as a traitor to his own race. Although he himself believed with Paul that "neither circumcision counts for anything, nor uncircumcision, but a new creation" (6:15), prompted by fear of others he had adopted a course of action that was totally inconsistent with that conviction. And because of his influence, he had carried with him the rest of the Jewish Christians, including Barnabas (2:13), thereby destroying Christian fellowship and denying the truth of the gospel, according to which all barriers that separate people have been abolished for those who have been incorporated into Jesus Christ (3:28).

Peter's action showed how real was the danger facing the apostolic church to be divided into two "denominations"—a Jewish Christian church and a Gentile Christian church, each with its own emphases, serving its own homogeneous unit. The situation was so serious that a meeting was held in Jerusalem to discuss the problem with the apostles and elders of the local church and with Paul and Barnabas as delegates from Antioch (Acts 15:1ff.). The circumcision party that had provoked the Jewish-Gentile incident in Antioch presented its case, but the "council" vindicated Paul and Barnabas and sent them back to Antioch with a letter summarizing the decision that had been reached (vv. 22-29).

The "Jerusalem Decree" provided the basis for Jewish and Gentile Christians to live in unity, as equal members of the body of Christ. It clearly exemplifies the apostolic practice in the face of problems arising out of racial, cultural, and social differences among Christians. In the first place, the Gentile converts would not have to be circumcised in order to be accepted as full members of the people of God. Faith in Jesus Christ was thus affirmed as the only condition for salvation. And the repudiation of the attempt made by the conservative party of the Jerusalem church to impose circumcision on the Gentile Christians was archetypical of the Christian rejection of every form of "assimilationist racism" (to use Wagner's expression). Clearly the apostles would have agreed with the claim that "any teaching to the effect that Christianity requires a person to adapt to the culture of another homogeneous unit in order to become an authentic Christian is unethical because it is dehumanizing."[18]

In the second place, it was taken for granted that Jewish and Gentile Christians would continue to have regular social intercourse as members of interracial local congregations, and provision was therefore made to prevent conflicts arising out of cultural differences. There is nothing at all in the book of Acts or the Epistles to lend support to the theory that the apostles ever contemplated the idea of adopting Peter's approach as described in Galatians 2:11-14: the separation of Jews and Gentiles in different one-race churches that would then endeavor to show their unity in Christ exclusively in "the supracongregational relationship of believers in the total Christian body over which Christ himself is the head."[19] The apostles rejected imperialistic uniformity, but they also rejected segregated uniformity. It was precisely because they assumed that Christians, whether Jews or Gentiles, would normally eat and worship *together* that they took measures to remove the most obvious obstacle to Christian fellowship in interracial churches. As F. F. Bruce has rightly observed,

> The Jerusalem decree dealt with two questions — the major one, "Must Gentile Christians be circumcised and undertake to keep the Mosaic law?" and the subsidiary one, "What are the conditions with which Gentile Christians should comply if Jewish Christians are to have easy social relations with them?" The second question would not have been raised had the first question been answered in the affirmative. If Gentile Christians had been required to follow the example of Gentile proselytes to Judaism, then, when these requirements were met, table-fellowship and the like would have followed as a matter of course. But when it was decided that Gentile Christians must not be compelled to submit to circumcision and the general obligations of the Jewish law, the question of table-fellowship, which had caused the recent trouble in Antioch, had to be considered.[20]

18. Wagner, p. 99.
19. Wagner, p. 132.
20. Bruce, *New Testament History* (Garden City, N.Y.: Doubleday, 1969), p. 288.

The decision reached was that the Gentiles would abstain from practices that were particularly offensive to the Jews — namely (according to the most probable reading), eating the flesh of animals that had been offered in sacrifices to idols, eating meat with blood (including, therefore, the flesh of animals that had been strangled), and engaging in "unchastity" in the sense of the degrees of consanguinity and affinity mentioned in Leviticus 18: 16-18.[21] If the Jerusalem "Council," having set out to deal with the question of circumcision, ended with regulations related to table fellowship, the obvious explanation is that once the matter of principle was settled, the effort was made to provide a *modus vivendi* for churches in which Jews and Gentiles would continue to have table fellowship together. And it is quite likely that the regulations included in this arrangement were basically the same as those that had always provided a basis for intercourse between Jews and "God-fearing" Gentiles in synagogues throughout the empire.[22]

According to Alan R. Tippett, the Jerusalem Decreee "against the forcing of the cultural pattern of the evangelizing people on the unevangelized, is written into the foundation of the Church and cries aloud today at the expressly westernizing missionary."[23] True. But a closer look at the historical situation shows that the Jerusalem Decree also cries aloud at every attempt to solve the conflicts arising out of cultural differences among Christians by resorting to the formation of separate congregations, each representing a different homogeneous unit. The regulations given by the Jerusalem conference were for-

21. Bruce, p. 287.
22. On this point, see W. M. Ramsay, *St. Paul the Traveller and the Roman Citizen*, 3d ed. (1898; rpt., Grand Rapids: Baker Book, 1960), p. 169. We should also note at this point the fact that Wagner recognizes that "most synagogue communities in the Roman provinces were made up of a core of Hellenistic Jewish residents, some Gentile proselytes who had converted to Judaism and been circumcised, and a number of so-called God-fearers who were Gentiles attracted to the Jewish faith but who had not wished to be circumcised and keep the Jewish law" (*Our Kind of People*, p. 127). If that kind of pluralism was possible in a Jewish context, Wagner's thesis that New Testament churches were homogeneous unit churches can be dismissed a priori as an unwarranted assumption.
23. Tippett, *Church Growth and the Word of God* (Grand Rapids: William B. Eerdmans, 1970), p. 34.

mulated on the assumption that table fellowship between Jewish and Gentile Christians was to continue despite the difficulties. Unity in Christ is far more than a unity occasionally expressed at the level of "the supracongregational relationship of believers in the total Christian body"; it is the unity of the members of Christ's body, to be made visible in the common life of local congregations.

The working arrangement represented by the Jerusalem Decree was entirely consistent with Paul's attitude expressed later in 1 Corinthians 8:7ff. and Romans 14:13ff. There was no compromise on a matter of principle, but the Gentiles were asked to forego their freedom with regard to practices that caused offense to their Jewish brothers and sisters. At least for Paul, the way to solve the conflicts in the church was neither imperialistic uniformity nor segregated uniformity but love, for love alone "binds everything together in perfect harmony" (Col. 3:14).

THE GENTILE MISSION

A well-attested fact regarding evangelism in the early church is that almost everywhere the gospel was first preached to both Jews and Gentiles *together*, in the synagogues. Luke provides no evidence to support McGavran's claim that family connections played a very important role in the extension of the faith throughout the Roman Empire,[24] but there is no doubt that the "God-fearers" on the fringe of the Jewish congregation served in every major city as the bridgehead into the Gentile world.[25] That these Gentiles who had been attracted to Judaism should be open to the Christian message is not surprising. If (according to the Mishnah) even the proselytes could only refer to God as "O God of *your* fathers," how much less would the "God-fearers" — who were not willing to be circumcised and comply with food laws — be regarded as qualified for membership in the chosen people. In F. F. Bruce's words,

> By attending the synagogue and listening to the reading and exposition of the sacred scriptures, these Gentiles, already wor-

24. See McGavran, *The Bridges of God*, pp. 27-31.
25. See Bruce, pp. 276-77.

shippers of the "living and true God," were familiar with the messianic hope in some form. They could not inherit this hope and the blessings which accompanied it until they became full converts to Judaism, and this was more than most of them were prepared for. But when they were told that the messianic hope had come alive in Jesus, that in him the old distinction between Jew and Gentile had been abolished, that the fullest blessings of God's saving grace were as readily available to Gentiles as Jews, such people could not but welcome this good news just as every ancestral instinct moved Jews to refuse it on these terms.[26]

A cursory study of the Pauline mission shows that time after time on arriving in a city the apostle would first visit the synagogues and then, when the break with the Jewish authorities was produced, he would start a Christian congregation with the new Gentile believers and a handful of converted Jews (Acts 13:5; 14:1; 17:1, 10, 17; 18:4, 19; 19:8). Such an approach had a theological basis: the offer of the gospel was to be made "to the Jew first" (Rom. 1:16; 2:9-10; Acts 3:26) according to a conviction going back to Jesus himself, and the Gentile could be incorporated into the Kingdom only after Israel had had the opportunity to return to the Lord.[27] But it also made it possible for the church to start almost everywhere with a nucleus of believers who already had the background provided by Judaism, with all the obvious advantages that this background implied. From that nucleus the gospel would then spread to Gentiles with a completely pagan outlook.

It would be ridiculous to suggest that Jews and Gentiles heard the gospel *together* in the synagogues and that those who believed were then instructed to separate into segregated house churches for the sake of the expansion of the gospel. Such a procedure would have been an open denial of apostolic teaching concerning the unity of the church. It would also have meant that the door of the church was made narrower than the door of the synagogue, where Jews and Gentiles could worship

26. Bruce, pp. 276-77
27. On this point, see Jeremias, *Jesus' Promise to the Nations*, pp. 71-72; see also Manson, *Jesus and the Non-Jews* (London: Athalone, 1955).

together. The suggestion is so farfetched that it can hardly be taken seriously.

All the New Testament evidence points in the opposite direction — namely, toward an apostolic practice that aimed at forming churches that would live out the unity of the new humanity in Jesus Christ. The apostles knew very well that if they were to get beyond a mere lip service to the ideal of accepting people "as they are," they would have to do so at the level of the local congregations. Accordingly, they sought to build communities in which Jew and Gentile, slave and free, poor and rich would worship together and learn the meaning of their unity in Christ right from the start, although they often had to deal with difficulties arising out of the differences in background and social status among the converts. A survey of New Testament accounts of the dealings of the apostles with the churches in the Gentile world attests that this was indeed the case. For the sake of brevity, two examples will suffice.

The Church at Corinth

It is in the context of a chapter dealing with the diversity not of homogeneous unit *churches* but of the *members* of the church that Paul states, "For just as the body is one and has many members, and all the members of the body, though many, are one body, so it is with Christ. For by one Spirit we were all baptized into one body — Jews or Greeks, slaves or free — and all were made to drink of one Spirit" (1 Cor. 12: 12-13). The emphasis on the nature of the oneness of Christians representing various racial and social groups can best be understood when it is viewed in relation to the situation of the church in Corinth.

According to Luke's report in Acts, the initiation of the church in that city followed the pattern characteristic of the Gentile mission. Paul began his preaching ministry in the synagogue, where Jews and Gentiles heard the gospel *together* (Acts 18: 4). Later on he was compelled to leave the synagogue, but by then there was a nucleus of converts, including "God-fearing" Gentiles such as Gaius Titius Justus (Acts 18: 7; 1 Cor. 1: 14) and Stephanas and his household (1 Cor. 1: 16; according to 1 Cor. 16: 15 they were the first converts in Achaia), and

Jews such as Crispus, the ruler of the synagogue, and his household (Acts 18:8; 1 Cor. 1:14). Gaius's house was located next door to the synagogue (Acts 18:7), and it became the living quarters for Paul and the meeting place for "the whole church," consisting of Jews such as Lucius, Jason, and Sosipater, and Gentiles such as Erastus and Quartus (Rom. 16:21, 23).

There are other hints regarding the constituency of the Corinthian church given in 1 Corinthians. The clear inference from 1:26 is that the majority of the members came from the lower strata of society; they were not wise or powerful or of noble birth "according to worldly standards." At least some of the members were slaves, while others were free (7:21-22). On the other hand, the community also included a few well-to-do members, notably Gaius (presumably a Roman citizen), Crispus (the ex-ruler of the synagogue), Erastus (the city treasurer according to Rom. 16:23), and possibly Chloe (the "dependents" referred to in 1 Cor. 1:11 may have been her slaves).

It would be absurd to take Paul's exhortation to each Corinthian Christian to remain "in the state which he was called" (1 Cor. 7:20) as lending support to the idea that each one was to belong to a homogeneous unit church representing his or her own race or social class.[28] The whole point of the passage (1 Cor. 7:17-24) is that in the face of God's call both race and social status have become irrelevant; the only thing that really matters is faithfulness to Jesus Christ. The apostle is not teaching here that slaves should remain in slavery or that they should take freedom if presented with the opportunity for manumission; rather, he is saying that the Christian's experience is not determined by legal status but by the fact that one has been called by God. The slave's slavery is irrelevant because he is "a freedman of the Lord"; the free man's freedom is equally irrelevant because he is "a slave of Christ" (v. 22). This is not a piece of advice to reject or accept manumission, to leave or remain in one's homogeneous unit, but an exhortation to see that whatever one's social status may be, one is to "remain with God" (v. 24). In S. Scott Bartchy's words, "Since God had called the Corinthians into *koinonia* with his crucified Son, it was *this*

---

28. See Wagner, p. 133.

fellowship and not any status in the world which determined their relationship to God."[29] This relationship to God was in turn to be the basis for the relationship among Christians.

The racial, social, and cultural diversity among the people that made up the church in Corinth goes a long way toward explaining the problems of dissension that Paul addresses in 1 Corinthians 1:10ff. Although the Christians continued to meet together at Gaius's house (Rom. 16:23), they tended to divide into at least four groups, each claiming to follow a different leader (1 Cor. 1:12). We cannot be certain about exactly what claims each group was making individually; the most we can say is that the Petrine party was made up of Jews who insisted on the food regulations formulated by the Jerusalem Council (1 Cor. 8:1ff.; 10:25ff.), while the "Christ party" was probably made up of Gentiles who regarded themselves as "spiritual men," opposed Jewish legalism, and denied the Jewish doctrine of the resurrection.[30] To complicate things even further, the communal meals, in the course of which the believers participated in the Lord's Supper, had become a sad picture of the division of the church according to economic position. C. K. Barrett is probably right in inferring from the text that "the members of the church were expected to share their resources, the rich, presumably, to bring more than they needed and to make provision for the poor."[31] Instead of sharing, however, the rich would go ahead and eat their own supper and even get drunk, while the poor would go hungry. The natural result was that the poor felt ashamed and the supper became a display of a lack of brotherliness (1 Cor. 11:20-22).

It seems clear that despite the division, the whole Christian community in Corinth continued to come together regularly in one assembly (11:17, 20; 14:23, 26; Rom. 16:23). There may be some exaggeration in Johannes Munck's description of

29. Bartchy, *First Century Slaves and I Corinthians* (Missoula, Mont.: University of Montana Press, 1973), p. 182.

30. Manson, "The Corinthian Correspondence (I)," in *Studies in the Gospels and the Epistles*, ed. Matthew Black (Philadelphia: Westminster Press, 1962), pp. 190-209.

31. Barrett, *A Commentary on the First Epistle to the Corinthians* (London: Adam & Charles Black, 1971), p. 263.

the Corinthian church as "the church without factions,"[32] but it is undeniable that although there is evidence of substantial disunity and bickering in the church, there is no evidence that there were separate churches representing the various positions in conflict.

The important thing to notice here is that the whole Epistle exemplifies again the apostolic practice in the face of problems of division caused by racial, cultural, or social differences among the members of the church. Not the least suggestion is ever made that the solution to such problems is to be found in homogeneous unit churches that would then seek to develop "intercongregational activities and relationships."[33] Again and again the emphasis falls on the fact that believers have been incorporated into Jesus Christ and that as a result all of the differences deriving from their different backgrounds are now relativized to such a degree that in the context of the Christian community they can be viewed as nonexistent. Indeed, the call to unity is central to the whole Epistle.

The Church in Rome

The church in Rome, in contrast to the church in Corinth, seems to have broken up into separate groups, some of which may have been formed on the basis of different social backgrounds. In Bruce's words, "Perhaps some local groups consisted of Jewish Christians and others of Gentile Christians, and there were few, if any, in which Jewish and Gentile Christians met together."[34] It may well be that it was because of this situation that Paul addressed his Epistle to the Romans "to all God's beloved in Rome" (1:7) rather than "to the church of God which is at Rome." A better indication of the situation, however, can be found in the fact that in Romans 16 mention is made of at least five house churches, associated with the names of Prisca and Aquila (v. 3), Aristobulus (v. 10), Narcissus (v. 11), Asyncritus (v. 14), and Philologus (v. 15).

If this reconstruction of the situation of the church in Rome

32. Munck, *Paul and the Salvation of Mankind* (1959; rpt., Atlanta: John Knox Press, 1971), pp. 135-67.
33. See Wagner, p. 150.
34. Bruce, p. 394.

is correct, are we then to conclude that it lends support to the theory that the apostolic practice was aimed at the formation of homogeneous unit churches? To conclude such a thing would be to disregard completely what was undoubtedly Paul's main purpose in writing the Epistle — namely, "to bring about the obedience of faith" (1:5) in congregations in which, as Paul S. Minear has argued, Christians representing a given position would not worship side by side with Christians representing another position.[35] But one would have to read Minear's work very selectively in order to suppose that the evidence he adduces could be used to support the theory that the apostolic church consisted largely of homogeneous unit congregations or that the situation of the church in Rome reflected the apostolic practice.[36] Quite to the contrary, Minear's claim is that the Epistle to the Romans was written with the hope that "a larger number of segregated house churches would at last be able to worship together — Jews praising God among Gentiles and Gentiles praising God with his people."[37] Accordingly, he shows how the entire Epistle develops the idea that through the coming of Jesus Christ all human distinctions have broken down, and he concludes that faith required the various groups in Rome to welcome one another regardless of their differing views on foods and days. Thus, Minear holds that the situation Paul deals with in chapters 14 and 15 is "the target of the whole epistle."[38]

Paul's approach to the problem in Rome was consistent with the apostolic practice with regard to churches threatened by division. There is no evidence that he would have approved of the modern device of forming segregated congregations to solve the problem of disunity. All his letters make it overwhelmingly clear that he held oneness in Christ to be an essential aspect of the gospel and therefore made every effort to see that Christians would together "with one voice glorify the God and Father of our Lord Jesus Christ" (Rom. 15:5).

35. See Minear, *The Obedience of Faith: The Purpose of Paul in the Epistle to the Romans* (London: SCM Press, 1971).
36. See Wagner, pp. 130-31.
37. Minear, pp. 16-17.
38. Minear, p. 33.

Other New Testament writings reflect the same apostolic concern for church unity across all the barriers separating people in society. No research is necessary to verify that the congregations that resulted from the Gentile mission normally included Jews and Gentiles, slaves and free, rich and poor, and were taught that in Christ all the differences stemming from their respective homogeneous units had become irrelevant (Eph. 6: 5-9; Col. 3: 22-4: 1; 1 Tim. 6: 17-19; Philem. 16; James 1: 9-11; 2: 1-7; 4: 13; 1 Pet. 2: 18; 1 John 3: 17).

The impact that the early church made on non-Christians because of Christian brotherhood across natural barriers can hardly be overestimated. The abolition of the old separation between Jew and Gentile was undoubtedly one of the most amazing accomplishments of the gospel in the first century. Equally amazing, however, was the breaking down of the class distinction between master and slave. As Michael Green comments, "When the Christian missionaries not only proclaimed that in Christ the distinctions between slave and free man were done away as surely as those between Jew and Greek, but actually lived in accordance with their principles, then this had an enormous appeal."[39] In F. F. Bruce's words, "Perhaps this was the way in which the gospel made the deepest impression on the pagan world."[40]

AN EVALUATION OF THE "HOMOGENEOUS UNIT PRINCIPLE"

In light of the preceding discussion of the apostolic teaching and practice regarding the unity of the church, how are we to evaluate the use of the homogeneous unit principle advocated by Donald McGavran and his followers?

Before we attempt to answer that question, we should be clear on two points. In the first place, it cannot be denied that from a biblical perspective the quantitative growth of the church

39. Green, pp. 117-18.
40. Bruce, *Commentary on the Epistle to the Colossians* (London: Marshall, Morgan & Scott, 1957), p. 277.

is a legitimate concern in the Christian mission.[41] If God "desires all men to be saved and to come to the knowledge of the truth" (1 Tim. 2:4), no Christian is in harmony with God's desire unless he or she also longs to see all coming to Jesus Christ. Moreover, it is clear that this longing will have to be expressed in practical terms (which may well include the use of anthropological and sociological insights) so that the gospel is in fact proclaimed as widely as possible. The issue in this evaluation, therefore, is not whether we should employ principles that can help in the expansion of the church. In the second place, it is a fact that hardly needs verification that the growth of the church takes place in specific social and cultural contexts and that people generally *prefer* to become Christians without having to cross the barriers between one context and another. This, again, is not the issue in this evaluation.

The real issue is whether church planting should be carried out so as to enable people to become Christians without crossing barriers and whether this principle is in fact "essential for the spread of the Gospel" as well as biblically and theologically defensible.[42] Enough has been said in the two previous sections on the apostolic teaching and practice bearing on the subject for me to draw the following conclusions, all of which are amply supported by exegesis:

1. In the early church the gospel was proclaimed to all people, whether Jew or Gentile, slave or free, rich or poor, without partiality. More often than not during the Gentile mission, Jews and Gentiles heard the gospel together. The New Testament provides no indication that the apostolic church had a missionary strategy based on the premise that church planting would be "more effective" if carried on within each separate homogeneous unit and was therefore to be conducted along racial or social lines.

2. The breaking down of the barriers that separate people in the world was regarded as an essential aspect of the gospel, not merely as a result of it. Evangelism therefore involved a call

41. On this point, see Orlando E. Costas, "Church Growth as a Multidimensional Phenomenon," in *Christ Outside the Gate: Mission Beyond Christendom* (Maryknoll, N.Y.: Orbis Books, 1982), pp. 43-57.

42. See McGavran, *Understanding Church Growth*, pp. 198-215.

to be incorporated into a new humanity that included all kinds of people. Conversion was never a merely religious experience; it was also a means of becoming a member of a community in which people find their identity in Christ rather than in race, social status, or sex. The apostles would have agreed with Clowney's dictum that "the point at which human barriers are surmounted is the point at which a believer is joined to Christ and his people."[43]

3. The church not only grew, but it grew across social barriers. The New Testament contains no example of a local church with a membership that had been taken by the apostles from a single homogeneous unit, unless the term *homogeneous unit* means no more than a group of people with a common language. By contrast, it provides plenty of examples of how the barriers had been abolished in the new humanity.

4. The New Testament clearly shows that the apostles, while rejecting "assimilationist racism," never contemplated the possibility of forming homogeneous unit churches that would then express their unity in terms of interchurch relationships. Each church was meant to portray the oneness of its members regardless of their racial, cultural, or social differences, and in order to reach that aim the apostles suggested practical measures. If "authentic unity is *always* unity in diversity,"[44] the unity fostered by the apostles could never have denied the pluralism in the membership of the local churches. Unity was not to be confused with uniformity either among local congregations or among individual church members. In Ignatius's words, "Where Jesus Christ is, there is the whole Church." Each local congregation was therefore to manifest both the unity and the diversity of the body of Christ.

5. There may have been times when the believers were accused of traitorously abandoning their own culture in order to join another culture, but there is no indication that the apostles approved of adjustments made merely in order to avoid that charge. They regarded Christian community across cul-

43. Clowney, "The Missionary Flame of Reformed Theology," in *Theological Perspectives on Church Growth*, ed. Harvie M. Conn (Nutley, N.J.: Presbyterian and Reformed Publishing Co., 1976), p. 145.
44. Wagner, p. 96; emphasis mine.

tural barriers not as an optional blessing to be enjoyed whenever circumstances were favorable to it or as an addendum that could be omitted if it were deemed necessary to do so in order to make the gospel more palatable, but rather as essential to Christian commitment. They would have readily included any attempt to compromise the unity of the church among those "adjustments which violate essential Christian teachings."[45]

If these conclusions are correct, it is quite evident that the use of the homogeneous unit principle for church growth has no biblical foundation. Its advocates have taken as their starting point a sociological observation and developed a missionary strategy; only then, a posteriori, have they made the attempt to find biblical support. As a result, the Bible has not been allowed to speak. A friendly critic of the Church Growth movement has observed that "lack of integration with revelation is the greatest danger in Church Growth anthropology."[46] The analysis we have made here leads to the conclusion that the Church Growth emphasis on homogeneous unit churches is in fact directly opposed to the apostolic teaching and practice in relation to the expansion of the church. No missionary methodology can be built without a solid biblical theology of mission as a basis. What can be expected of a missiology that exhibits dozens of books and dissertations dealing with the Church Growth approach but not one major work on the theology of mission?

We must admit that at times "the witness of separate congregations in the same geographical area on the basis of language and culture may have to be accepted as a necessary, but provisional, measure for the sake of the fulfilment of Christ's mission."[47] But the strategy of forming homogeneous unit churches for the sake of mere quantitative church growth reflects "the fear of diversity and the chauvinistic desire to ignore, barely tolerate, subordinate or eliminate pluralism" that, according to C. Peter Wagner, "has perhaps done more to harm

45. McGavran, *The Clash between Christianity and Culture*, p. 20.
46. J. Robertson McQuilkin, *How Biblical Is the Church Growth Movement?* (Chicago: Moody Press, 1973), p. 43.
47. Lesslie Newbigin, "What Is 'A Local Church Truly United'?" *The Ecumenical Review* 29 (April 1977): 124.

church life in America than has heretofore been recognized."[48] Because of its failure to take biblical theology seriously, it has become a missiology tailor-made for churches and institutions the main function of which is to reinforce the status quo. What can this missiology say to a church in an American suburb in which the bourgeois is comfortable but remains enslaved to the materialism of a consumer society and blind to the needs of the poor? What can it say to a church in which a racist feels at home because of the unholy alliance of Christianity with racial segregation? What can it say in situations of tribal, caste, or class conflict? Of course it can say that "men like to become Christians without crossing racial, linguistic and class barriers," but what does that have to do with the gospel concerning Jesus Christ, who came to reconcile us "to God *in one body* through the cross"?

The missiology that the church needs today ought to be perceiving the people of God not as a quotation that simply reflects the society of which it is a part but as "an embodied question-mark" that challenges the values of the world. As John Poulton has said, referring to the impact of the early church on society, "When masters could call slaves brothers, and when the enormities of depersonalizing them became conscious in enough people's minds, something had to go. It took time, but slavery went. And in the interim, the people of God were an embodied question-mark because here were some people who could live another set of relationships within the given social system."[49]

Only a missiology in line with the apostolic teaching and practice with regard to the extension of the gospel will have a lasting contribution to make to the building up of this kind of church — the firstfruits of a new humanity made up of persons "from every tribe and tongue and people and nation" who will sing in unison a new song to the Lamb of God (Rev. 5:9).

---

48. Wagner, p. 147.
49. Poulton, *People under Pressure* (London: Lutterworth Press, 1973), p. 112.

New Testament Perspectives on Simple Lifestyle

A paper on any topic related to lifestyle is likely to show more about the writer than about the subject matter. One's lifestyle cannot be separated from one's person; in writing about lifestyle, therefore, one can hardly avoid exposing oneself, with one's values and ambitions.

That being the case, it is legitimate to ask whether an authoritative word on the question of lifestyle can ever be given. Show me a person's lifestyle and I will tell you what he is likely to say on the question of lifestyle.

The problem is not readily solved when the question of lifestyle is viewed as a topic of Bible study. Does Jesus' poverty, for instance, have any relevance to Christian discipleship today, or should it be regarded as totally incidental to his ministry? Should "blessed are the poor in spirit" be interpreted in the light of "blessed are the poor" or vice versa? What did Jesus mean when he introduced himself as one coming to preach good news to the poor? Does the "love communism" of the primitive church have meaning for people living in "the Age of Plenty" in their relationship to people living in "the Age of Hunger," or should it be cast aside as no more than an interesting experiment inspired by the idealism of people living in "the Age of the Spirit"? All these and many other questions bearing on lifestyle will find different answers from different interpreters. But are all the answers equally valid? Is there not a way to let the Bible speak without imposing our own ideology on it?

For the Christian, to raise questions about lifestyle is to

raise questions about the kingdom of heaven. It is to ask not speculative questions but questions about what kind of life is appropriate in the New Age that has already come in Jesus Christ. And here too, it is those who know they are spiritually poor who will see the kingdom of heaven.

I approach my subject as one who recognizes the ease with which one can spiritualize the gospel in order to avoid its demands concerning lifestyle. I do not share the optimism of those who believe that if we Christians only understood what the Bible says on this question, we would readily submit to its demands in order to put our lives in line with them. At the same time, I recognize the possibility of reading the Bible in order to find support for a lifestyle conformed to a leftist ideology. My honest desire is to hear and to help others hear what the Spirit of God is saying to the church today on the question of simple lifestyle, for the sake of obedience. First I would like to examine briefly the meaning of Jesus' poverty in relation to Christian discipleship, then I would like to take a look at the way in which Jesus' teaching and example were reproduced in the early church, and finally I would like to explore the teaching of the apostles bearing on the question of riches.

I. JESUS AND POVERTY

1. Jesus' Poverty

The picture of Jesus that emerges out of the Gospels is that of a person who knew economic poverty throughout his entire life. His birth took place without the normal comforts, in a feeding trough for animals (Luke 2:7). The offering that Joseph and Mary brought on the occasion of his presentation in the Temple was the one that the Old Testament stipulated for poor people—namely, two doves or pigeons (Luke 2:23). Quite early in his life Jesus was a refugee (Matt. 2:14). He grew up in Galilee, an underdeveloped region of Palestine (Matt. 2:22-23), in the home of a carpenter, and this placed him in a position of disadvantage in the eyes of many of his contemporaries (see John 1:46; Matt. 13:55; Mark 6:3). During his ministry, he had no home he could call his own (Luke 9:58);

he depended on the generosity of a group of women for the provision of his needs (Luke 8: 2).

Jesus' poverty is a hard historical fact unanimously portrayed in all four Gospels. In order to understand its significance, we must view it in the light of Jewish piety in Jesus' day, which usually held that poverty was a curse and that wealth was evidence of God's favor.[1] At the same time, however, we must also view it in its relation to what Martin Hengel has rightly called "Jesus' free attitude to property,"[2] evidenced in his contact with well-to-do women (Luke 8: 2-3; cf. Luke 10: 38-39) and his willingness to attend banquets organized by the rich (Luke 7: 36ff.; 11: 37; 14: 1, 12; Mark 14: 3ff.) and to incur the label of "a glutton and a drunkard" (Luke 7: 34). Obviously, Jesus was not a propounder of rigorous asceticism. With this qualification in mind, we still have to ask whether his willingness both to defy Jewish piety by identifying himself with the poor and at the same time to maintain a free attitude to riches throws any light on the question of what kind of lifestyle is appropriate to the Kingdom of God, or whether Jesus' example in this matter is totally irrelevant to Christian discipleship.

Our answer to that question should also take into account Jesus' special concern for the poor, to which we will return shortly. At this point it will suffice to note that if Jesus was poor and at the same time regarded himself as sinless, he could not have thought of poverty as a direct result of personal sin. It would seem that he could have considered poverty to be something desirable for his disciples throughout the ages, perhaps as a virtue or as a means to improve their relationship to God. Such an idealization of poverty, however, can hardly be maintained in view of Jesus' "free attitude toward property." Whatever the motivation for his own poverty might have been, it is quite obvious that he did not intend to depict it as a positive value. As Julio de Santa Ana has insisted, all through the Bible poverty is not a virtue but an evil that must be elim-

---

1. See Martin Hengel, *Property and Riches in the Early Church: Aspects of a Social History of the Early Church* (London: SCM Press, 1974), pp. 12-22.

2. Hengel, p. 26.

inated and with regard to which God is specially concerned.[3]
All the evidence suggests that Jesus shared that attitude.

2. Jesus' Concern for the Poor

As we have seen, the Gospel records clearly show that Jesus
was materially poor. Equally, they show that he was especially
concerned for the poor, the needy, the oppressed. *Prima facie*,
it is most unlikely that at a time when people were subjected
to hard taxation linked to both their temple obligations and the
Roman government Jesus could go about cities and villages
without taking notice of the poverty that afflicted the masses.
The diseases and infirmities of which he healed many were only
one aspect of the destitute condition of the crowds that earned
his compassion because "they were harassed and helpless, like
sheep without a shepherd" (Matt. 9:36).

Jesus' attitude toward the poor is clearly stated in Luke's
version of one of the Beatitudes: "Blessed are you poor, for
yours is the kingdom of heaven" (Luke 6:20). To be sure, the
reference to material poverty can be and has in fact been denied
by appealing to Matthew's modification, according to which
the poor who are blessed are the "poor in spirit" (Matt. 5:3).
This disagreement calls for the following observations:

First, poverty is not equated with a mere absence of material resources in the Bible; it is safe to assume that behind the
use of the term *poor* in the New Testament ofttimes lies an
earlier Jewish tradition in which *poor* is almost synonymous with
pious and *righteous*.[4] In Luke 6:20, however, the poor stand in
contrast to the rich, on whom Jesus pronounces a woe because
they have already received their consolation — namely, the
comforts provided by wealth (6:24). No one would claim that
the riches of the rich to whom Jesus refers are spiritual riches;
why then should the poverty of the poor be regarded as spiritual poverty (i.e., poorness in spirit)?

---

3. Santa Ana, *Good News to the Poor: The Challenge of the Poor in the History
of the Church* (Maryknoll, N.Y.: Orbis Books, 1979). On God's concern for
the poor, see Ronald J. Sider, *Rich Christians in an Age of Hunger: A Biblical
Study* (1977; Downers Grove, Ill.: InterVarsity Press, 1984), pp. 53-78.
4. See *Dictionary of New Testament Theology*, ed. Colin Brown (Exeter:
Paternoster Press, 1971), 2: 824-25.

Second, if the Beatitude in Luke 6:20 is prematurely spiritualized, the very basis for interpreting the Matthean version of Jesus' saying is removed. For what does it mean to be "poor in spirit" if it is not primarily to share the outlook of the materially poor? If every time that the term *poor* is used in the Gospels it is taken to mean "poor in spirit," then the Beatitude in its Matthean form has no reference to concrete reality. To be poor in spirit is to be like those who, being materially poor, acknowledge their needs and are willing to receive help.

Third, the Beatitude is pronounced from the perspective of a poor man and addressed to the poor; its spiritualization, by contrast, usually reflects a way of thinking characteristic of people who have all their material needs met and are therefore unable to claim for themselves the blessedness of the materially poor. Unless one is willing to become literally poor, the literal interpretation of Jesus' saying is too threatening for one to prefer it to a spiritualistic reading.

If the literal interpretation is accepted, however, how are we to understand that Jesus should describe as "blessed" those who are so poor as to have to beg (which is the meaning of *hoi ptochoi*)? What kind of link does Jesus see between the Kingdom of God and the poor?

Latin American theologian Enrique Dussel has claimed that since the Kingdom of God stands in contrast to the prevailing system, and since the poor are not constituent parts of the system, they are the people of God and thus "the active subjects and carriers of the Kingdom of God". Quoting the Beatitude in Luke 6:20, he writes,

> For inasmuch as the poor are not subjects of the system, owners of capital and holders of power, they are both a negative factor (the pure negativity of the oppressed) and at the same time, positively (the positivity of the *exteriority*), they are the subject-carriers of the Kingdom who co-labour to build it. By being oppressed (and by that non-sinners, thus righteous) and active liberators (as members of the people), the poor are the subjects of the Kingdom. [5]

5. Dussel, "The Kingdom of God and the Poor," *International Review of Mission* 68 (April 1979): 124.

But if being materially poor is equivalent to being righteous, one is tempted to ask why anyone should fight poverty. Let poverty abound so that righteousness may also abound! The poor are blessed not because they are poor and as such righteous but because the Kingdom of God is *already* (*estin*) theirs. God has given them a share in his Kingdom through Jesus Christ. Already the Kingdom of God belongs to the poor, because Christ is in their midst, as one of them, bestowing on them the blessings of the Kingdom. The New Age announced by the prophets has arrived and is being manifested among the poor. Neither their material condition nor their own merits but rather Jesus' concern for them is the source of their blessedness.

That particular concern for the poor on Jesus' part is amply documented. Right at the beginning of his ministry, in the manifesto on his mission he presented in the synagogue of Nazareth, he read the prophetic pronouncement in Isaiah 61: 1-2 and went on to claim that he who would fulfill it had arrived. The fact that he applied that passage to himself makes it obvious that Jesus understood his mission in terms of the inauguration of a new era — "the day of the Lord's favor" — marked by the proclamation of good news to the poor, release for the captives, sight for the blind, and liberty for the oppressed. Seen in the light of the Old Testament background, Jesus' view of his mission implies that he, as the Messiah, is bringing in "the acceptable year of the Lord" — that is, the year of jubilee, of the structuring of society according to the demands of justice and love.[6] He is the bearer of the blessings of the Kingdom, and these blessings will be released among people living in conditions of deprivation and oppression, poverty and exploitation.

This interpretation of Jesus' mission should not be taken to mean that he was exclusively or even primarily concerned with material prosperity and physical or economic oppression. What it does mean is that Jesus understood his mission in terms of the fulfillment of Old Testament promises with a concrete historical content related to the reestablishment of justice in the messianic age, and consequently the poverty and oppression

6. See John Howard Yoder, *The Politics of Jesus* (Grand Rapids: William B. Eerdmans, 1972), and Robert Sloan, *The Favorable Year of the Lord: A Study of Jubilee Theology in the Gospel of Luke* (Austin: Scholars Press, 1977).

referred to in the definition of his mission cannot be limited to a spiritual condition. The blessings of the Kingdom ushered in by Jesus relate to the totality of human existence. Because this is so, when John the Baptist, having heard about the deeds of Christ, sent his disciples to ask "Are you he who is to come, or shall we look for another?" he replied, "Go and tell John what you hear and see: the blind receive their sight and the lame walk, lepers are cleansed and the deaf hear, and the dead are raised up, and the poor have good news preached to them" (Matt. 11:1). The listing of the "poor" along with the blind, the lame, the lepers, the deaf, and the dead makes it clear that this poverty is just as literal a condition as all the others. And just as Jesus' ministry means the end of suffering for all the others, so also for the poor: his proclamation is good news because it means the end of poverty through the establishment of a new order characterized by justice and love.

Does that mean that anyone who is literally poor automatically shares in the blessings of the Kingdom by virtue of his poverty? Are the poor "the active subjects and carriers of the Kingdom of God"? The answer is that the good news of the Kingdom should not be objectivized but kept in strict relation to Jesus' call to discipleship. Neither the poor nor the rich have a part in the Kingdom unless, regardless of their deprivation or material possessions, they are "poor in spirit" and as such totally dependent on God's grace.

According to his answer to John the Baptist, Jesus' concern for the poor, expressed in word and deed, is a sign that he is the Messiah. In order to meet John's doubts regarding this messiahship, Jesus acts on behalf of the poor, the sick, the oppressed. The clear implication is that his mission is related to those people in a very special way. He is not a conquering Messiah who establishes his rule by means of violence. He is rather the Messiah-Servant who comes as a poor man among the poor and the needy and announces to them the end of their suffering. According to the expectations expressed in the Magnificat, he comes to put down the mighty from their thrones and to exalt those of low degree; to fill the hungry with good things and to send the rich away empty (Luke 1:52-53). But he does this in the role of "the servant of Yahweh" who takes the side of the poor for the sake of bringing in the Kingdom. Is salvation then restricted to the poor? Is there hope for the rich? It is quite clear that no one is saved or condemned because of the quantity of material possessions he has or does not have. Jesus' special concern for the poor does not mean that he does not care for the rich; Jesus came to proclaim good news to the poor, but the rich are not excluded. Jesus' identification with and special concern for the poor does not limit salvation to a social class. The fact remains, however, that the good news is addressed to "the poor"—that is, "to those who are literally poor, or who share the outlook of the poor."[7] Consequently, it can be a word of salvation to the rich only when they set aside their riches as a means to find their identity and adopt instead the attitude of the poor. As Paul Gauthier has put it, "The point is not to leave the rich unevangelized but, on the contrary, to proclaim to them the whole gospel, in season and out of season."[8]

A more extended discussion of this topic would have to deal carefully with the meaning of Jesus' solidarity with the poor—the hungry, the thirsty, the stranger, the naked, the sick, and the prisoner, according to Matthew 25:31-46. In all probability this passage should be interpreted in the light of the biblical concept of *corporate personality*, "the least of these my brethren" meaning Jesus' disciples.[9] Even so, it clearly shows Jesus' special concern for the poor and needy: he identifies

7. I. Howard Marshall, *Commentary on Luke*, New International Greek Testament Commentary (Grand Rapids: William B. Eerdmans, 1978), p. 249.

8. Gauthier, *Los pobres, Jesús y la Iglesia* (Barcelona: Editorial Estela, 1965), p. 20.

9. The concept of "corporate personality" holds that a given group of individuals is a unit much like a person, and that the whole group is represented by each individual member of the group, just as each individual is a projection of the whole group. For a discussion of the concept of corporate personality and its relevance to the interpretation of Scripture, see Russell P. Shedd, *Man in Community* (London: Epworth Press, 1958).

The interpretation of "the least of these my brethren" is basic to the interpretation of Matt. 25:31-46. That the expression points to Jesus' solidarity with his own disciples is underscored by Matt. 10:40-42 (cf. Mark 9:41), in which the cup of cold water and the reward that are mentioned also show that the passage belongs to the same circle of ideas discussed in Matt. 25:31-46.

himself with them to the extent that he claims that what is done to them is done to him. It also shows the very close connection between salvation and concern for the poor and needy: the saved (i.e., "the righteous," the truly "poor in spirit") are identified with those who feed the hungry, give a drink to the thirsty, welcome the stranger, clothe the naked, and visit the sick and the imprisoned.

Interpreters may differ in their understanding of Jesus' solidarity with the poor and the oppressed, but no one can deny, without setting aside the evidence, that Jesus conceived of his ministry as the ushering in of a new era in which justice would be done to the poor.

3. Poverty and Discipleship

Jesus was poor and he showed special concern for the poor. Does that mean, then, that the rich are automatically excluded from the Kingdom of God? Is poverty an unavoidable condition for Christian discipleship?

In Luke 14:33 the renunciation of all possessions appears as a straightforward demand Jesus makes to those who want to follow him: "So, therefore, whoever of you does not renounce all that he has cannot be my disciple." This is the price that one must count as part of the cost of discipleship, together with the bearing of one's cross and the breaking away from one's family (Luke 14:26-32). Evidently the Twelve accepted that demand in a literal sense, as Peter pointed out when Jesus spoke about the hindrance of riches in relation to entering the Kingdom: "Lo, we have left everything and followed you" (Mark 10:20; cf. Mark 1:10ff. and par.; Luke 5:11, 28). When Jesus sent out his disciples, he sent them out in complete poverty (Luke 9:3; 10:4; cf. Mark 6:7ff.). On another occasion he told them to sell their possessions and give alms, in order to provide themselves with "purses that do not grow old" (Luke 12:33). His demand to the rich young ruler follows the same pattern: "You lack one thing; go, sell what you have, and give to the poor, and you will have treasure in heaven; and come, follow me" (Mark 10:21 and par.).

In light of the preceding passages, we can hardly avoid the conclusion that Jesus regarded poverty to be essential to Christian discipleship. The radical nature of his position is summed up in his comment "How hard it will be for those who have riches to enter the kingdom of God!" which is followed by the well-known simile of the needle's eye: "It is easier for a camel to go through the eye of a needle than for a rich man to enter the kingdom of God" (Mark 10: 23-24). Quite clearly this saying was toned down in some manuscripts through the addition of words that leave the way open for the rich to enter the Kingdom without necessarily giving up their riches: "How hard it is *for those who trust in riches* to enter the kingdom of God" (v. 24).[10] Such an addition provides a comforting interpretation of Jesus' saying, but it must not be allowed to take away the bite inherent in Jesus' demand concerning earthly possessions: If the disciples were "exceedingly astonished" after Jesus told them how difficult it is for a rich man to enter the Kingdom, it is quite clear that they did not understand him to be saying the obvious — namely, that trust in riches is incompatible with life in the Kingdom. Their astonishment was rather their response to an affirmation that stood in total opposition to the common belief — namely, that it is relatively easy to combine riches and piety, that as long as one is willing to give alms to the poor, one need not worry about how much one keeps for oneself. Rejecting this opinion, Jesus holds that riches constitute a real obstacle to the germination of God's Word in the human heart (see Matt. 13: 22), dismisses the attempt to serve both God and money as impossible (see Matt. 6: 24), and warns against the foolishness of accumulating wealth in order to secure one's future (Luke 12: 13-20). It is not surprising, then, that he should regard salvation as practically impossible for the rich.

Jesus' command to the rich young ruler to sell everything he had and give it to the poor applies to the multitudes as well as to an individual. It is a general call to renounce all in order to follow him. It is at root a call to be like him in his solidarity with the poor for the sake of the gospel, a call to servanthood that can be understood only in the context of discipleship. We should not assume that Jesus was not speaking to us when he said to the rich young ruler, "You lack one thing; go, sell what

10. The words *tous pepoithotas epi chremasin* should be eliminated in a number of ancient manuscripts, as they have been from the RSV and NIV.

you have, and give to the poor"; nor should we suppose that his command to renounce all things was not literal but simply a demand for inward detachment from earthly possessions. If it is clear that Jesus did at times demand literal poverty as a condition of discipleship, why should we take it for granted that in our case his demand to renounce all possessions should be interpreted figuratively? True inward detachment from riches can be experienced only by those who are willing literally to give all they have for the sake of the gospel. The renunciation of all we have is genuine to the extent that it is concretely expressed, as it was expressed in the case of Jesus and his disciples. Such a renunciation is a *sine qua non* of spiritual poverty. It derives its significance from its connection to a personal commitment to him who, being rich, for our sake became poor so that by his poverty we might become rich.

II. THE PRIMITIVE CHURCH AND THE POOR

1. The Constituency of the Primitive Church

A number of passages in the New Testament suggest that the Christian communities formed from Pentecost on were predominantly made up of poor people. Paul's words addressed to the Corinthian church, for instance, suggest that only a few members of it may have belonged to the upper classes: "Consider your call, brethren," he writes; "not many of you were wise according to worldly standards, not many were powerful, not many were of noble birth" (1 Cor. 1:26). Some exceptions are obvious in Acts and the Pauline Epistles: the "most excellent" Theophilus (Luke 1:3; Acts 1:1) for whom Luke writes his two works; the centurion Cornelius (Acts 10:1ff.); Manaen, a member of the court of Herod the tetrarch (Acts 13:1); Sergius Paulus, proconsul of Cyprus (Acts 13:7); Dionysius the Areopagite and a woman named Damaris (Acts 17:34); Philemon of Colossae (Philem. 2); Erastus, the city treasurer (Rom. 16:23); and Crispus, the ruler of the synagogue in Corinth (Acts 18:8). But it is obvious that the large majority of Christians were of humble origin. Paul interpreted this situation as a means by which God was working to confound the world, "so that no human being might boast in the presence of God" (1 Cor. 1:27ff.). Jesus Christ is a crucified Messiah; his church is the church of the weak and the poor.

2. *Concern for the Poor in the Primitive Church*

Jesus' concern for the poor was emulated in the early church, especially in the context of the Christian community. Obviously, they conceived themselves to be a community modeled on the Messiah-Servant.

Luke shows the effect of Jesus' message and lifestyle on the church in Jerusalem, the "love communism" of which (described in Acts 2:40-47 and 4:32-37) has attracted the attention of friends and foes down through the centuries. According to Luke's report, "all who believed were together and had all things in common; and they sold their possessions and goods and distributed them to all, as any had need" (2:44-45); "no one said that any of the things which he possessed was his own but had everything in common" (4:32). How are we to understand this "love communism"?

The common ownership of goods was one of the results of the outpouring of the Holy Spirit on the day of Pentecost. It was an accomplishment made possible not through human engineering but through the outflow of spiritual life that welded the believers together in "one heart and soul" (4:32).

The sharing of goods was also practiced by the Essenes, but in their case it was strictly enforced by law.[11] By contrast, in the early Christian community it was entirely on a voluntary basis. The sin of Ananias and Sapphira was not that they kept a part of the proceeds of the sale of their land for themselves but that they brought only a part as if it had been all. Sharing was not compulsory. As Peter made clear, they did not have to sell their land, and if they did sell it, they were free to use the money as they wished (5:4). Private property was not totally eliminated (Mary the mother of John Mark, for instance, kept her house as a meeting place according to 12:12), but it was made subservient to the needs of the whole community.

11. See Hengel, p. 32.

The basic criterion for the distribution of the goods was that each person receive according to his or her needs (2:45; 4:35), and the immediate result was the elimination of poverty, so that "there was not a needy person among them" (4:34). The agelong ideal that there be no poor among God's people (Deut. 15:4) was thus fulfilled. In the dawn of "the Age of the Spirit" the barriers of possessions had been broken down and the New Society had come into existence. Consequently, "the Lord was adding to their number day by day those who were being saved" (2:47).

Neither Acts nor the New Testament Epistles ever refer to the "love communism" of the early Jerusalem church as normative for the church throughout the ages. It is quite clear, however, that concern for the poor was for the early Christians an essential aspect of the life and mission of the church. When the church in Jerusalem faced economic distress because of the great famine that took place under Claudius in the forties, the church in Antioch sent relief by the hand of Barnabas and Saul (see Acts 11:29-30). Later on Paul organized a great collection in the Gentile churches for the purpose of helping "the poor among the saints in Jerusalem" (Rom. 15:26; cf. Gal. 1:10). The careful instructions that the apostle lays down for the collection, especially in 2 Corinthians 8 and 9, show the great significance he attaches to economic sharing as an expression of Christian unity across racial and national boundaries. He sees material contributions as concrete "fellowship" (koinonia, Rom. 15:26) and as a means to respond to the grace of God manifested in Jesus Christ (2 Cor. 8:8-9). Money is thus divested of its demonic power and turned into an instrument of service that supplies the needs of the poor and brings glory to God (see 2 Cor. 9:11ff.).

Concern for the poor in the primitive church was a normal aspect of Christian discipleship. Translated into action, it made visible the life of the Kingdom inaugurated by Jesus Christ. Its root was neither in the idealization of poverty nor in the desire to gain merits before God, but in "the grace of our Lord Jesus Christ, that though he was rich, yet for our sake became poor, so that by his poverty you might become rich" (2 Cor. 8:9).

III. APOSTOLIC TEACHING REGARDING RICHES

The same prophetic note present in those teachings of Jesus about riches that are contained in the Gospels can also be found in the apostolic teaching contained in the Epistles. Paul, for instance, includes the greedy among those who will not inherit the Kingdom of God (1 Cor. 6:10; cf. 5:10-11; Rom. 1:29; Eph. 5:5), and he describes covetousness as idolatry (Col. 3:5) and the love of money as "the root of all evils" (1 Tim. 6:10). James goes even further and assumes that the wealth of the rich is related to oppression of the poor (James 2:1-7), exploitation of workers, and wastefulness (5:1-6). In the same vein, Revelation announces the destruction of a civilization dedicated to the consumption of luxuries and indifferent to the Gospel (chapter 18).

All these warnings echo Jesus' warning about how hard it will be for those who have riches to enter the Kingdom of God. They leave us in no doubt as to the danger facing the rich man who attempts to gain the whole world but does not take care to avoid forfeiting his life.

There is, however, another strand of teaching in the Epistles that suggests it is possible to combine riches with Christian discipleship in a lifestyle characterized by inner freedom from any enslavement to material possessions and by generosity toward the poor. The most illuminating passage on the question of inner freedom is found in Philippians 4:10-13, in the context of a series of remarks Paul makes concerning the material gift he has received from the church in Philippi. "I have learned," he writes, "in whatever state I am, to be content. I know how to be abased, and I know how to abound; in any and all circumstances I have learned the secret of facing plenty and hunger, abundance and want. I can do all things in him who strengthens me" (4:11-12). The basic attitude described here is one of contentment, of inner freedom or detachment (*autarkeia*); this calls for some additional consideration.

First, we should note that this detachment was an ideal held in high regard in the popular Greek philosophy of Paul's time.[12] According to Xenophon, it was taught by Socrates,

12. See Hengel, pp. 54-56.

whom he quotes as saying, "My belief is that to have no wants is divine; to have as few as possible comes next to divine." Placed in a Christian context, however, contentment is no mere ideal but, as Jesus taught, the faith response to a heavenly Father who knows the needs of his children (see Matt. 6:25-34). True contentment is possible only where both abundance and scarcity can be seen in the light of God's purpose of love. In the final analysis, therefore, anxiety over material things is unbelief, a sign that one has lost one's perspective on the values of the Kingdom.

Second, we should note that contentment is a polar opposite to greed. The latter is unable to recognize limits and boundaries; the former is possible only when the limits and boundaries of the human condition are fully acknowledged. "There is great gain in godliness with contentment; for we brought nothing into the world, and we cannot take anything out of the world" (1 Tim. 6:7). It was this kind of contentment that the rich fool of Jesus' parable lacked. Whenever greed is allowed to take the place of contentment, life itself is under threat of destruction (1 Tim. 6:9). We are exhorted therefore to keep our lives "free from love of money" and to be content with what we have (Heb. 13:5).

Third, we should note that contentment is intimately related to sobriety, or temperance, one of the marks of the lifestyle for which the grace of God has appeared in Jesus Christ (Titus 1:11) and a fruit of the Spirit (Gal. 5:23). As Paul claims, it is possible through the resurrection power of Christ (Phil. 4:13).

Fourth, we should note that contentment is an essential qualification for leadership in the church (1 Tim. 3:2-3; Titus 1:17; 1 Pet. 5:2).

Generosity toward the poor goes hand in hand with contentment or inner freedom. One can give only to the extent to which one recognizes that all things belong to God and can be possessed only when they are put in relation to the Kingdom of God and his righteousness. In his instructions for rich Christians, therefore, Paul exhorts Timothy to teach them not to be conceited or to fix their hope in the uncertainty of riches but to show concern for the poor, "to do good, to be rich in good deeds, liberal and generous, thus laying up for themselves a good foundation for the future, so that they may take hold of the life which is life indeed" (1 Tim. 6: 17-19). A clear inference from these injunctions is that rich Christians ought to see themselves as no more than stewards of God's gifts summoned to live in the light of God's generosity toward all men and his special concern for the poor. The same assumption lies behind John's claim that the rich man who fails to share with the needy does not know God's love manifest in Jesus Christ (1 John 3: 16-17). Solidarity with the poor on the part of the poor is not a mere option but an essential mark of participation in the life of the Kingdom.

Jesus was poor and came to proclaim good news to the poor. His followers are those who in response to his love give up all their possessions and even their lives for the sake of the Kingdom of God. Blessed are the poor and those who share the outlook of the poor, for theirs is the Kingdom of God.

The Mission of the Church in Light of the Kingdom of God

Every attempt to define the relationship between the Kingdom of God and the church on the one hand and between the Kingdom of God and the world on the other will be necessarily incomplete. To speak of the Kingdom of God is to speak of God's redemptive purpose for the whole creation and of the historical vocation that the church has with regard to that purpose here and now, "between the times." It is also to speak of an eschatological reality that is both the starting point and the goal of the church. The mission of the church, therefore, can be understood only in light of the Kingdom of God.

THE PRESENCE OF THE KINGDOM

The central thrust of the New Testament is that Jesus has come to fulfill Old Testament prophecy and that in his person and work the Kingdom of God has become a present reality.

One of the basic concepts of Jewish eschatology during the time of Jesus and the apostles was that of the two ages, clearly expressed in a formula common to rabbinic literature: "this age" and "the age to come."[1] The dualism of Jewish eschatology

---

1. There is no certainty regarding the use of the formula among the rabbis before A.D. 70. Along with P. Volz, W. D. Davies believes that we may assume that the idea is "older than the terms used to define it" (*The Setting of the Sermon on the Mount* [Cambridge: Cambridge University Press, 1964], p. 183). We must not dismiss the possibility that Jesus was the first to use the terminology of the two ages. See Mark 10:30; Luke 18:30; Matthew 12:32; etc.

reflects the profound pessimism into which the Jewish people had fallen during the rule of pagan emperors in the postexilic period. The voice of God was silent; the messianic kingdom promised by the prophets had not appeared. Instead, the faithful in Israel were victims of the Gentiles' hate and persecution. Out of this setting a concept of history emerged in Israel with an exaggerated interest in the future and a persistent scorn for the present. History was divorced from eschatology. Although the Jews still expected God to establish a new creation, they saw that action taking place in the future. The present, by contrast, was abandoned to the dominion of evil and suffering.

Such an eschatology stands in opposition to that of the Old Testament prophets, for whom the fulfillments of God's purposes within history held the utmost importance. As George Eldon Ladd has pointed out, "The prophetic message is addressed to the people of Israel in a specific historical situation, and the present and the future are held together in an eschatological tension."[2]

Throughout the New Testament the doctrine of the two ages is presupposed but interpreted in light of the death and resurrection of Jesus Christ. The fundamental premise is that in the life and work of Christ, God has acted definitely to fulfill his redemptive purpose. The main actor has appeared and the eschatological drama of Jewish hope has begun. Eschatology has invaded history. The impact of the former upon the latter has produced what Oscar Cullmann has aptly called "the new division of time."[3] In contrast to Judaism, New Testament Christianity holds that the midpoint of the timeline is not in the future but in the past: it has arrived in Jesus Christ. The new era ("the coming age") of Jewish hope has been initiated in advance; here and now men and women can enjoy the blessings of the Kingdom of God.

Although the midpoint of the timeline has appeared, the consummation of the new age still remains in the future. The same God who has intervened in history to initiate the drama

2. Ladd, *The Presence of the Future: The Eschatology of Biblical Realism* (Grand Rapids: William B. Eerdmans, 1974), p. 93.
3. Cullmann, *Christ and Time*, trans. Floyd V. Filson (London: SCM Press, 1962), pp. 81ff.

is still acting and will continue to act in order to bring the drama to its conclusion. The Kingdom of God is, therefore, both a present reality and a promise to be fulfilled in the future: it has come (and is thus present among us), and it is to come (and thus we wait for its advent). This simultaneous affirmation of the present and the future gives rise to the eschatological tension that permeates the entire New Testament and undoubtedly represents a rediscovery of the Old Testament "prophetic-apocalyptic" eschatology that Judaism had lost.[4]

The most recent investigations of the eschatology of the New Testament emphasize that the oldest tradition of Jesus' preaching combines the affirmation of the coming Kingdom as a present reality with the expectation of the future completion of God's redemptive purpose. Yet the basic premise of Jesus' mission and the central theme of his preaching is not the hope of the Kingdom's coming at some predictable date in the future but the fact that in his own person and work the Kingdom is already present among men and women in great power. He affirms that no one knows the day and hour at which the eschatological drama will come to its conclusion—"not even the angels in heaven, nor the Son, but only the Father" (Mark 13:32). But he also affirms that the beginning of the last act of the drama ("the last days") has already begun in him. The Kingdom has to do with God's dynamic power through which "the blind receive sight, the lame walk, those who have leprosy are cured, the deaf hear, the dead are raised, and the good news is preached" (Matt. 11:5). It has to do with the Spirit of God, the finger of God, which casts out demons (Matt. 12:28; Luke 11:22). It is seen in liberation from demon possession (Luke 8:36), from blindness (Mark 10:56), from bleeding (Mark 5:34), and even from death (Mark 5:23). The kingdom of darkness that corresponds to "this age" has been invaded; the "strong man" has been disarmed, conquered and plundered (Matt. 12:29; Luke 11:22). The hour announced by the prophets has arrived: the Anointed One has come to preach good news to the poor, to announce freedom for the prisoners and recovery of sight to the blind, to release the oppressed, to proclaim the year of the Lord's favor (Luke 4:18-19). In other words, Jesus' historical

---

4. See Ladd, *The Presence of the Future*, pp. 318ff.

mission can be understood only in connection with the Kingdom of God. His mission here and now is the manifestation of the Kingdom as a reality present among men and women in his own person and action, in his preaching of the gospel and his works of justice and mercy.

Accordingly, the Kingdom of God is God's dynamic power made visible through concrete signs pointing to Jesus as the Messiah. It is a new reality that has entered into the flow of history and affects human life not only morally and spiritually but also physically and psychologically, materially and socially. In anticipation of the eschatological consummation at the end time, it has been inaugurated in the person and work of Christ. It is active among people, although it can be discerned only from the perspective of faith (Luke 17:20-21). The completion of God's purpose still lies in the future, but a foretaste of the eschaton is already possible.

It is in the light of the visible manifestations of God's Kingdom that Jesus' proclamation of the Kingdom can best be understood. His announcement "The time is near, the kingdom of God is near; repent and believe the good news" (Mark 1:15) is not a verbal message given in isolation from the signs that corroborate it; rather, it is good news concerning something that can be seen and heard. As Jesus' words imply, (1) it is news concerning a historical fact, an event that is taking place and that affects human life in every way; (2) it is news that is of public interest, having to do with the whole of human history; (3) it is news related to the fulfillment of Old Testament prophecy (the *malkuth Yahveh* announced by the prophets and celebrated by Israel has become a present reality); (4) it is news calling for repentance and faith; and (5) it is news resulting in the formation of a new community, a community of people who are personally called.

The exact sense in which the Kingdom of God has come can be seen in the unfolding story of Jesus' work. It is in him and through him that the Kingdom has become a present reality.

THE KINGDOM AND THE CHURCH

The New Testament presents the church as the community of the Kingdom in which Jesus is acknowledged as Lord of the universe and through which, in anticipation of the end, the Kingdom is concretely manifested in history.

The terms *Messiah* and *messianic community* are correlative: if Jesus was the Messiah, as indeed he claimed he was, then it is not at all strange that among other things he should surround himself with a community that recognized the validity of his claim. Even a superficial analysis of the evidence leads us to conclude that this is in fact what he did. In his ministry he called men and women to leave everything and follow him (Luke 9: 57-62; 14: 25-33; Matt. 10: 34-38). Those who respond to his call become his "little flock," to whom God desires to give the Kingdom (Matt. 26: 31; Luke 12: 32). They are the ones whom he will acknowledge before his Father who is in heaven (Matt. 10: 32ff.). They are his family, closer to him than his own brothers and mother in the flesh (Matt. 12: 50).

Jesus' reference to this messianic community as "my church" (Matt. 16: 18) fits perfectly with one purpose of his mission — his intention to surround himself with a community of his own in which the promises of God's covenant with Israel could be fulfilled. The context of Jesus' revelation that he will establish a "church" that will be characteristically his own by itself suggests the relation between the church and his messiahship: only after the disciples have realized that he is the Messiah does he announce his intention. He is the Messiah in whom the Kingdom of God has become a present reality. The church is the community that comes into existence as a result of his kingly power. That being the case, it is quite obvious that the church must not be equated with the Kingdom. As Ladd puts it,

> If the dynamic concept of the Kingdom is correct, it is never to be identified with the church. . . . In the biblical idiom, the Kingdom is not identified with its subjects. They are the people of God's rule who enter it, live under it, and are governed by it. The church is the community of the Kingdom but never the Kingdom itself. . . . The Kingdom is the rule of God; the church is a society of men.[5]

5. Ladd, *A Theology of the New Testament* (Grand Rapids: William B. Eerdmans, 1974), p. 111.

In God's purpose after Pentecost, the Kingdom of God was to continue to be a present reality through the gift of the Holy Spirit. This is made clear by the fact that when Jesus' disciples asked "Lord, are you at this time going to restore the kingdom to Israel?" he answered "It is not for you to know times or dates that the Father has set by his own authority. But you will receive power when the Holy Spirit comes on you" (Acts 1: 6-8). The Holy Spirit is thus the agent of eschatology in the process of fulfillment. The Kingdom of God that has broken into history in Jesus Christ continues to act through the Holy Spirit.

The church is the result of God's action through his Spirit. It is the body of Christ and, as such, the sphere in which the life of the new era initiated in Jesus Christ operates; the Holy Spirit is the agent through whom that life is imparted to the believers (2 Cor. 3: 6; Gal. 5: 25; Rom. 8: 2, 6). Likewise, the Spirit gives the church the *charismata* that make possible its existence as a missionary community (1 Cor. 12: 4ff.). This means that the church is not primarily an *organization* but an *organism*, the members of which are united by the action of the Spirit. "One body" corresponds to "one Spirit" (Eph. 4: 3).

The importance of this relationship between the Holy Spirit and the church for the correct understanding of the relationship between the Kingdom of God and the church can hardly be exaggerated. The church is dependent on the Spirit for its very existence. Its words and deeds are merely the means for the present manifestation of God's Kingdom; they cannot be fully explained as human deeds and words. The Kingdom of God does not belong exclusively to the future. It is also a present reality manifested in the Christian community, which is "a dwelling place of God in the Spirit" (Eph. 2: 22). The church is not the Kingdom of God, but it is the concrete result of the Kingdom. It still bears the marks of the Kingdom's historical existence, the marks of the "not yet" that characterize the present time. But here and now it participates in the "already" of the Kingdom that Jesus has set in motion.

As the community of the Kingdom indwelt by the Holy Spirit, the church is clearly called to be a "new society" that stands alongside both Jews and Gentiles (1 Cor. 10: 31). The church must not be equated with the Kingdom, but it must not be separated from it either. Here and now it is intended to reflect the values of the Kingdom by the power of the Holy Spirit. This is not to say that the church is already "the church victorious" but to recognize that the church is "the Israel of God" (Gal. 6:16), the people of God called to confess Jesus Christ as Lord and to live in the light of that confession. As Lesslie Newbigin has put it,

> It is the community which has begun to taste (even only in foretaste) the reality of the Kingdom which alone can provide the hermeneutic of the message. . . . Without the hermeneutic of such a living community, the message of the Kingdom can only become an ideology and a programme; it will not be a gospel. [6]

The result of Pentecost was not merely power to preach the gospel but also "many wonders and miraculous signs" done by the apostles, and a community of people who "devoted themselves to the apostles' teaching and to the fellowship, to the breaking of bread and to prayer," who "were together and had everything in common" (Acts 2:42-44; cf. 4:32-37). Pentecost, therefore, meant power for a new lifestyle, including a new economy. The powers of the new age, released by Jesus Christ, were present through his Spirit among God's people, enabling them to be a credible sign of the Kingdom.

MISSION AND GOOD WORKS

Because the Kingdom has been inaugurated in Jesus Christ, the mission of the church cannot be properly understood apart from the presence of the Kingdom. The mission of the church is an extension of the mission of Jesus. It is the manifestation (though not yet complete) of the Kingdom of God, through proclamation as well as through social service and action. The apostolic witness continues to be the Spirit's witness to Jesus Christ as Lord through the church. God, who placed the whole universe under Jesus, "appointed him to be the head over everything for the church, which is his body, the fullness of him

6. Newbigin, *Sign of the Kingdom* (Grand Rapids: William B. Eerdmans, 1980), p. 19.

who fills everything in every way" (Eph. 1:22-23). As the community of the Kingdom, the church confesses and proclaims the Lord Jesus Christ. It also performs good works that God prepared in advance for it to do and for which God created it in Christ Jesus (Eph. 2:10). It is true that "through the apostolic writings, Jesus and the apostles continue to speak";[7] it is equally true that through the church and its good works the Kingdom becomes historically visible as a present reality. Good works are not, therefore, a mere addendum to mission; rather, they are an integral part of the present manifestation of the Kingdom: they point back to the Kingdom that has already come and forward to the Kingdom that is yet to come.

This does not mean, of course, that good works — the signs of the Kingdom — will necessarily persuade unbelievers of the truth of the gospel. Even the works that Jesus performed were sometimes rejected. Nor were his works alone rejected; some turned away from his words as well. We must, therefore, posit no interpretation of the Christian mission that leaves the impression that the verbal proclamation is "in itself persuasive to the unbelievers" while visible signs — good works — are not.[8] Neither seeing nor hearing will always result in faith. Both word and deed point to the Kingdom of God, but "no one can say 'Jesus is Lord' except by the Holy Spirit" (1 Cor. 12:3).

THE KINGDOM OF GOD AND THE WORLD

According to the New Testament, the whole world has been placed under the Lordship of Jesus Christ. The Christian hope is related to the consummation of God's purpose to bring all things in heaven and on earth together under him as Lord and to liberate humanity from sin and death in his Kingdom.

The Christ whom the church acknowledges as Lord is the Lord of the whole universe. It is in the affirmation of his universal Lordship that the church finds the basis for its mission.

7. Arthur P. Johnston, "The Kingdom in Relation to the Church and the World" (paper presented at the Consultation on the Relationship between Evangelism and Social Responsibility, Grand Rapids, 19-26 June 1982), p. 28.

8. Johnston, p. 29; cf. p. 44.

Christ has been enthroned as King, and his sovereignty extends over the totality of creation. As such, he commissions his disciples to make disciples of all nations (Matt. 28:18-20).

The church is the expression of the universal Lordship of Jesus Christ — the concrete manifestation of the Kingdom of God. The fact that Jesus is "Lord of all" means not only that he is sovereign over all men and women but also that at present he grants the blessings of the Kingdom of God to all who call upon his name (Rom. 10:12). The fact that he is "head over all things" is important because as such he has been granted dominion over the church so that it may be filled with his fullness (Eph. 1:22). As the exalted Lord whose authority extends to the whole universe, he has given his people gifts that enable them to grow into an organic unity so that they can imitate the model of humanity perfectly realized in his person (Eph. 4:10ff.). He who is the firstborn of the old creation by virtue of his role as the wisdom of God is at the same time the firstborn of the new creation by virtue of his resurrection (Col. 1:15, 18). He who is "the head of all rule and authority" (Col. 2:10) is also "the head of the body, the church" (Col. 1:18; cf. Eph. 5:23), the head from which the church receives its life (Col. 2:19). By Christ's death God desired "to reconcile to himself all things" (Col. 1:20), and by his physical body he reconciled the believers in order to present them "holy and blameless and irreproachable before him" (Col. 1:22). The fact that he is "at the right hand of God" not only affirms his preeminence as the mediatorial King of all creation but is also a statement of his ministry of intercession on behalf of his people (Heb. 1:3 and 10:12; Rom. 8:24).

This whole thrust of the New Testament leads us to conclude that if the church is to be properly understood, it must be seen in the context of God's universal purpose in Christ Jesus. God's intention is "to bring all things in heaven and on earth under one head, even Christ" (Eph. 1:10). The "open secret" is already taking shape in the church, whose confession of Jesus Christ anticipates the fulfillment of God's purpose "that at the name of Jesus every knee should bow, in heaven and on earth and under the earth, and every tongue confess that Jesus Christ is Lord, to the glory of God the Father" (Phil. 2:10-11).

To speak of the Kingdom of God is to speak of a universal gospel — a message centered in the Son who was sent by the Father "to be the Savior of the world" (1 John 4:14). The fact that God's purpose includes the whole world does not mean that all men and women automatically belong to the Kingdom. The Kingdom of God is an eschatological order that one must enter, and one cannot enter without fulfilling certain conditions (Matt. 5:20; 7:21; 18:3; 19:23; Mark 10:23ff.). Consequently, the proclamation of the Kingdom of God is not merely the proclamation of an objective fact concerning which men and women should be informed; rather, it is simultaneously a proclamation of an objective fact *and* a call to faith.

Nevertheless, in light of God's universal purpose, the relationship of the world to the Kingdom cannot be understood exclusively in terms of God's providence. With the coming of Jesus Christ, the whole world has been placed under the sign of the Cross. The Cross spells not only judgment but also grace. Because Jesus Christ died and was raised from the dead, the world can no longer be seen as nothing more than humanity standing under the judgment of God. His "act of righteousness" has universal implications. For "just as the result of one trespass was condemnation for all men, so also the result of one act of righteousness was justification that brings life for all men" (Rom. 5:18). The gospel continues to be the proclamation of an event that affects the totality of human history.

It is not enough, therefore, to say that God "is providentially reigning supreme and will bring all history to the fulfillment of His purposes in His creation,"[9] as if the work of Christ were totally irrelevant to the way God will accomplish his purpose for history. Christ has been exalted as Lord. He must exercise his kingship — he must reign — until all his enemies, including death, have been placed under his feet. "When he has done this, then the Son himself will be made subject to him who put everything under him, so that God may be all in all" (1 Cor. 15:28).

The God of redemption is also the creator and judge of all humanity who wills justice and reconciliation for all. His pur-

9. Johnston, p. 17.

pose for the church, therefore, cannot be separated from his purpose for the world. The church is properly understood only when it is seen as the sign of God's universal Kingdom, the firstfruits of redeemed humanity. Here and now, in anticipation of the end, *in* the church and *through* the church, the whole world is placed under the Lordship of Christ and therefore under God's promise of a new heaven and a new earth in the Kingdom of God. One cannot read the New Testament and still try to understand the church apart from God's purpose for humanity and history, from which it derives its significance. The universality of the gospel does not mean that all men and women will participate in the Kingdom of God, however, but rather that the church will proclaim the Kingdom to all men and women (cf. Acts 1:8; 19:8; 28:23). The redemption of creation is inseparable from the "revealing of the sons of God"; its liberation is inseparable from the "glorious liberty of the children of God" (Rom. 8:19, 21). In other words, from the New Testament perspective the meaning of general history is closely linked with the cosmic meaning of the church. The church is not a sect composed of a few souls rescued from the tumultuous sea of history but the cosmic manifestation of the manifold wisdom of God, who created all things (Eph. 3:9-10), of the "new man" in whom the image of the Second Adam is reproduced (Eph. 2:15 and 4:13; 1 Cor. 15:45), of the first-fruits of a new humanity (James 1:18).

To speak of the Kingdom of God in relation to the world is not simply to affirm the providence of God but to speak of the Mediator-King Jesus Christ, whose reign is made visible (though not yet in its fullness) in the community that confesses his name. It is also to confirm that God has a goal for history, a goal that provides meaning and direction for the mission of the church here and now. God is at work to bring about his purpose for creation. The church in the power of the Spirit proclaims salvation in Christ and plants signs of the Kingdom, always giving itself fully to the work of the Lord, knowing that its labor in the Lord is not in vain (1 Cor. 15:58).

CONCLUSIONS

From the preceding discussion the following conclusions emerge:

1. Both evangelism and social responsibility can be understood only in light of the fact that in Jesus Christ the Kingdom of God has invaded history and is now both a present reality and a future hope, an "already" and a "not yet." Accordingly, the Kingdom of God is neither "the progressive social improvement of mankind whereby the task of the church is to transform earth like unto heaven and do it now" nor "the present inner rule of God in the moral and spiritual dispositions of the soul with its seat in the heart."[10] Rather, it is God's redemptive power released in history, bringing good news to the poor, freedom to prisoners, sight to the blind, and liberation to the oppressed.

2. Evangelism and social responsibility are inseparable. The gospel is good news about the Kingdom of God. Good works, on the other hand, are the signs of the Kingdom for which we were created in Christ Jesus. Both word and deed are inextricably united in the mission of Jesus and his apostles, and we must continue to hold both together in the mission of the church, in which Jesus' mission is prolonged until the end of the age. The Kingdom of God is not merely God's rule over the world through creation and providence; were that the case, we could not regard it as having been inaugurated by Jesus Christ in any significant sense. Rather, the Kingdom is an expression of God's ultimate kingship over creation, which, in anticipation of the end, has become present in the person and work of Jesus Christ. Both the proclamation of the Kingdom and the visible signs of its presence made through the church are brought about by the power of the Spirit—the agent of eschatology in the process of realization—and point to its present and its future reality.

10. Of these two views, Johnston rejects the former and accepts the latter. As Joachim Jeremias has rightly observed, "Neither in Judaism nor elsewhere in the New Testament do we find that the reign of God is something indwelling in men, to be found, say, in the heart; such a spiritualistic understanding is ruled out both for Jesus and for the early Christian tradition" (*New Testament Theology: The Proclamation of Jesus*, trans. John Bowden [London: SCM Press, 1971], 1: 101).

The widest and deepest human need is for a personal encounter with Jesus Christ, through whom the Kingdom is mediated. "The same Lord is Lord of all and richly blesses all who call on him, for 'Everyone who calls on the name of the Lord will be saved' " (Rom. 10: 12b-13). From this perspective, and this perspective only, "in the church's mission of sacrificial service evangelism is primary" (Lausanne Covenant, par. 6), and the gospel must be proclaimed diligently. But the gospel is good news concerning the Kingdom, and the Kingdom is God's rule over the totality of life. Every human need, therefore, can be used by the Spirit of God as a beachhead for the manifestation of his kingly power. That is why in actual practice the question of whether evangelism or social action should come first is irrelevant. In every concrete situation the needs themselves provide the guidelines for the definition of priorities.

As long as both evangelism and social responsibility are regarded as essential to mission, we need no rule of thumb to tell us which comes first and when. On the other hand, if they are not seen as essential, the effort to understand the relationship between them is a useless academic exercise. It would be as useless as the effort to understand the relationship between the right and left wings of a plane when one believes that the plane can fly with only one wing. And who can deny that the best way to understand the relationship between the two wings of a plane is by actually flying it rather than by merely theorizing about it?

3. According to God's will, the church is called to manifest the Kingdom of God here and now in what it is as well as in what it proclaims. Because the Kingdom of God has already come and is yet to come, "between the times" the church is both an eschatological and a historical reality. If it does not fully manifest the Kingdom, that is not because God's dynamic reign has invaded the present age "without the authority or the power of transforming it into the age to come"[11] but because the consummation has not yet arrived. The power that is active in the church, however, is like the working of God's mighty strength, "which he exerted in Christ when he raised him from

11. Johnston, p. 23.

the dead and seated him at his right hand in the heavenly realms, far above all rule and authority, power and dominion, and every title that can be given, not only in the present age but also in the one to come" (Eph. 1:20-21). The mission of the church is the historical manifestation of that power through word and deed, in the power of the Holy Spirit.

4. Because of his death and resurrection, Jesus Christ has been enthroned as Lord of the universe. The whole world, therefore, has been placed under his Lordship. The church anticipates the destiny of all mankind. Between the times, therefore, the church — the community that confesses Jesus Christ as Lord and through him acknowledges God as "both the Creator and the Judge of all men" — is called to "share his concern for justice and reconciliation throughout human society and for the liberation of men from every kind of oppression" (Lausanne Covenant, par. 5). Commitment to Jesus Christ is commitment to him as the Lord of the universe, the King before whom every knee will bow, the final destiny of human history. But the consummation of God's Kingdom is God's work. As Wolfhart Pannenberg has put it, "The Kingdom of God will not be established by man. It is most emphatically the Kingdom of God. . . . Man is not to be exalted but degraded when he falls victim to illusions about his power."[12]

---

12. Pannenberg, *Theology of the Kingdom of God*, ed. Richard John Neuhaus (Philadelphia: Westminster Press, 1974), p. 91.